Praise for

packaging terrorism

"Susan Moeller trains her scholarly eye on the role of the media in our understanding of modern-day terrorism. What she has produced is a valuable, important, and timely study—essential reading for all of us."
Marvin Kalb, *Edward R. Murrow Professor Emeritus at Harvard University*

"This is a sober and timely analysis of the toxic mix of politics, terrorism, and the media since 9/11. It lays bare the price paid by the West, but also points to a better way forward."
Richard Sambrook, *Director, BBC Global News*

"*Packaging Terrorism* is an urgently needed meditation on how journalism has too often failed to ask the hard questions about the 'War on Terror' and become instead a weapon of propaganda. Susan Moeller's timely book is a must-read for all concerned journalists and citizens."
John Owen, *Professor of International Journalism, City University, London*

"An outstanding in-depth analysis of one of the most difficult and controversial issues in modern journalism. Moeller critically dissects the roles of government and media, laying bare the spin, manipulation of language, and vested interests that all too often distort the true story and deceive the public."
Stephen Jukes, *Dean of the Media School at Bournemouth University; former Global Head of News at Reuters*

"If you need a thoughtful, thorough, and challenging survey of recent media treatment of terrorism, then this is it. Susan Moeller is a clever and realistic analyst of how journalism treats this vital subject. She has both an insider's understanding of the media and the intelligence and research to mount a critical attack on those who misrepresent the true nature of political violence."
Charlie Beckett, *London School of Economics; Director, POLIS*

"Susan Moeller has exploded a bomb, splintering the 'War on Terror.' This thoroughly researched book provides an X-ray image of the US and British media as they have grappled with reporting the news of terrorism and war. It is a stinging rebuke of this largely profit-driven profession and also a primer for students of journalism on how to cover war and violence to make us better informed citizens in a democracy."
Nayan Chanda, *Yale Center for the Study of Globalization*

D0150205

Communication in the Public Interest

Communication has never been more important than in our current cultural moment. From the growing monopolization of global media, to human rights issues, health campaigns, and issues of free speech and society, communication has real political and ethical consequences. The books in this ICA Wiley-Blackwell *Communication in the Public Interest* series are accessible and definitive treatments of subjects central to understanding communication and its intersections to the wider world; they will widen understanding, encourage discussion, and illuminate the importance of communicating about issues that affect people's lives.

Already published

Susan Moeller: *Packaging Terrorism: Co-opting the News for Politics and Profit*

Forthcoming

Roxanne Parrott: *Talking about Health: Why Health Communication Matters*
Nadia Caidi: *Right to Know: Information Post 9/11*
Karen Ross and Stephen Coleman: *Them and Us: The Media and the Public*
Michael Delli Carpini: *Beyond the Ivory Tower: Communication and the Public Interest*

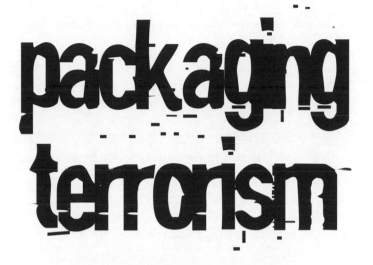

packaging terrorism

co-opting the news for politics and profit

susan d. moeller

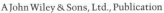

WILEY-BLACKWELL

A John Wiley & Sons, Ltd., Publication

This edition first published 2009
© 2009 Susan D. Moeller

Blackwell Publishing was acquired by John Wiley & Sons in February 2007. Blackwell's publishing program has been merged with Wiley's global Scientific, Technical, and Medical business to form Wiley-Blackwell.

Registered Office
John Wiley & Sons Ltd, The Atrium, Southern Gate, Chichester, West Sussex, PO19 8SQ, United Kingdom

Editorial Offices
350 Main Street, Malden, MA 02148-5020, USA
9600 Garsington Road, Oxford, OX4 2DQ, UK
The Atrium, Southern Gate, Chichester, West Sussex, PO19 8SQ, UK

For details of our global editorial offices, for customer services, and for information about how to apply for permission to reuse the copyright material in this book please see our website at www.wiley.com/wiley-blackwell.

The right of Susan D. Moeller be identified as the author of this work has been asserted in accordance with the Copyright, Designs and Patents Act 1988.

Library of Congress Cataloging-in-Publication Data

Moeller, Susan D.
   Packaging terrorism : co-opting the news for politics and profit / Susan D. Moeller.
     p. cm.
   Includes bibliographical references and index.
     ISBN 978-1-4051-7366-7 (hardcover : alk. paper) — ISBN 978-1-4051-7365-0 (pbk. : alk. paper)   1. Terrorism—Case studies.   2. Terrorism and mass media—Case studies.   I. Title.
   HV6431.M632 2009
   363.325—dc22

                                                                                      2008039272

A catalogue record for this book is available from the British Library.

Set in 9.5/12.5pt Photina by Graphicraft Limited, Hong Kong
Printed in Singapore by Ho Printing Pte Ltd

01   2009

This book is dedicated to my father
and is for Stephen,
the love of my life, forever and always

contents

abbreviations

ANC	African National Congress
AP	Associated Press
CENTCOM	United States Central Command
CISSM	Center for International and Security Studies at Maryland
DHS	US Department of Homeland Security
DU	depleted uranium
FDNY	New York Fire Department
FEMA	Federal Emergency Management Agency
GSAVE	global struggle against violent extremism
GWOT	global war on terror
IAEA	International Atomic Energy Agency
ICMPA	International Center for Media and the Public Agenda
LBC	Lebanese Broadcasting Corporation
MSF	Médecins Sans Frontières (also known in English as "Doctors Without Borders")
NCTC	National Counterterrorism Center
NGO	non-governmental organizations
NPR	National Public Radio
NSA	National Security Agency
PIPA	Program on International Policy
PRI	Public Radio International
VNR	video news release
WMD	weapons of mass destruction

introduction: a very simple idea

Packaging Terrorism is the account of very simple idea. The idea is this: that it's not the acts of terrorism that most matter in the post-9/11 world, it's what we are told to think about the acts of terrorism. Politicians tell us what to think. The media tell us what to think.[1] Even terrorists tell us what to think. They all want to attract our attention. They all have reasons for wanting us to think in a certain way. They all want to tell us why an act of terrorism matters. They all have agendas. They all are packaging terrorism for our consumption. We are the audience for all those disparate actors.

I

what is terrorism?

the american experience:
the agenda of the "war on terror"

President George W. Bush's "War on Terror" publicly began on September 11, 2001.

We think of wars beginning with a cataclysmic event—everything up to that moment could have gone either way until "the moment" occurs that makes a war inevitable. It is that clap of thunder, we believe, that coalesces events into something that we recognize as "war."

The designation that a series of events has become a "war" wonderfully concentrates public and official support behind a situation that had not previously generated unanimity. Henry Cabot Lodge and Congressional Republicans needed the sinking of the *Maine*, Woodrow Wilson needed the *Lusitania*, FDR needed Pearl Harbor.

Bush needed 9/11. The astonishing loss of life that single September morning validated his declaration of war against the Al Qaeda terrorists. But his "War on Terror" encompassed more than the fight against Osama bin Laden and his minions and in many ways it began well before 9/11. Bush declared war against disparate enemies; in his estimation the "War on Terror" was not only properly fought in Afghanistan once the Taliban refused to give up Al Qaeda leaders, but included battles of all kinds—most notably against Saddam Hussein.

In quick order, with everyone watching (but few willing to criticize), the September 11-initiated war became a war to create the new moral order articulated by President Bush and his Vulcans, as author James Mann compellingly defined the administration's foreign policy team of Donald Rumsfeld, Dick Cheney, Colin Powell, Richard Armitage, Condoleezza Rice, and Paul Wolfowitz.

The "War on Terror" was more than a response to the terrorists attacks of September 11. The 9/11 cataclysm gave President Bush the opportunity to realize all the Vulcans' unilateralist, interventionist foreign policy goals, by uniting them into one comprehensive, Ur-policy that connected the 9/11 terrorists, weapons of mass destruction (WMD), Iraq, and other "Axis of Evil" countries. As Vice President Dick Cheney declared within days of September 11, "the administration intended to work 'the dark side.'" What that meant, writer Philip Gourevitch chillingly explained in his book *Standard Operating Procedure*, was that "the vice president's legal counsel, David Addington, presided over the production of a series of secret memorandums, which argued against several centuries of American executive practice and constitutional jurisprudence by asserting that the president enjoyed essentially absolute power in wartime, including the authority to sanction torture."[1]

Three months after the attacks on the World Trade Center, on the sixtieth anniversary of the attack on Pearl Harbor, President Bush defined his public conception of terrorism before more than 8,000 sailors and Marines and their families assembled on the vast deck of the nuclear-powered aircraft carrier the USS *Enterprise*. "We're fighting to protect ourselves and our children from violence and fear. We're fighting for the security of our people and the success of liberty," Bush said. "We're fighting against men without conscience but full of ambition to remake the world in their own brutal images."[2]

Bush described these men as "a movement, an ideology that respects no boundary of nationality or decency. . . . They celebrate death, making a mission of murder and a sacrament of suicide." And he compared the 9/11 "terrorists" to the enemies of World War II: "They have the same will to power, the same disdain for the individual, the same mad global ambitions. And they will be dealt with in just the same way. . . . Like all fascists, the terrorists cannot be appeased; they must be defeated."[3]

By linking terrorism to fascism, the terrorist threat to the one posed by World War II, President Bush was suggesting that this current evil was as heinous and as threatening as those two generations ago. And by naming not just the 9/11 conspirators, but a much larger conception of "the enemy" as "terrorists" and naming America's cause as a "global war against terrorism," rather than a more limited effort to eradicate Al Qaeda or to capture Osama bin Laden, President Bush attempted to forestall and even pre-empt media and public criticism. The Bush administration succeeded at labeling its foreign policy objectives as part of his "War on Terror," thus making it very difficult for political opponents or media commentators to challenge the President without coming off as not only "soft" on defense, but as cavalier about the lost American lives of 9/11.

The media responded as directed—and as they always have at the start of a national crisis.[4] They rallied in support of the President and appropriated his characterization of the situation. At the end of October 2001, the then CNN chairman Walter Isaacson wrote a memo to his staff members that ordered them to balance the broadcast images of civilian devastation in Afghanistan with reminders of the American lives lost at the World Trade Center and the Pentagon.[5] Isaacson suggested language for his anchors, including: "The Pentagon has repeatedly stressed that it is trying to minimize civilian casualties in Afghanistan, even as the Taliban regime continues to harbor terrorists who are connected to the September 11 attacks that claimed thousands of innocent lives in the U.S." It "seems perverse," Isaacson said, "to focus too much on the casualties or hardship in Afghanistan."[6]

Isaacson was wrong. The American public deserved to know more about the casualties and hardship in Afghanistan. The public needed to know more about the meaning and the effect of the President co-opting 9/11 and co-opting the patriotic, broad-based interest in responding through a "War on Terror." "In the wake of

9/11," noted *New York Times* col
adopted fear-mongering as a po
what it was—an atrocity commi
adversary—the administration p(
every direction."[7]

The reason Americans didn't u
a lot to do with how they get their 1
Trojan horse—his "War on Terror
the presidency.[8]

And those problems persist.

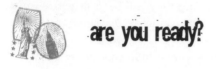

are you ready?

Duct tape and plastic. It all came down to that. If you just had enough of each you'd be safe.

In February 2003, before the start of the Iraq war, the US Department of Homeland Security (DHS) raised the official national terrorism alert to the Code Orange (high risk) level, citing "recent intelligence reports." DHS announced that Americans should prepare for another terrorist attack. To get ready, Americans needed to assemble a household disaster supply kit that included duct tape and plastic sheeting to be used to seal a room against radiological, chemical, and/or biological contaminants.[9]

DHS insisted that its new home preparedness tips would increase Americans' sense of security by giving them ways to keep their families safe.

But the "Duct and Cover" strategy, as it was called on radio talk shows and late-night comedy reports, struck many as the twenty-first-century equivalent of 1960s schoolchildren being asked to shelter from an atomic blast underneath the flimsy protection of their desks. The joke was in the general assessment that Americans could not begin to protect themselves—at least by hardware supplies —against most threats posed by terrorists.

Despite the run on the hardware stores, chemical and bioterrorism researchers noted that plastic sheeting and duct tape were unlikely to help in the case of a biological or chemical attack for two reasons. First, in order for a "safe room" to be effective, one has to be able to get to the room and seal it quickly. "You wouldn't have time to get that in place," said Dr. Monica Schoch-Spana, a senior fellow at the Johns Hopkins Center for Civilian Biodefense Strategies, to the *New York Times*.

"You won't be tipped off that something's going to happen." And second, even if doors, windows, and vents in a room were well sealed by duct tape and plastic before an attack, outside air would completely cycle through the room in a matter of hours.[10]

Then there were terrorism experts who pointed out that almost all terrorist attacks had occurred outside the United States and were overwhelmingly characterized as conventional bombings.[11]

A year and a half later those criticisms didn't stop DHS and the Federal Emergency Management Agency (FEMA) from relaunching a "revised, updated, and enhanced" version of their *Are You Ready?* pamphlet. Once again, almost three years after September 11, 2001, and a year after the coalition forces failed to find weapons of mass destruction in Iraq, the *Are You Ready?* guide instructed its readers what to do in a chemical attack: "Close doors and windows and turn off all ventilation, including furnaces, air conditioners, vents, and fans; Seek shelter in an internal room and take your disaster supplies kit; Seal the room with duct tape and plastic sheeting; Listen to your radio for instructions from authorities."[12]

Once again the guide served to remind Americans of the threat of a chemical, biological, or nuclear attack on the United States.[13] Scientists continued to say that it was uncertain whether individuals could effectively protect themselves from a terror attack. The media noted that even if Americans survived the initial assault, there was no viable local or national policy in place for handling the days and weeks that would follow. And terrorism experts argued that Americans were more likely to be killed driving to the hardware store for duct tape than they were to be killed by a terrorist.

It was not lost on any of these groups that the release of the updated guide came in August 2004, in the midst of a tightly fought re-election campaign for the White House. Four days before the election, on October 29, 2004, the Arab television network Al Jazeera broadcast excerpts from a videotape of Osama bin Laden, and posted transcripts of the speech in Arabic and English on its website: "I am amazed at you," Al Jazeera quoted bin Laden as saying. "Even though we are in the fourth year after the events of September 11th, Bush is still engaged in distortion, deception and hiding from you the real causes. And thus, the reasons are still there for a repeat of what occurred . . . the wise man doesn't squander his security, wealth and children for the sake of the liar in the White House."[14]

That evening, after details of the speech were broadcast by American TV networks, *Newsweek* conducted an overnight poll that gave Bush 50 percent of the vote and his Democratic opponent Senator John Kerry 44 percent. A similar poll conducted a week earlier gave the President 48 percent and Kerry 46 percent of the vote.[15]

According to Ron Suskind, a Pulitzer Prize-winning former reporter for the *Wall Street Journal*, CIA analysts determined that "bin Laden's message was clearly designed to assist the President's reelection."[16]

words and trojan horses

Let's go back and start at the beginning with the word "terrorism."

It's one of those words, frequently used, by politicians and people on the street alike, that seem to be transparent in their meaning.

Like "human rights." "obscenity." "weapons of mass destruction."

"Terrorism." That's about terrorists committing acts of terror.

Right?

For most of us, most of the time, precise definitions of words don't matter. The points that are being made are conversational, not legal. The ramifications of what is being said over coffee or written via email are casual, not cataclysmic.

But that carelessness about language can sometimes spill over into occasions and venues where precision does matter. A lot.

And sometimes others, usually political "others," take advantage of our careless understanding and hide agendas within the meaning of words, like Trojan horses. They know that certain words have exact legal meanings that can trigger specific consequences. Governments are loath, for example, to employ the word "genocide" to a crisis because under the 1948 UN Convention on the Prevention and Punishment of the Crime of Genocide, nations are obligated to prevent and punish genocide wherever it occurs. So governments try to use phrases, such as "acts of genocide," that have no legal meaning or obligation, but sound alike to an untrained ear. And governments know that certain other words, such as "terrorism," for example, are imprecise and legally undefined. Those kinds of words can be used freely—with the only consequence being that they may trigger emotional responses in their audience. Just hearing the word "terrorism," for instance, can cause listeners to be fearful, to be concerned for their own and others' safety.

Sometimes speakers want their audiences to be scared.

The powerful set the terms of public debate. Media, including independent, privately owned media, usually confirm the political and social agenda of governments. Even when they challenge politicians' spin on events, the media usually report on what the government says is important. The level of recognition that politicians give to an issue usually matches the level of coverage given to that issue by the media. When the White House suggests that Americans need to fear terrorists, then there are stories online, in print, and on TV about the terrorist threat.

That's why we must think more about "terrorism," the word, before we think about "terrorism," the act. What do we know, or think we know, about "terrorism"? And is our own understanding of that word generally shared by others?

I used to think that words, like butterflies, could be pinned to a page. Sure, they normally flew around and one rarely stopped to define what a word meant in a passing conversation, but I imagined that important words, words that underlay relations between states, for example, were similarly understood by the players involved.

Then I was asked by a UN-sponsored agency to conduct a study of how three different groups of players—government, non-governmental organizations (NGOs), and the media—prioritized human rights. Human rights had become a familiar and essential component of both global communications and international diplomacy; it had found its way, for example, into both the media's assessment of foreign affairs and governments' justifications for their actions. So the agency that hired me wanted to know just how important different groups considered human rights to be. The agency assumed that I would find something like this: governments prioritize human rights fairly low—they are more concerned with the security and economic well-being of their citizens; NGOs prioritize human rights fairly high—they are most concerned with issues of fairness and equity especially of underclasses; and the media, well, they prioritize human rights somewhere in the middle—they are concerned with the most exciting story, and sometimes that happens to be a story about injustice or abuse.

The UN-sponsored agency's assumptions, actually, were pretty much on target. But it turned out that that analysis was not the major take-away of the report that I wrote. What turned out to be the major conclusion was this: those who speak of human rights do not all prioritize human rights in the same manner, nor do they even define "human rights" in the same terms. When pressed, people in all the groups I spoke to could reference the last century and a half of international documents on the subject, but for the purposes of their jobs they had an operating definition of human rights often quite different than that found in the formal documents.

I had expected to find political and cultural distinctions. But I found something different. As I traveled to interview UN and NGO officials, government bureaucrats, policy advisors and former military officers, human rights lawyers, print, broadcast, and online journalists, editors and producers, I discovered that I could anticipate their operating definition of human rights by simply looking at their job titles. Here's what they told me. Let me give you first their job title and then what they said:

- A former wire service reporter in Vietnam and then foreign correspondent for a major newspaper: "Human rights always in my mind means killing—war, torture, and killing."

- A professor of international law at an Ivy League school: "Human rights are related to a particular set of political events—there can be systematic human rights violations of the 1980s Latin American type, and there can be mass human rights violations, such as war crimes like genocide."
- The executive director of a major human rights organization: "Human rights is the language of duty and communitarianism; we have to move from moral outrage to global responsibility."
- A senior official at the World Bank: "In the World Bank you have the situation where the bank is governed by its members, and many of them, of course, really don't want the World Bank to dabble in human rights. The bank in theory is only supposed to make decisions based on economic criteria. So then you have a problem—human rights and money don't mix."
- The president of a major foundation: "Human rights has become a rhetoric by which people discuss their values—it may be just hypocrisy, but even so it is a discussion of values."

You can see how each person's job began to match up with how each one viewed human rights. Ultimately, the study led to two realizations: each of the different "cultures"—NGOs, governments, the media—was unaware that the others had a different professional interpretation of human rights. As a result, they each misunderstood the language and the underlying values used by the others. And even more importantly, the study documented that there were ramifications to "human rights" being variously defined. What one set of actors defined as "human rights" shaped the responses of those actors to a situation—and as those definitions were different, so were the responses different.

Since I conducted that study, the world has become more sophisticated. Michael Moore's movies and Jon Stewart's *The Daily Show*, for example, have made a practice of juxtaposing the comments of multiple speakers on the same subject to expose the various priorities and spin that would otherwise be overlooked. While the technique can be milked for political satire, there is genuine value in the exercise. Even when we think we understand someone else, we may not. We likely will have different reactions to the same issue that may in part be traceable to our different understanding of that issue. We may not understand even though we share a common language, if our definitions are different. We may not understand even though we share a common language, if that other is intentionally trying to deceive us.

"Everyone agrees terrorism is evil—at least when committed by the other side," noted Professor Ronald Steel. "But it did not pop up yesterday. As a method of warfare it goes back to the dawn of civilization. It is new to Americans because nothing is truly real until it happens to us. To be sure, acts of terrorism against us must be dealt with and, if possible, prevented. But first we have to agree on what it is and what inspires it. That means recognizing that terrorism is not an enemy in itself, as we thought of the Soviet Union during the cold war."[17]

 ## political correctness: can i use the word "terrorist?"

Four days after the London Underground and bus bombings on July 7, 2005 the BBC re-edited its coverage of the attacks "to avoid labeling the perpetrators as 'terrorists.'" Editors changed the word "terrorists" in archived website stories to the more neutral term "bombers,"[18] and in ongoing coverage across BBC's TV, radio, and online news, reporters and presenters began to use the word "bombers" to refer to the attackers.

Opinion exploded around the world. "Only a news organization such as BBC . . . could apply political correctness to terrorist mass murderers," jeered one audience member from Switzerland. "The term is terrorist, not bomber. If you had a loved one that was killed or injured, you would probably understand," mocked another from the United States. "Isn't it time to develop some moral courage and use the word 'terrorist' for terrorists?" scorned a third from the UK.

One of the few positive responses was from an Arab man living in France: "Al-Jazeera are discussing your decision to not use 'terrorist' about the London bombings. I thank you for your choice, because it shows that you are an objective channel [and] a very civilised people . . ."[19]

Politicians who speak of terrorism rarely hesitate over their words, rarely suggest that there is debate over the terms or admit to any ambiguities about their use: Such-and-such a person is a terrorist. This event is terrorism. Only by comparing different statements by different speakers, by juxtaposing a statement made today with one made a year ago, or by going back in history and evaluating an event with some historical perspective, does it become apparent that political assessments differ and policies change.

But mainstream media have learned to be circumspect in their usage of the terms "terrorism" and "terrorist."

Before 9/11, a number of media outlets had a policy in place about when their reporters could use the terms "terrorism" and "terrorist." The Associated Press, according to its spokesman Jack Stokes, used a variety of terms and permitted the use of the word "terrorist" for those in non-governmental groups who carry out attacks on the civilian population.[20] Other news organizations shunned the words in reference to the Israeli–Palestinian conflict, aware of the politicization of the terms, but had no compunctions about using them in other circumstances.

The assistant managing editor, Roger Buoen, of the *Minneapolis Star Tribune*, for example, explained in a pre-9/11 statement to his paper's ombudsman that:

> Our practice is to stay away from characterizing the subjects of news articles but instead describe their actions, background and identity as fully as possible, allowing readers to come to their own judgments about individuals and organizations. In the case of the term "terrorist," other words—"gunman," "separatist" and "rebel," for example— may be more precise and less likely to be viewed as judgmental. Because of that we often prefer these more specific words.[21]

Six months after September 11, the *Washington Post* wrote formal guidelines into its internal style manual to govern the paper's usage of the words "terrorist" and "terrorism." The guidelines developed in the context of pressure from watchdog groups concerned about the paper's coverage of the Israeli–Palestinian conflict. Post ombudsman Michael Getler cited the manual extensively in a column written a year and a half later. He quoted the guidelines:

> The language we use should be chosen for its ability to inform readers. Terrorism and terrorist can be useful words, but they are labels. Like all labels, they do not convey much hard information. We should rely first on specific facts, not characterizations. Why refer to a "terrorist attack in Tel Aviv" when we can be more informative and precise: "The bombing of a disco frequented by teenagers in Tel Aviv," for example. Our first obligation to readers is to tell them what happened, as precisely as possible.
>
> When we use these labels, we should do so in ways that are not tendentious. For example, we should not resolve the argument over whether Hamas is a terrorist organization, or a political organization that condones violence, or something else, by slapping a label on Hamas. Instead, we should give readers facts and perhaps quotes from disputing parties about how best to characterize the organization.

The guidance also quotes Foreign Editor David Hoffman:

> If the Israelis say they have assassinated a terrorist, we should not embrace their labeling automatically. We may say he was a suspected terrorist, or someone the Israelis considered a terrorist, or someone the Israelis say participated in a terrorist act. In other words, we should always look independently at whether the person has committed an act of terrorism, whether we know sufficient facts to say he has or has not and what the facts are. We should always strive to satisfy our own standards and not let others set standards for us.

Getler then noted: "That last sentence is central to the editing process here. The terrorist label is very powerful and the paper takes care in avoiding language that is preferred by one side or another in the Middle East."[22]

why do news standards matter?

In the years following September 11, news outlets have struggled with how to use the "terrorist" label—some media are leery of using the word "terrorist" to describe the perpetrators of acts most members of the public wouldn't hesitate to label as such. The 9/11 bombers, for example. A no-brainer for calling "terrorists," right? Not for some media.

Washington Post media columnist Howard Kurtz reported on an internal memo from the British news agency Reuters written after the 9/11 attack by Stephen Jukes, the agency's global head of news. "One man's terrorist is another man's freedom fighter," said Jukes. "Reuters upholds the principle that we do not use the word terrorist." As he told Kurtz, "To be frank, it adds little to call the attack on the World Trade Center a terrorist attack. . . . We're there to tell the story. We're not there to evaluate the moral case."

In September 2001, when Jukes spoke to Kurtz, Jukes was pilloried by many, especially in the United States, for Reuters' rejection of the term "terrorists" to identify the World Trade Center bombers. Howard Kurtz, for example, chided him for his (and Reuters') "value-neutral approach."[23]

But, in hindsight, Reuters' caution in applying the term was prescient; its caution is now reflected in many newsroom guidelines. Many prominent news outlets have come to agree with Jukes that not only should journalists not take moral positions on the stories they cover, but that using the label "terrorism" or "terrorist" is in effect doing so.

Newsrooms' hesitation to apply the term "terrorism" across the board remains controversial to audiences, however. There are many who find that judgment too "politically correct" at best and cowardly, perhaps traitorous, at worst. In summer 2007, in response to hostile questions on its editor in chief's blog, Sean Maguire, acting editor for politics and general news, made public the guidelines in Reuters' internal handbook of standards.

Terrorism—We may refer without attribution to terrorism and counter-terrorism in general but do not refer to specific events as terrorism. Nor do we use the word terrorist without attribution to qualify specific individuals, groups or events. Terrorism and terrorist must be retained when quoting someone in direct speech. When quoting someone in indirect speech, care must be taken with sentence structure to ensure it is entirely clear that they are the source's words and not a Reuters label. Terrorism and terrorist should not be used as single words in inverted commas (e.g. "terrorist") or preceded by so-called (e.g. a so-called terrorist attack) since that can be taken to imply that

Reuters is making a value judgment. Use a fuller quote if necessary. Terror as in terror attack or terror cell should be avoided on stylistic grounds.

This is part of a wider and long-standing policy of avoiding the use of emotive terms. Reuters does not label or characterise the subjects of news stories. We aim to report objectively their actions, identity and background. We aim for a dispassionate use of language so that individuals, organisations and governments can make their own judgment on the basis of facts. Seek to use more specific terms like "bomber" or "bombing," "hijacker" or "hijacking," "attacker" or "attacks," "gunman" or "gunmen" etc. It is particularly important not to make unattributed use of the words terrorism and terrorist in national and territorial conflicts and to avoid using those terms in indirect speech in such a context.[24]

Reuters, like the BBC, the CBC in Canada, and ABC in Australia, have all emphasized that digital media and satellite television have turned formerly local viewers into global ones—word choices are now scrutinized by a larger and more diverse audience.[25] Following the criticism of the BBC's coverage of the 2005 bombings, the BBC's governors met that September to review its editorial guidelines on the use of the terms, and revisions were issued that December. Rather than retreat from the moderated use of "terrorism," the new internal guidelines reinforced the value of using it sparingly:

Careful use of the word "terrorist" is essential if the BBC is to maintain its reputation for standards of accuracy and especially impartiality . . . that does not mean we should emasculate our reporting or otherwise avoid conveying the reality and horror of what has occurred; but we should consider the impact our use of language may have on our reputation for objective journalism amongst our many audiences . . . we must be careful not to give the impression that we have come to some kind of implicit—and unwarranted—value judgment.[26]

The *New York Times*, too, has repeatedly admitted that it tiptoes through the language minefield. "Nothing provokes as much rage as what many perceive to be *The Times*'s policy on the use of 'terrorist,' 'terrorism' and 'terror.' There is no policy, actually, but except in the context of Al Qaeda, or in direct quotations, these words, as explosive as what they describe, show up very rarely," wrote former public editor Daniel Okrent in the lead to one of his columns. But in his estimation, he wrote, "given the word's history as a virtual battle flag over the past several years, it would be tendentious for *The Times* to require constant use of it, as some of the paper's critics are insisting. But there's something uncomfortably fearful, and inevitably self-defeating, about struggling so hard to avoid it."[27]

Terrorism or not terrorism, that is the question. Almost all of the media debate has been focused on whether journalists should use the term at all, not on the question of what it means when they do use it.

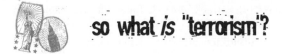

so what *is* "terrorism"?

"When I use a word," Humpty Dumpty said, in a rather scornful tone, "it means just what I choose it to mean, neither more nor less."

"The question is," said Alice, "whether you can make words mean so many different things."

"The question is," said Humpty Dumpty, "which is to be master—that's all."[28]

To Be Master: Defining "Terrorism"
to Support One's Point of View

The American government has undertaken a public diplomacy effort to educate Americans and the world about its view of terrorism. As part of that effort, the website of the National Counterterrorism Center (NCTC), has put out an annual "Counterterrorism Calendar" in either a handy online interactive form or a down-loadable Daily Planner version. Handsomely designed, each calendar marks dates "according to the Gregorian and Islamic calendar, and contains significant dates in terrorism history as well as dates that terrorists may believe are important when planning 'commemoration-style' attacks."

In the Daily Planner version, page-length overviews of major groups on the State Department's list of terrorist organizations and a page's-worth of details on major terrorists ("Usama Bin Ladin" has an "Olive" complexion, weighs "160lbs/72kg" and "is left-handed") are opposite a week's-worth of dates. Each day has its own "This Day in History" set of facts; for example Monday, February 19, 2007, or 1 Safar, was not just President's Day in the United States, but was the day in 2001 when the Terrorism Act in the UK was enacted and when Hamas official Mahmud Madani was shot in the West Bank.

Occasional pages offer readers "technical" information. The page opposite the week of February 19, 2007, for instance, gave "Bomb Threat Stand-Off Distances"—a grid of how far one needs to evacuate in case of a bombing, from a pipe bomb to a semi-trailer bomb. Other pages that same year offered information on "Medical Symptoms of Exposure to Nerve Agents" or about the "Indicators of Suspicious Financial Activity" (the first indicator is "Account transactions that are inconsistent with past deposits or withdrawals"). Another page was on Ramadan: "Muslims are banned from fighting other Muslims during Ramadan, but they may engage in combat with non-Muslims." Several dates during Ramadan are mentioned as being "especially auspicious for a terrorist attack." The CT Calendar, accessible from the Center's homepage, is "oriented primarily to readers in the United States, but we hope that we have also made it useful for citizens of other countries."[29]

Despite the authority with which the CT Calendar gives its information on individual terrorists, on terrorist groups, and on the acts they might commit, there is in fact no universally agreed-upon legal definition of "terrorism" and no universally agreed-upon list of terrorist groups.[30] And any listing of what acts "terrorists" might commit with either conventional or unconventional weapons is certain to be incomplete.

As the mere existence of the CT Calendar demonstrates, the word "terrorism" is not always equally understood by those who use it and those who hear it. "Terrorism" actually is a kind of jargon. Lots of institutions, from governments to the military to international organizations, have developed their own gobbledygook, sometimes to simplify their own bureaucratic paper-shuffling, but at times also to obfuscate their actions to an outside audience. In the lexicon of the United Nations, for example, there is something called "bluespeak," the UN's in-house term for the careful phrasings of their diplomats. So, over the last several decades or so, we have heard generally about "peacekeeping" missions, and learned specifically about "armed humanitarian interventions" in Somalia and "safe havens" in Bosnia.

Jargon used to be what insiders used to communicate complicated ideas to each other. Jargon has become a way to gloss over the intolerable and unspeakable. We have become familiar with hearing about "collateral damage" when what is meant is that civilians were killed, "surgical strikes" when what is meant is that a target was completely obliterated, and "renditions" when what is meant is that terrorist suspects were captured and clandestinely shipped to another country for interrogation and torture. We've come to learn about "sleep management," which sounds like a way to handle insomnia, but is a form of torture that deprives a prisoner of sleep for a hundred hours or so. Then there's "water-boarding," which is not something that one does while wearing a Hawaiian shirt, and "stress positions," which are not a rigorous form of yoga.

These bits of jargon are euphemisms—a way to speak abstractly about situations that are not at all abstract, and a way to give a certain veneer of disinterestedness and neutrality to what can be a far from neutral policy.

It's a brave new world of spin. Jargon allows its users to take a word and have it mean something else—something that suits the user of the jargon. Sometimes both the speaker and the listener know the meaning, and the use of jargon is an inside joke of sorts. Sometimes the point of jargon is to confuse the listener.

"Terrorism" is that latter kind of "confusing" jargon. When you hear politicians or journalists use the word "terrorism," stop and think about what they are really saying.

"Terrorism" and "terrorist" often have little "real" meaning—they are instead political epithets. When used, they can confuse more than illuminate a political event or environment—especially because politicians and media only rarely explain that "terrorism" is a contested concept and that the language used to make the moral case on terrorism is typically loaded. A month and a half before September 11, 2001, reporter Cameron Barr of the *Christian Science Monitor* wrote that "perhaps no word in modern political usage is more controversial than 'terrorism.' The United Nations spent 17 years trying to come up with a universally accepted definition, and failed."[31] One study discovered 109 different definitions of the word.[32]

What is contested about the definition? The international community has not be able to reach agreement on a common definition of "terrorism" for two main reasons.

First, some governments have had little interest in closely defining it, preferring either to keep the definition vague or to only proscribe certain actions. Is terrorism the act only of "non-state actors"—in other words, the terrorists aren't part of a government in power? Or can "states" practice terrorism? Some nations have committed acts that have been considered the moral equivalent of terrorism—the American dropping of atomic bombs on Hiroshima and Nagasaki is often cited as a case where a government deliberately targeted a civilian population. Other states have sponsored terrorism abroad or given safe haven to external groups that commit terrorist acts abroad such as the Taliban Afghan government's support for Al Qaeda. Many international analysts are loath to lump "state" terrorism, which they believe is generally driven by foreign policy concerns, together with the terrorism conducted by "non-state" groups that have entirely different motivations. This, then, is a point of contention in the definition.

A second issue is that many governments are flatly unwilling to define terrorism at all because they are concerned with how a formal definition would reflect on the legitimacy of self-proclaimed wars of national liberation.[33] "In some countries, the word [terrorist] has become almost synonymous with 'political opponent,'" William Schulz, executive director of Amnesty International, has said. "The Chinese, for example, consider peaceful Tibetan Buddhists vicious terrorists; Robert Mugabe regards the democratic opposition in Zimbabwe in a similar vein."[34] In fact when governments claim that an individual or a group has engaged in terrorism it can be an attempt by that government to try and stake out the moral high ground for itself.

The political definition of terrorism directs both government policy on terrorism and how government sells its policy to its citizens. The definition of terrorism leads inexorably to the packaging of it. Three questions loom large:

1 Is terrorism a tactic or an ideology?
2 Is an act of terror a "crime" or an "an act of war"?

3   Much terrorism crosses nation-state lines. Can outside states forcibly, pre-
    emptively intrude in a country to stop what they think is terrorism?

Let us take those questions one by one.

1   The Definition Matters

The argument for terrorism as a "tactic"

Historically, experts from think tanks and universities have focused on tactics
as the defining element of terrorism. Focusing on tactics and means allows for
a culturally neutral conversation about terrorism and the ways to confront it.
"Terrorism is not a movement, terrorism is not a state, terrorism is a tactic," affirmed
British academic and former foreign correspondent Anatol Lieven.[35]

On one hand, "Terrorism" is a method of engaging an enemy, one of a long list
of tactics that includes such familiar military practices as land-mining a territory,
strategic bombing or guerrilla warfare, as the NCTC Daily Planner outlines. But
what sets terrorism apart from even other forms of political violence such as
guerrilla warfare are three key factors:

1   Terrorism deliberately targets civilians.
2   The victims and the intended audience of a terrorist act are not the same.
3   The psychological impact of a terrorist act is intended to be greater than the
    physical damage caused. The goal of terrorism is to send a message, not defeat
    the enemy.[36]

Let me repeat that last point. The goal of terrorism is to send a message, not
defeat the enemy. Wars have historically been about gaining territory. Terrorism
is about getting the public's attention. It is that last factor that has changed the
post-9/11 world. On September 11, the entire world, through the marvels of both
old and new media, became eyewitness to the deaths of 3,000 people.[37] After
September 11, "terrorism" was no longer some rather ordinary event that killed
a few random people with quiet and depressing regularity in such places as
Northern Ireland or Indonesia or Israel. Terrorism could now be catastrophic—
and be part of the active conversation across the globe.

The whole world could be sent a message.[38]

Terrorism as a technique—the deliberate targeting of civilians—is a violation
of every religious tradition as well as a violation of both domestic and international
law—some crimes of terrorism are so serious that they are considered international

crimes: piracy, aggression, torture, war crimes, genocide, crimes against humanity.[39] But historian Walter Laqueur, who fled the Nazis and lost his parents to the Holocaust, noted in his book *Terrorism* that "it is not the magnitude of the terrorist operation that counts, but the publicity." The terrorist is inseparable from his or her beholder.[40]

Laqueur and others note that terrorism is more than simple violence which requires only two parties, the perpetrator and the victim. Terrorism needs a third party; it needs an audience. That understanding of terrorism and terrorists crosses professional bounds. Reporter Melvin Maddocks has argued, "A terrorist without an audience is inconceivable."[41] And Rand terrorism expert Brian Michael Jenkins famously wrote: "Terrorism is theater."

> What sets terrorism apart from other violence is this: terrorism consists of acts carried out in a dramatic way to attract publicity and create an atmosphere of alarm that goes far beyond the actual victims. Indeed, the identity of the victims is often secondary or irrelevant to the terrorists who aim their violence at the people watching.[42]

In the wake of September 11, media outlets in the United States noted that while terrorism had long been part of the international news repertoire, the coverage of the World Trade Center bombing had brought terrorism to the country in a way that even the Oklahoma City bombing had not. The planes that struck the Twin Towers in New York City, the media capital of the world, were timed so that when the second plane hit, every news program on the planet that wanted to could have run the pictures from the cameras already trained on them. And the TV cameras were still running live images when first one, then the other building imploded, with all the loss of life that their collapse implied. Terrorism live, terrorism conducted explicitly so the whole world could watch was different than an act where the intent was simply to destroy something or someone. It was clear that Al Qaeda wanted the world to watch. The tactics of catastrophic terrorism and the technology that allowed media to cover the breaking story live fed the terrorists' agenda of attracting global attention. It wasn't just the deaths of thousands that terrified us, it was that those deaths were packaged so that we all became witnesses to them.

"Terrorism isn't about violence," insisted Baroness O'Neill, a crossbench member of the House of Lords and a former professor of philosophy at Cambridge. "Yes, most terrorists use violence but what it's ultimately about is terror, intimidation. We talk about the victims of terror and we mean that, whether on 11 September or some other time, the real victims of terror are the people who have survived and who are intimidated in one way or another."[43]

We all are the victims of terror.

The argument for terrorism as an "ideology"

Post-9/11 a number of media outlets took it upon themselves to give their audiences a hasty education in the history of terror. Most of these efforts focused on the *actions* of terrorists in the past, rather than on the way in which terrorists throughout history have *publicized* their actions. "The word originated during the French Revolution when enemies of the state were guillotined in the Reign of Terror," reporter Jim Auchmutey reminded the readers of the *Atlanta Journal and Constitution*. " 'Those hellhounds called terrorists . . . are let loose on the people,' 'British politician Edmund Burke wrote in one of the earliest usages cited by the Oxford English Dictionary.' "[44]

But what few media early made clear was that the "terroristes" of the French Revolution weren't the insurgents of their day, they weren't the rebels—they were the government. Finally, in the fall of 2007, historian François Furstenberg bluntly educated Americans in a *New York Times* op-ed:

> If the French Terror had a slogan, it was that attributed to the great orator Louis de Saint-Just: "No liberty for the enemies of liberty." Saint-Just's pithy phrase (like President Bush's variant, "We must not let foreign enemies use the forums of liberty to destroy liberty itself") could serve as the very antithesis of the Western liberal tradition.
>
> On this principle, the Terror demonized its political opponents, imprisoned suspected enemies without trial and eventually sent thousands to the guillotine. All of these actions emerged from the Jacobin worldview that the enemies of liberty deserved no rights.
>
> Though it has been a topic of much attention in recent years, the origin of the term "terrorist" has gone largely unnoticed by politicians and pundits alike. The word was an invention of the French Revolution, and it referred not to those who hate freedom, nor to non-state actors, nor of course to "Islamofascism."
>
> A terroriste was, in its original meaning, a Jacobin leader who ruled France during la Terreur.[45]

What mattered, in Furstenberg's estimation, was how completely the Jacobin leaders dominated the political conversation in France. Those who opposed their way of thinking had to be destroyed—intellectually and physically. Alternative ideologies were anathema to those government "terroristes." The effect was to create not just a tyranny of ideology, but a terrorism of ideology. The Jacobin leaders didn't bother with fancy packaging of their ideas. The selling point was that it was fatal to dissent.

Following "le Terreur," other political groups adopted the terminology. Geoff Nunberg, on NPR's *Fresh Air*, traced the meanings through time:

For the next 150 years, the word "terrorism" led a double life. A justified political strategy to some; an abomination to others. The Russian revolutionaries who assassinated Czar Alexander II in 1881 used the word proudly. And in 1905, Jack London described terrorism as a powerful weapon in the hands of labor, though he warned against harming innocent people. . . . By the mid 20th century, terrorism was becoming associated more with movements of national liberation than with radical groups and the word was starting to acquire its universal stigma . . . most of the Third World movements that resorted to political violence in the 1950s and 1960s didn't call themselves terrorists. They preferred terms like freedom fighters or guerrillas or mujahaddin. Terrorism became a condemnation, a word used only by the colonial powers. That's the point when news organizations like Reuters started to become circumspect about using the word to describe groups like the IRA and the African National Congress. It seemed to be picking sides and perhaps a little imprudent, particularly when you consider that former terrorists like Nelson Mandela and Menachem Begin had ended their careers as winners of the Nobel [Peace] Prize.

By the 1980s, terrorism was being widely applied to all manners of political violence . . . [and] the word "terrorism" had acquired a kind of talismanic force, as if refusing to describe something as terrorism was the next thing to apologizing for it.[46]

By the end of the twentieth century, therefore, "terrorism" had already been long identified as an ideology synonymous with "evil," and was dissociated from any specific beliefs or goals. The scale and the inhuman impunity of the September 11 attack only served to solidify that sense held by many that what defined "terrorists" was their crazed, single-minded commitment to a generic ideology of hate and fear. In a speech in Washington in August 2004, US National Security Advisor Condoleezza Rice articulated the Bush administration's understanding of the post-9/11 world:

Since the beginning of the war on terror, the President has recognized that the war on terror is as much a conflict of visions as a conflict of arms. One terrorist put it succinctly. He said, "You love life, we love death." True victory will come not merely when the terrorists are defeated by force, but when the ideology of death and hatred is overcome by the appeal of life and hope, and when lies are replaced by truth.[47]

The choice of the tactics used by "terrorists" was seen to be of secondary importance to the terrorists' dogma of "death and hatred." The world aligned up according to who shared that doctrine and who didn't. The clash of civilizations, the "conflict of visions," the us-versus-them attitude that President Bush had challenged the world with in the weeks following the World Trade Center attack remained: "You're either with us or against us in the fight against terror."[48] The Bush administration "sold" its policies to the world by defining its position in opposition to that of the generic "terrorists": You can't agree with the terrorist's belief system, so you must come on board with us.

Indeed, even late in the fall of 2007, on the homepage of the White House's website a prominent box outlined the President's policy in the "Global War on Terror": "President Bush's top priority is the safety and security of the American people. Though America and its allies are safer since 9/11, we are not yet safe. We have important challenges ahead as we wage a long-term battle not just against terrorists, but against the ideology that supports their agenda."[49]

And the problem with defining "terrorism" as an ideology is?

"Terrorism" is often used both intentionally and unintentionally to muddle distinct causes and acts into one singular problem. In Rice's definition of terrorism as an ideology there were no distinctions made among any terrorist individuals, groups, or states. That's a problem. When terrorists are talked about as a monolithic enemy rather than as distinctive actors looking to achieve specific political ends, when terrorists are portrayed as brainwashed religious fanatics not as rational political actors, terrorism seems inexplicable.[50] Terrorists must be defined narrowly if there's any hope of understanding them.

This is a key consequence for defining all terrorism as an ideology dedicated to death and hatred. When a government, say, calls someone or some group a "terrorist" the government has limited how it and others can deal with that person or group. Governments don't—or can't, in political terms—negotiate with terrorists; nor do accused terrorists have any incentive to negotiate if all their actions are declared to be war crimes. Further, if governments claim that the accused are not only "terrorists" but are evil, they make it difficult for any players in the civilized community of nations to engage with them. And even attempts to explain the "terrorists'" possible motivations "may be viewed as tacit acceptance of what is judged to be pernicious and reprehensible," as Sean Anderson and Stephen Sloan, authors of the *Historical Dictionary of Terrorism*, have noted.[51]

But those consequences may be desirable—a government may want an individual or group to be isolated from the world community. If an individual or group is seen and treated as a pariah, then the government making that claim is advantaged. "If one party can successfully attach the label terrorist to its opponent, then it has indirectly persuaded others to adopt its moral viewpoint," Rand's public policy expert Brian Michael Jenkins noted.[52] And there are other reasons for a government to emphasize the ideological fervor of terrorists. Doing so helps to legitimate an at least equal, but opposite, moral fervor on the side of the "good guys"—a "crusade" as the President briefly called his "War on Terror."[53]

But such didactic language causes terrorism experts to tear their hair out. When Bush and Blair spoke about terror as the "evil in plain sight," experts argue, it played directly into Al Qaeda's agenda.[54] "Apocalyptic language is the language on which fundamentalism prospers. It is rooted," noted British academic Jacqueline Rose, "in a fear; but it also thrives on the prospect of annihilation. So we have to think very carefully about what we're doing by using this vocabulary."[55]

Clearly the Bush administration thought about it. Much of the force of President Bush's sales pitch came from his use of strident, almost apocalyptic, terms. This is what he said in Washington in the fall of 2006:

> The terrorists who attacked us on September the 11th, 2001, are men without conscience—but they're not madmen. They kill in the name of a clear and focused ideology, a set of beliefs that are evil, but not insane. These al Qaeda terrorists and those who share their ideology are violent Sunni extremists. They're driven by a radical and perverted vision of Islam that rejects tolerance, crushes all dissent, and justifies the murder of innocent men, women and children in the pursuit of political power. They hope to establish a violent political utopia across the Middle East, which they call a "Caliphate"—where all would be ruled according to their hateful ideology. Osama bin Laden has called the 9/11 attacks—in his words—"a great step towards the unity of Muslims and establishing the Righteous . . . [Caliphate]."[56]

The words the President used to describe the terrorists' motivations—"evil," "violent," "perverted," "hateful"—may be the truth, at least as most define those words. But what President Bush was doing in this speech was framing a broad swathe of terrorist groups in ways that demonized them as one collective enemy—"men without a conscience . . . beliefs that are evil"—which effectively precluded any American actions not directed at absolute victory over terrorism writ large.[57]

"Far from trying to educate the public, U.S. leaders played to their fears," observed Louise Richardson, dean of the Radcliffe Institute for Advanced Study. "Rather than attempting to put the terrible atrocity of 9/11 into perspective, it fanned the outrage. Rather than countenance the possibility that certain of its actions might have fueled resentment toward it, it divided the world into good and evil, and those who were not with the United States were with the terrorists."[58]

The irony, as a number of observers have noted, is that Bush and Blair used the same cosmic, divisive terms as Osama bin Laden. In a public roundtable discussion hosted by the *London Review of Books*, Jacqueline Rose asked her colleagues: "If I just give you a few quotations I want you to guess who says which one. 'A wind of change is blowing to remove evil from the peninsula.' 'The ways of the wicked will not prosper.' 'Those who promote evil will be defeated.' 'Out of terror will come good.' 'The shadow of evil will be followed by good in the world.' 'We will either be defeated or we will defeat.' Now the point is that one of those is Osama bin Laden, one of them is Tony Blair and one of them is Ariel Sharon, and they share a vocabulary."[59]

Terrorist recruitment is changing, and when politicians use polarizing, ideological language, those who already feel marginalized may become further radicalized. "Officials worldwide have been preoccupied for more than two years by a fear of terror groups consisting of 'self-starters'—men who become radicalized on their own and decide to conduct operations without the support of an extremist network, or with only tenuous connections," noted the *Chicago Tribune* in a 2006 article. "Instead of taking orders from al-Qaida leaders, these terrorists act on what they believe is al-Qaida's behalf. Although bin Laden has always seen the incitement of terrorism as one of his primary roles, al-Qaida has been viewed for the past couple of years as more of a global ideology than an actual terror network. The March 11, 2004 synchronized bombings of trains at the height of rush hour in Madrid, attacks that left 192 people dead, were generally viewed as the first significant such assault."[60]

"Which is the greater threat: terrorism, or our reaction against it?" asked political scientist John Mueller. "A threat that is real but likely to prove to be of limited scope has been massively, perhaps even fancifully, inflated to produce widespread and unjustified anxiety."[61] Those fears were founded on the new kind of terrorism brought to American shores, but they were stoked by the choices that the Bush administration made to emphasize ideology over tactics and heightened by an emotionally charged political rhetoric.

And the advantage of defining "terrorism" as an ideology is?

There are, of course, advantages to considering the ideology of terrorism as its defining element. One advantage is that doing so can help distinguish terrorism from organized crime, which is generally driven by financial or material benefit —although there are many who consider violent drug traffickers such as the Medellín cartel and their counterparts in Afghanistan and eastern China to be terrorists.

Others define terrorism in ideological terms because, like Irish politician Conor Cruise O'Brien, they believe terrorism can only occur in a democratic state.[62] In a democratic state, opponents of the government can work within the political process. If actors choose to use violence instead of the ballot box, they are terrorists. By that argument members of the IRA were terrorists because they had political options open to them in Northern Ireland but decided not to use them, while members of the ANC, who were fighting the apartheid regime in South Africa, were not terrorists (even though President P. W. Botha called them so) because blacks were excluded from the political process.

But claiming that kind of division not only forces one to ignore the fact that the ANC committed acts that killed innocents, but strains the consideration of other global cases even more. "I don't think that [approach is] very helpful," Harvard professor Louise Richardson has noted, "because in a sense it means that the Basque ETA in Spain were *not* terrorists when they blew up tourists under Franco, but *were* terrorists when they continued to blow up tourists under the democratic regime."[63]

Emphasizing tactics prompts a more "neutral" consideration of events, while emphasizing ideology stresses any divisions without offering ways to bridge them. Focusing on tactics helps keep moral valuations out of the condemnation of given acts. Focusing on ideology actively raises the question of when violence can be "justified."[64] There might very well be general agreement that members of the French Resistance were justified in attacking the Nazis in Paris, but defending violence can get very sticky, Harvard terrorism expert Jessica Stern has cautioned. "Every terrorist I have interviewed has told me he is certain his ends are just . . . the justness of terrorists' ends is inherently subjective. If we focus on the means, we run into a lot less trouble."[65]

For those reasons, many of the terrorism experts are perfectly happy to put the question of whether violence is ever justified off to the side of the debate. Everyone can get caught up in it, and everyone can get tripped up by it because there is no agreement about it.

Who has the right to say what is just? The US military learned this lesson when it tried to sell the initial phase of the post-9/11 war against the Taliban by calling it "Operation Infinite Justice." It quickly shelved the name in favor of "Operation Enduring Freedom" when Muslim Americans protested that only Allah renders infinite justice.

2   Is an Act of Terror a "Crime" or an "Act of War"?

We have reached a critical moment in the war on terror. Sorry, let me rephrase that, we have reached a critical moment in our efforts to counter the terrorist threat. No. We are at an important juncture in the continuing process of countering Islamism . . . no . . . Islamic militancy . . . er . . . modern Muslim radicalism . . . Al Qaeda . . . no, make that Al Qaeda-inspired violence . . . er . . . on second thoughts . . .

What are we fighting? Who are we fighting against?

"The semantics of the post-9/11 era have never been easy," as Jason Burke, author of *Al Qaeda: The True Story of Radical Islam*, wrote in a column in the *Observer* shortly before the sixth anniversary of September 11. "The battle fought to ensure a language that more or less accurately describes the phenomenon that we have seen emerging in recent years . . . is far from over . . . but as language often determines thoughts and, thus, policies, it is an essential process . . . It is a counterterrorist effort as valuable as any other."[66]

The terms used to describe the "War on Terror" were set early on by President George W. Bush, and repeated—sometimes blindly, sometimes with caveats—by media. Then, three years after announcing his "War," the President revisited the terminology. On August 6, 2004, he spoke to 7,000 members of the media attending the "Unity: Journalists of Color" convention in downtown Washington, DC. In response to a question from the floor asking "What is the mission at this point" for the American forces in Iraq, the President tried to define his declared "War on Terror": "We actually misnamed the 'war on terror,'" he said. "It ought to be the—'the struggle against ideological extremists who do not believe in free societies, who happen to use terror as a weapon, to try to shake the conscious [sic] of the free world.'"[67] "Or, if you prefer to abbreviate," as reporter Dana Milbank of the *Washington Post* noted in his article covering the speech, "SAIEWDNBIFSWHTUTAAWTTTSTCOTFW."[68]

While people all over the world guffawed at this new Bushism, others noted that there was real news embedded in this longer and unwieldy moniker—the Bush administration was beginning to take at least passing note of the many legal experts and most of the international community who were unhappy with the use of the word "war."[69]

Most commentators rightly link the language used in the debate on terrorism to the policy about terrorism.[70] Redefining terms has the power to shift not only the focus of the debate but the response to questions that arise. Think about my human rights study, outlined above. If human rights is about "war, torture and killing" as my journalist said, then no one's going to pay much attention to the struggle waged about Pakistan's sweatshops. If human rights is about "duty and communitarianism" as my activist said, then it is unlikely that bankers are going to feel that they need to get professionally engaged in an Amnesty International letter campaign. Defining one's terms matters. So when the Bush administration briefly attempted in 2005 to rename the conflict the "Global Struggle against Violent Extremism" or when many in the US armed forces came to call the effort a "global counterinsurgency," political and military opportunities changed. David Kilcullen, an Australian lieutenant colonel "on loan" to the US government, put the reason for the US military's attempt to shift the name simply: a terrorist is "a kook in a room" who is beyond persuasion, an insurgent "has a mass base whose support can be won or lost through politics."[71]

One of the few to make an early comment on the President's choice of words was Anne-Marie Slaughter, the dean of the Woodrow Wilson School at Princeton University. "From a legal perspective, the difference between calling what has happened war and calling it terrorism is considerable," she wrote in the

Washington Post the Sunday after 9/11. "Terrorism is a matter for the courts and prosecutors. War is up to our military forces. But which best describes what we face now?"[72] So that was one question—a definitional one. But as Slaughter, a lawyer, recognized, some definitions come with consequences. And the differences between calling something a "war" and calling it "terrorism" have legal consequences.

"I've increasingly come not to just dislike, but to fear that expression," said Peter Goldsmith, Attorney General of England and Wales from 2001 to 2007. "If you talk about a people as engaged in a 'War on Terror' you risk not only dignifying their cause, you risk treating them as soldiers and not as criminals." He continued:

> [As] a legal diagnosis . . . a "War on Terror" justifies two things: first of all it justifies detaining people until this amorphous war comes to an end—and who is going to say when it has? When do you determine when a war on a tactic has come to an end? Because "terror" is not a person. It's not a country. It's not even a group— "a war on al Qaeda." It's war on a tactic. And secondly, because it is said to be a "war" . . . the decisions about how to conduct the war are for the executive (i.e. the president) to determine.[73]

One key problem with the phrase "War on Terror" is that it *does* have specific legal meaning distinct from its rhetorical power. "By literalizing its 'war' on terror," agreed Human Rights Watch director Kenneth Roth, "the Bush administration has broken down the distinction between what is permissible in times of peace and what can be condoned during a war."[74]

So the President's phrase, which to many Americans in September 2001 seemed a stirring statement of the commitment the United States would bring to its confrontation with the terrorists, actually went far beyond a rhetorical call to arms to become a blueprint for an American military engagement first in Afghanistan and then in Iraq.

That's where the problems started to arise, because as analyst Grenville Byford explained in his famous 2002 article in *Foreign Affairs* magazine, there's one more very, very simple problem with the phrase. A "War on Terror" is not a militarily realistic option:

> Wars have typically been fought against proper nouns (Germany, say) for the good reason that proper nouns can surrender and promise not to do it again. Wars against common nouns (poverty, crime, drugs) have been less successful. Such opponents never give up. The war on terrorism, unfortunately, falls into the second category.[75]

One can easily see why calling something a "war" so armed forces could get involved would be attractive—especially because the executive branch of government—the

President—retains much of the control of those operations. But calling something a "war" that's not winnable seems a very short-term strategy. Sooner or later, you're going to get caught out.

And there were additional complaints about the phrase—these in keeping with the concerns expressed about terrorism as an ideology. If you call something a "War on Terror" and are sufficiently vague about just who the terrorists are— such that many Muslims the world over feel themselves to be that "enemy"—it's hard to convince some of that group that you actually want them on your side. But defining terrorism as a tactic leaves more opportunity to create alliances—all you have to do is find a connection around mutual distaste for terrorist acts.

This was the shift that the UK has tried to negotiate. In December 2006, with Prime Minister Tony Blair still in power, the British Foreign Office told cabinet ministers to drop the phrase "War on Terror." In fact, neither Blair nor Margaret Beckett, Blair's Foreign Secretary, had used the term "War on Terror" in a formal speech since June 2006. In the aftermath of the London bombing on July 7, 2005, British intelligence became increasingly concerned about the radicalization of British Muslims, not only about the existence of terrorists "over there" some- where. The use of "extreme" terms such as "War on Terror" allowed militants at home and abroad, British intelligence believed, to use the sense of war and the "clash of civilizations" to recruit supporters.[76] "The whole aim of terrorism is to get us to overreact," observed Harvard expert Jessica Stern.[77]

After that July 2005 attack, the distinctions between American and British approaches to terrorism widened. Whereas the Americans continued to speak about a "war" that would defeat the aberrant ideology of terrorists, the British began talking about the "crimes" that were committed and the need to discover "shared values" with the communities in which terrorists operate. When, in December 2006, the Foreign Office phased out the use of the phrase "War on Terror," its explana- tion, according to a spokesperson, was that "We tend to emphasise upholding shared values as a means to counter terrorists."[78] Months later, after Gordon Brown became prime minister in 2007, and after the failed terrorist attacks in Glasgow and London, Brown said the words "Muslim" or "Islam" were to be avoided as well. Noted Home Secretary Jacqui Smith, "Let us be clear—terrorists are criminals, whose victims come from all walks of life, communities and religions. Terrorists attack the values shared by all law-abiding citizens. As a Government, as communities, as individuals, we need to ensure that the message of the terrorists is rejected."[79] This new approach rejected the knee-jerk reaction to respond to terrorism with force, and instead committed to a process, that, in Louise Richardson's words, "is more intangible, is likely to take a long time to produce results, appears to reward those close to the terrorists, and insufficiently repudiates the evil of the atrocity."[80] It is, however, the only method of confronting terrorists likely to achieve a measure of success.

You can see how the British government eventually came around to selecting that method. But it's equally clear why, in the immediate aftermath of 9/11, such a moderated approach had little appeal. That approach would have hardly achieved all of the foreign policy goals of President Bush—and those of Prime Minister Blair who joined him. Aggressive military action, as was befitting in a "war," seemed the obvious choice. It was only after that method essentially failed to halt terrorism, after the war in Iraq became so bloody, and after Brown became prime minister, that considering a terrorist act to be a crime, not a battle in a larger war, became, for Britain at least, a more politically palatable step.

Shortly after the 2007 Glasgow and London attacks, the Brown government began to put resources into community policing, where crime prevention is based on authorities and citizens sharing an interest in the security and the health of their neighborhoods. By Brown's emphasizing the criminality of terrorism, as David Rieff has noted, "he effectively changed the terms (and temperature) of the British debate: he redefined a world historical threat as a manageable danger."[81] The "War on Terror" had led the Bush administration to focus on military responses and a search for victory and surrender. The language of warfare argues the need for immediate combat and an all-out effort. The language of crime raises images of police, law, the courts and a deliberative legal process that results in a verdict of guilt or innocence. Focusing on crime opened a way for the British authorities to consider solutions that would be unacceptable against an "enemy." Emphasizing crime allows local authorities to play a larger role and gives communities the responsibility for the terrorism in their midst: How do they stop those terrorists? How do they break the cycle of terrorism?

But on the other side of the Atlantic, in the United States, little changed during the second four years of the George W. Bush administration. By 2008, only months before the presidential election, the administration had tinkered with the language the State Department and other federal officials used to refer to terrorists, but expressed no significant second thoughts on the "War on Terror" itself. In a report circulated by Homeland Security, federal officials were counseled not to use the terms "jihadists," "mujahedeen" and "Islamofascism." Using such words, the report said, results in "unintentionally portraying terrorists, who lack moral and religious legitimacy, as brave fighters, legitimate soldiers or spokesmen for ordinary Muslims." Another similar document, titled *Words That Work and Words That Don't: A Guide to Counterterrorism Communication*, written by the Extremist Messaging Branch of the NCTC, observed "Don't compromise our credibility" by using language that "may ascribe benign motives to terrorists." Noted the Associated Press, which obtained the documents, "At least at the top level, it appears to have made an impact. Secretary of State Condoleezza Rice, who once frequently referred to 'jihad' in her public remarks, does not appear to have used the word . . . since last September."[82]

The two US documents mirrored those government memos that circulated in Britain and the European Union the year before, following protests from local Muslim communities about the way in which the "War on Terror" was being represented and recognition from the intelligence services that using such terminology actually damaged counterterrorism efforts. But the Bush administration, unlike its European counterparts, did not reappraise either the phrase "War on Terror" or its fundamental assessment of the war—even after the government and military's packaging of the conflict had been repeatedly exposed. First there was the revelation of the WMD intelligence failures in Iraq. Then there were repeated challenges that the war was being misrepresented: as *Nightline* anchor Terry Moran wondered in a live shot with a reporter in Baghdad following the 2006 attack on the Golden Dome mosque in Iraq: "Kimberly, I'm going to go out—back to what this Army spokesman is saying when he says that the Army does not sense that the people of Iraq have any heightened sense of 'unsecurity,' as he called it. I mean, how can somebody say that with what is going on there? Do you get the sense that he was saying what he had been told to say on orders from above?"[83] And then there was the *New York Times* exposé in April 2008 of the Pentagon's six-year campaign to cultivate several dozen military analysts as "surrogates" to deliver the administration's "themes and messages" on terrorism during literally tens of thousands US television and radio appearances.[84]

Although in the latter case the Pentagon announced after the *New York Times'* disclosures that it was suspending its private high-level briefings for the retired military analysts, the Bush White House admitted no failures and stayed on message. A spokesman for the State Department had already declared that there was no question of dropping the phrase "War on Terror": "It's the President's phrase, and that's good enough for us."[85]

3   Is Pre-emption an Acceptable Method of Stopping Terrorism?

How many terrorists are there in the world?

At last count, there were 325,000 on the American master list put together from reports supplied by the CIA, the FBI, the National Security Agency (NSA), and other international agencies.

But, actually, the number may not be exactly 325,000 terrorists. Officials have admitted that the same person may appear on different lists under different spellings or aliases, so the number may be closer to 200,000. And those on the master list are not actually all "terrorists," but rather "international terrorism suspects or people who allegedly aid them."[86] But there *might* be 325,000 terrorists out there. Or more. Who really knows?

Yet just knowing that there are terrorists out there—or suspected or alleged terrorists out there—raises the question of what governments should do about them. How do you stop terrorists?

On August 14, 2004, US Vice President Richard Cheney, on the campaign re-election trail in Nevada, bluntly stated the White House's assessment of what needed to be done in the "Global War on Terror":

> Today we face an enemy every bit as determined to destroy us as the Axis powers in World War II, or the Soviet Union during the Cold War. . . . [A]s we saw on the morning of 9/11, this enemy is perfectly prepared to slaughter anyone—man, woman, or child—who stands in the way. This is not an enemy we can reason with, or negotiate with, or appease. This is, to put it quite simply, an enemy that we must destroy. . . . September 11th showed us, as surely as anything can, that we must act against gathering dangers—not wait to be attacked. That awful day left some 3,000 of our fellow citizens dead, and everything we have learned since tells us the terrorists would do worse if they could, that they will use chemical, biological, or even nuclear weapons against us of they can.[87]

Cheney, one of the Bush administration's key architects of the "War on Terror," was the most impassioned defender of the White House's broad doctrine of pre-emption—a policy well beyond a doctrine of self-defense. Cheney and President Bush's comparison of the "War on Terror" to World War II and the Cold War made the case that the "war" must be won by any means necessary —to fail to do so would be to repeat the mistakes of the nations that tried to appease Hitler in the 1930s.[88] "History teaches that underestimating the words of evil and ambitious men is a terrible mistake," said President Bush in a major speech from Washington in late 2006 in which he reasserted the doctrine of pre-emption.

> In the early 1900s, an exiled lawyer in Europe published a pamphlet called "What Is To Be Done?"—in which he laid out his plan to launch a communist revolution in Russia. The world did not heed Lenin's words, and paid a terrible price. The Soviet Empire he established killed tens of millions, and brought the world to the brink of thermonuclear war. In the 1920s, a failed Austrian painter published a book in which he explained his intention to build an Aryan super-state in Germany and take revenge on Europe and eradicate the Jews. The world ignored Hitler's words, and paid a terrible price. His Nazi regime killed millions in the gas chambers, and set the world aflame in war, before it was finally defeated at a terrible cost in lives.
>
> Bin Laden and his terrorist allies have made their intentions as clear as Lenin and Hitler before them. The question is: Will we listen? Will we pay attention to what these evil men say? America and our coalition partners have made our choice. We're taking the words of the enemy seriously. We're on the offensive, and we will not rest, we will not retreat, and we will not withdraw from the fight, until this threat to civilization has been removed.[89]

Cheney in his campaign address and Bush in his speech over two years later underscored the terrorist targeting of innocent civilians, the great numbers of those killed, and above all, the ultimate security of America: If the terrorists are "determined to destroy us," "we" need to not just react but to take the "offensive" to stop terrorists' "threat to civilization." Pre-emption, in short, was a military necessity when nations were faced with the horror of a new Hitler or Lenin who could marshal the destructive power of weapons of mass destruction.

In the face of biological, chemical, or nuclear weapons, pre-emption could appear as a reasonable strategy and a war against Iraq could be justified and sold. As President Bush's carrier speech on May 1, 2003 defended the decision to go to war: "The liberation of Iraq is a crucial advance in the campaign against terror. We've removed an ally of al Qaeda, and cut off a source of terrorist funding. And this much is certain: No terrorist network will gain weapons of mass destruction from the Iraqi regime, because the regime is no more."[90] Homeland Security Secretary Tom Ridge underlined that argument when he moved the US terror alert up to Orange later that same month. Ridge noted that, while there was no specific threat against the US that had prompted the heightened status, "weapons of mass destruction, including those containing chemical, biological or radiological agents or materials, cannot be discounted."[91]

The endgame argument seemed compelling—only a few questioned the line of reasoning. One who did was Louise Richardson, who in early 2002 observed that "four [now five] people have died of anthrax and we have 285 million people in this country terrified. The fact that 20,000 people will die of flu this year is having much less impact. This demonstrates that terrorism is a very effective tactic of the weak against the strong, and shows that it's here to stay—precisely because it is such an effective tactic in sowing fear."[92]

The doctrine of pre-emption became politically viable because of that fear. It did not gain the equivalent moral authority, however, as a policy founded on strict self-defense. Other Western world leaders, in fact, not only rejected the necessity of a pre-emptive doctrine, but argued that implementation of the doctrine would itself overset the rule of law. And following the inability of troops in Iraq to find the weapons of mass destruction that were used as part of the rationale for going to war, talk against the doctrine of pre-emption grew blunt. At the opening of the UN General Assembly session in 2004, Secretary General Kofi Annan said that "unilateralism and the doctrine of pre-emption represented 'a fundamental challenge' to the principles on which world peace and stability have rested since 1945, and threatened to set precedents resulting in a proliferation of the 'lawless use of force, with or without justification.'" French President Jacques Chirac argued similarly: "In an open world, no one can live in isolation, no one can act alone in the name of all, and no one can accept the anarchy of a society without rules." Multilateralism, said Chirac, is the "guarantee of legitimacy and democracy in matters regarding the use of force."[93]

In an ideal world, the American President's role in times of international crisis is to establish the parameters of that crisis, to shape and direct the understanding of events, and to give dimension to the issues at stake. With luck, the President can propose action that is in proportion and that appeals to "the better angels of our nature," as President Abraham Lincoln hoped for in his first inaugural address on the eve of the American Civil War.

But most of the world argued that the pre-emptive war proposed and initiated by the Bush administration was neither in proportion to terrorists' threats nor appealed to "the better angels of our nature"—especially when the grounds were based on false evidence. "On Wednesday, President Bush finally got around to acknowledging that there was no connection between Saddam Hussein and the terrorist attacks of Sept 11, 2001," said a *New York Times* lead editorial in September 2003. "White House aides will tell you that Mr. Bush never made that charge directly. And that is so. But polls show that lots of Americans believe in the link. That is at least in part because the president's aides have left the implication burning." Why was that implication left "burning"? "Recent polls suggest that the American public is not as enthusiastic about making sacrifices to help the Iraqis as about making sacrifices to protect the United States against terrorism. The temptation to hint at a connection with Sept. 11 that did not exist must have been tremendous."[94]

Commentators in the press noted that not every terrorist attack can be prevented, but a nation's reactions to those that occur should be controlled. Pre-emption, which had started out as an argument for neutralizing terrorists before they could act, had been ultimately employed against a state that, while led by a dictator later tried and executed for crimes against humanity, was neither allied to the 9/11 terrorists nor had stocks of weapons of mass destruction. Pre-emption upset the moral imperative to avoid civilian casualties; Iraqi civilians had been killed by the thousands. Although Secretary of State Colin Powell had early argued that terrorists could only be attacked from "the highest moral plane," what little moral authority had attended the Americans because of their suffering the September 11 attacks, dissipated with Iraq, with Abu Ghraib, with Haditha, and with Guantánamo.[95] Other editorials, leader articles, and opinion pieces noted that the Bush administration had further undermined its moral authority by implying terrorist connections where none existed. And the Pentagon's cool rejection of civilian deaths in the theaters of operation further infuriated the watching world. "We know for a fact that these were legitimate military targets in that area that were struck," asserted Defense Secretary Donald Rumsfeld after an attack in Afghanistan that according to the international medical relief agency Médecins Sans Frontières killed at least 80, including women and children. Said Rumsfeld: "We know that there was terrific traditional, consistent planning to ensure that only these targets were struck. We know there were no off-target hits, so there were no collateral damage worries in this series of strikes."[96] Such statements in the face of outside observers' testimony seemed to be arrogant spin, at best, and most likely outright falsehoods.

As the war in Iraq worsened through 2006, the American ally in the Iraq war, Prime Minister Blair, began backpedaling, putting distance between his government and the Bush administration. Blair, who had literally and figuratively stood beside President Bush in support of pre-emption, belatedly argued that it wasn't 9/11 and Iraq, but the war in Kosovo and the 1997 collapse of the Asian markets which had taught him "that the rule book of international politics has been torn up." Challenges such as global warming and mass migration, he said, "can only be tackled together. And they require a pre-emptive not simply reactive response." Blair's tardy attempts to find a global foundation for a pre-emption doctrine were taken as spin. As the lead of a story in the conservative *Daily Telegraph* had it: "Tony Blair last night challenged the world to unite around a policy of 'progressive pre-emption' as he sought to shore up his legacy by linking the invasion of Iraq to a range of problems, from global warming and poverty to immigration."[97]

The political packaging of the doctrine of pre-emption, of the war in Iraq, and of the "War on Terror" itself, had come undone.

 ## what have we learned about terrorism?

Well, we've learned that there is no agreed-upon definition of terrorism. Although most would feel comfortable saying something like "Terrorism is the use of force involving the killing of civilians to advance a political cause," the word "terrorism" continues to have many meanings. "Terrorism" is a word trundled out to refer to heinous events as well as to damn political opponents. "Terrorists" can refer to the perpetrators of acts that receive legal condemnation as well as be used to smear quite disparate players whose behavior is rumored rather than confirmed.

Media have come to be painfully aware of the term "terrorism," but still do little to clarify what those who use it (including they themselves) mean when they do. In my early human rights study, I realized that different operating definitions of human rights changed the responses of individuals and institutions to given humanitarian crises. So too have different operating definitions of terrorism affected how governments and media have managed the politics of terrorism. How one frames the threat of terrorism suggests the possible ways to solve it. President Bush detailed a frightening world and promised to keep Americans secure by going on a global offensive. Prime Minister Brown argued that terrorism was criminal behavior, and as such could be controlled in part by community policing.

To speak about "terrorism" is to speak about contested turf. The three core questions of this first chapter—Is terrorism a tactic or an ideology? Is the way to fight "terrorism" through declaring a "war" on it? Should governments try to pre-emptively destroy terrorists?— introduce core debates about terrorism. These debates informed American and British government policy and President Bush and Prime Ministers Blair and Brown's selling of their policies.

What we know from these questions is that politicians and the media have come to emphasize one or another of the elements of that simple 16-word explanation: "Terrorism is the use of force involving the killing of civilians to advance a political cause." Sometimes there's an emphasis on the "killing" and other times on the "political cause." Sometimes there's a focus on the "civilian" victims, other times on the intended audience for whom the cause has been "advanced."

What we also know is that how post-9/11 governments initially played "terrorism" to look strong and decisive has proven in many cases to be counterproductive—both politically to those governments, and strategically in their attempts to defeat terrorism. As events unfolded, officials' packaging of news and policy became apparent: The Emperor Has No Clothes.

The next two chapters will take a look at how American and British politics have affected the coverage of terrorism. How has the American and British governments' attention to terrorism influenced reporting on terrorism? It turns out while some assumptions about how media cover terrorism are correct, there are many surprises when the coverage is systematically looked at.

Journalism—in print, on air, online—always seems so transparent. The words and pictures are out there for us all to see. But we rarely take the time to consider the choices that are made—the language that is selected, the voices that are heard, the images that are used, the stories that are told. Whose stories are these? Why are we hearing those and not another's? Why do we see what we see? And most of all, why does it all matter?

The balance of this book will explain why.

II

how is terrorism covered?

the politics of coverage

Shortly after World War I started in August 1914, when it became clear that the soldiers were not going to be home by Christmas, the French General Staff put their collective foot down: no unaccompanied reporters and photographers at the front. The General Staff regarded the press simply as a conduit of intelligence for the enemy. Bitter complaints were reprised about how reporters had lost the Franco-Prussian War of 1870 for the French by publishing information about the French generals' military plans and the condition and morale of the French troops. Historians were more likely to credit France's loss to the superior strategy and larger army of Prussian premier Otto von Bismarck together with his effective use of the most modern Krupp artillery, but the French General Staff of 1914 were unmoved by those arguments. The press had lost the 1870 war and reporters weren't going to be given the opportunity to lose this new Great War.

Fast forward to October 1983, two days after the suicide bombing of the US Marine headquarters in Beirut, Lebanon. On orders from the Reagan White House, American armed forces invaded the tiny Caribbean spice island of Grenada. Political upheavals on the island, including the arrest and murder of the prime minister, and the presence of 224 American medical students, were the argument for going in. President Reagan was unenthusiastic about the harder-line communism of the coup leader (the assassinated prime minister had also been a Marxist), and did fear a repetition of the Iranian hostage crisis, but more compelling motivations for the attack were the administration's need to deflect the sharp criticisms for the handling of the Beirut bombings and the administration's desire to provoke the Marxist Sandinistas in Nicaragua and demonstrate resolve to the El Salvadoran government fighting its own indigenous guerrillas.

Early news about what was happening came from the unverified reports from the US military—many of which turned out to be wildly wrong—because for several days after the invasion the Reagan administration flatly refused to let the media in to cover the fighting. White House officials blamed the American loss of world stature and credibility during the Vietnam era on US television.[1] According to them, TV had undermined public support by showing footage of American dead and wounded, among other horrors. Reagan wasn't going to let America be caught out again, no matter that researcher after researcher found that there had actually been very little Vietnam combat footage shown on the nightly news—and even less that had been graphic—and no matter that historians were writing that "the notion that the press lost the war in Vietnam remains, especially among military people, one of the most persistent and pernicious of the many myths of that war."[2]

Neither in World War I nor in the Grenada invasion did the media exactly cover themselves with glory, even regarding what they were able to witness. Reporters and photographers in both conflicts lacked access to the front, had to fight with their own editors and producers who wanted to place more patriotic spin on the coverage, and only recognized in hindsight many of the components of the wars that made them most dangerous: the administrative blunders, the new technologies that were poorly factored into the strategic planning, the hubris about the conflicts' outcomes.[3]

That should all sound very familiar. Many of those same problems faced in 1914 and 1983 have troubled the coverage of global terrorism since September 11, 2001: governments' hesitation to allow reporters and cameramen to freely cover zones of conflict, the tendency of newsrooms away from the field to give priority to the official government message, and, of course, the media's inadequate investigation of the government's failures, poor strategic assumptions, and political arrogance.

How have the media covered the new world of terrorism? Has government continued to co-opt reporting? Is the media's packaging of the news distinct from the government's spin of it? Like the French General Staff and the Reagan White House, we could make assumptions about how media have covered violence in the past—but better to analyze the coverage than rely on our memories of what we saw and heard and read.

  making terrorism the "big story"

Terrorism has been the main event of the twenty-first century. We've learned new meanings for old words: "9/11" is pronounced nine-eleven, not nine-one-one, the "Madrid train station" now calls to mind a site of horror rather than a place to meet friends traveling around Europe, Ground Zero no longer refers to the epicenter of an atomic bomb blast, and recently almost everyone (like Richard Nixon during Vietnam) has come to believe in the importance of winning "hearts and minds." We also can tick off on our fingers critical people and groups that weren't even part of our vocabulary before this: Bin Laden and Zarqawi, Al Qaeda and Jemaah Islamiyah.

Terrorism is so much in front of us, it has so deeply remade our sense of the world and our safety in it, that we could be forgiven for thinking that, since September 11, terrorism has been at the top of the news on every possible occasion. But terrorism does not always lead the TV newscasts or appear on the front pages of the paper. To get top billing, terrorism stories need to be framed by the question "What does this mean for *us?*"

If an event threatens "us" then the chance of it getting major coverage is high. So, for example, there was the January 13, 2003 *Time* magazine cover which asked "The Bigger Threat? North Korea's dictator is a nuclear menace. Why he may be more dangerous than Saddam." Or the headline to *Newsweek*'s cover story on the Madrid bombing in March 2004, which asked: "Europe's 9/11: A New Threat to America?" Or the *Economist* story following the failed bombings in London and Glasgow in the summer of 2007 which was titled, "Britain under Threat." "The great fear," the article said, "is that al-Qaeda will attempt to swamp Britain with repeated attacks—some professional, some amateurish, some relatively easily foiled, some not—making it ever more likely that a big one, such as these might have been, will one day succeed again."[4] With these headlines and copy the articles became not simple hard-news telling of the events, but commentaries on the meaning of these events for their readers. Threats, danger, fear. These words grab the attention of readers and that's what media want. Your attention. Be afraid. Be very afraid.

What does this kind of scaremongering mean for which stories of terrorism are covered—and how?

If a palpable sense of risk to the news outlet's audience is essential for top-of-the-news attention, a terrorist attack is likely to be framed so that its audience feels vulnerable. Audiences get hyped coverage of certain events so that they appear to directly engage or menace them. And the flipside of that is that terrorist attacks or threats where that audience cannot be represented as being at risk are under-covered. When was the last time you saw front-page or top-of-the-TV-news coverage of a terrorist attack in the Congo, Colombia, or even India?

If you're thinking that all this doesn't sound like entirely responsible reporting, you'd be right. This kind of reporting suggests the downsides to "Big Story" coverage. When one's knowledge of terrorism is limited to the big stories—and all of those share similarities, i.e., they all are stories about extraordinary violence in surprising locations of some political or economic or emotional connection to the audience, and they all are framed in a way to emphasize the threat—then one's understanding of terrorism as a phenomenon is distorted. And if the public's understanding is distorted, its sense of how to combat terrorism is distorted as well.

Most Western news outlets are concerned with their bottom lines. Money matters—the overnight ratings, the quarterly stockholder reports, loom in the background of every conversation about what to put on air or in print. Media agonize over how many people are watching, listening, or reading their stories and continually devise ways to try to retain or improve their market share of viewers, listeners, or readers. Literally hundreds of books and thousands of articles have been written about the business of media, and additional shelves of books and articles have been written about the impact of media mergers—the pressures mergers create for newsrooms to decimate their reporting staffs in order to show greater profit margins for the corporate owners, the fact that fewer independent media voices also means greater pack journalism pressure to follow a Big Story, and the fact that fewer corporate owners means greater oversight of news by fewer people, many of whom have ties to policymakers.

I don't intend to examine all that here. But it is pertinent to note that American and British mainstream media worry about what their audiences want. Do they want stock market reports or celebrity gossip, comic strips or political analysis? "Media" is a plural noun and there are no two news outlets that are alike in how they answer the questions related to what news they should cover. But all news outlets worry about attracting and keeping an audience and almost all worry about how to turn a profit. To do both of these, news organizations are chauvinistic: they focus on the news that is geographically and psychologically closest to their audience. The *New York Times* covers the Yankees baseball team more than it pays attention to the Chicago Cubs, the BBC covers cricket and largely ignores American football, CNN follows polls in the US presidential election more than it pays attention to the popularity of the prime minister.

With the general cutting of news budgets, the media (television especially) can't afford to cover all the disasters that occur. So they choose to cover what they think their audiences care most about. And they assume that their audiences care most about themselves. So for international stories, for example, the media don't necessarily cover crises on the basis of how many people are killed, although a high death toll, the involvement of someone famous, and attacks where white Westerners are killed can help propel a story to the top of the news. Oh, and access to good pictures is essential.

What matters is "American involvement" in the story, said former ABC *Nightline* anchor Ted Koppel. For US media, national security interests and the direct involvement of Americans trump the numbers. "Simply stated, no audience is perceived to be clamoring for foreign news, the exceptions being wars in their early months that involve American troops, acts of terrorism and, for a couple of weeks or so, natural disasters of truly epic proportions."[5] "I swear to you," said *Wall Street Journal* writer Walt Mossberg, "this applies to all the newspapers, some more, some less. Is it a place Americans know about? Travel to? Have relatives in? Have business in? Is the military going there? You're not going to get on page one with something about Bangladesh nearly as much as you do with something about some country where your readers have some kind of connection."[6]

Terrorist attacks are covered for political, strategic, and even commercial and historical considerations. But although there may be events that international editors think should be covered, where that event took place makes a difference. Some regions of the world "matter" more than other regions. An international event from a region that receives ongoing attention will usurp the coverage of a similar story from a region only rarely in the news.

The July 11, 2006 Mumbai, India, train bombings that killed 200 and injured over 700 is a perfect example. That story essentially stayed on top of the news in the United States for one day—and even then the *New York Times* only carried three stories that first day and the *Washington Post* only two. Most American coverage of the event came through the headline news on CNN and like outlets. Why did Mumbai get so little US coverage? Well, domestically, a portion of the Mass Pike I-90 tunnel in Boston had collapsed killing one person, and two dramatic murder cases were playing out in the courtroom, one involving a sex offender and the other involving a cousin of leading US Senator Edward Kennedy. Internationally, attention was focused on an unannounced trip of US Defense Secretary Donald Rumsfeld to Iraq and a meeting between German Chancellor Angela Merkel and President Bush on his way to the G8 Summit in Russia. But the main reason the Mumbai story disappeared was because the following day, July 12, the Hezbollah–Israeli war began with Hezbollah rocket attacks and the capture of two Israeli soldiers.[7]

The Mumbai bombing story was huge, the pictures were compelling (those in the Indian media were extremely graphic), but India is not on Americans' radar, at least compared to conflict in the Middle East. Consider the banality of the July 11 exchange on CNN between Daryn Kagan, the anchor, and Seth Doane, the reporter in India:

KAGAN: Mumbai is the financial capital of India. What else can you tell us about the city and where this happened?

DOANE: Well, this entire operation is complicated right now. The rescue operation is made more difficult. It is the middle of the monsoon here in India, and it is very—raining very heavily earlier during the day today. Mumbai is an extremely densely populated city. As you say, it's the financial capital, and it is a very crowded city. This is hitting at a very busy time of day.

KAGAN: All right. We'll continue to watch it as information, pictures come out of there.[8]

What do we learn from this scintillating exchange? That Mumbai is a very wet and very crowded city. We learn nothing about why bombers might have selected Mumbai to attack or what the implications of the bombing might be for the "financial capital" of India.

So as the coverage of Mumbai in the US media makes clear, you can't just look at a crisis in a vacuum and know whether it's going to lead the news. You must ask: "Which media outlet?" and "Who's the audience?" Once you know the answers to those questions, then you must ask: "What else is happening?" For local and national news outlets, coverage of major domestic incidents will typically trump that of almost any major international event. Domestic stories, by default, almost always lead the news. One example: on October 27, 2003, the first day of Ramadan, suicide bombers struck the Red Cross headquarters in Baghdad as well as several Baghdad police stations, killing 40 and injuring 200. In addition, the deputy mayor of Baghdad was assassinated. Yet the San Bernardino forest fires in California dominated the top headlines and the number one broadcast slots in the United States, even though the American network ABC called the Ramadan attacks the "bloodiest day in Iraq." Why? Well, there were great images from the forest fires, they posed an immediate threat to California residents and there was, in addition, no moral ambiguity about what needed to be done in response to the crisis.

Domestic news trumps international news. But as the Mumbai story demonstrated, the competition for time and space doesn't have to come from a domestic story. A dramatic—especially an unusually "deviant"—international affair will trump a more familiar kind of foreign story.

Coverage of the terrorist attacks on October 7, 2004 at several Red Sea resorts in Egypt's Sinai Peninsula is a case in point. The coordinated suicide bombings killed 34 people and injured more than 100. Many of the victims were Egyptians vacationers, but Israelis and Europeans on holiday were also among the casualties. The death toll alone should have compelled extraordinary coverage, as too should have the fact that the attack was targeted at Western and Israeli tourists. But while the news did make the front pages of the *New York Times*, the *Washington Post*, the *Los Angeles Times*, the *Guardian*, and the *Telegraph* that first day, others, such as *USA Today*, virtually ignored the bombing. CNN and the BBC covered it in some detail, but domestic networks, such as NBC, led with it once, then attention to it dropped sharply. Why did all the media not prominently cover the story?

The answer is simple. The following morning it was announced that Kenneth Bigley, the British hostage held by Abu Musab al-Zarqawi, had been killed and that his beheading had been videotaped, and news also broke that magazine entrepreneur Martha Stewart had slipped into the Alderson Federal Prison Camp in West Virginia in the early morning, evading camera crews, to begin her five-month sentence for insider trading. The day after that, October 9, all the international desks of the news outlets turned to yet another foreign story: the long-awaited direct elections for president in Afghanistan (interim president Hamid Karzai was declared the winner). For news outlets that have a finite amount of time or space for international news, the beheading video and the upbeat story of the Afghan elections (where a number of the outlets had with forward planning placed correspondents) seemed more compelling. And the Martha story was a must-do for coverage after months of news attention to every detail of the insider trading scandal.

If there hadn't been "stronger" stories to compete with the Red Sea bombing, the Egypt story would likely have gotten more play and longer play. But that's not true of all stories. There are some that never seem to make the top news by themselves no matter how slow a news day it is. The number of casualties, whether or not victims are civilians, seemingly makes no difference. The reason in those cases has to do with the acts themselves—or more precisely, with the *context* of the acts. They are not one-offs. For example, an attack—or two or three—is nothing particularly unusual in countries that have a high baseline level of violence. So on almost all occasions in Iraq, and for periods of time in Afghanistan and in Israel, suicide bombings have been poorly covered. That is *not* to say that suicide bombings haven't been covered at all, just that the coverage is terse and there is no specific follow-up reporting on a given attack.

Actually, even during the years when Iraq consistently dominated the news,[9] one could argue that, of all the terrorism in the world that *is* covered, the most poorly examined terrorist acts are the suicide bombings in Iraq. When the coverage of them is analyzed, there are surprisingly few that led the news across the media on the day they occurred, much less became major ongoing stories. Even back in 2003, before the number of suicide bombings in Iraq rose exponentially, there was little attention to the individual attacks. And even those that were pivotal in shifting the direction of the conflict were quickly subsumed into the "larger" story. In most cases, there were domestic and other non-Iraq international stories that seemed fresher. How many times can a suicide bombing make the news before readers and viewers say "Didn't we hear about that yesterday?"

For example, the death of over 125 in Iraq in a car bombing outside the Imam Ali mosque in August 2003, that also killed the Shiite leader Ayatollah Bakr al-Hakim, led the news in some outlets, but in the United States it shared the stage that day with the release of emergency-call transcripts from September 11 by the Port Authority of New Jersey and New York. A series of car bombings in mid-December 2003 that killed dozens was completely overshadowed by the breaking news of Saddam Hussein's capture. Word of Israeli prime minister Ariel Sharon's ill health and the Sago mine disaster in West Virginia stole the spotlight in early January 2006 from a series of bombings across Iraq that killed 150. And the February 2006 bombing of the Golden Mosque and the following coverage of the sectarian violence—would this lead to "civil war"?—had to share the limelight with the Winter Olympics and with the controversy over a Dubai corporation buying up the terminal facilities in US ports. The problem of course with reporting on terrorism in passing—through facile accounts or brief summaries of horrors—is that such coverage only serves to put the public on notice that there are threats to safety out there. But such superficial coverage doesn't give the public sufficient information to be able to reason its own way to a response.

Suicide bombings in Iraq have often been seen simply as data points on a graph, indicators of the relative wellbeing of the country. Few suicide bombings means things are looking up. Many bombings means the country is on its way to hell in that proverbial handbasket (and multiple bombings within a short span of time have often been taken to mean that current US policy is in error and its political and/or military leaders are at fault). In the effort to answer the "Why should I care?" question of their audiences, media turn these attacks into trend stories: CBS Evening News of October 9, 2003 covered an upbeat speech by Paul Bremer, Bush's appointed head of the Coalition Provisional Authority in Iraq, and then followed with news of the bombings of that day: "While US officials keep insisting the terrorists are on the run, America's enemies seem bent on proving them wrong."

But there's a problem with the media telling the news of multiple events in the same account: the causes and consequences of each one can be lost in the more generic point that today-there-were-suicide-bombings-in-the-Middle-East. Consider this CNN lead-in in November 2005 following the attacks on the hotels in Jordan: "A security lockdown today in Jordan after the deadliest terrorist bombing ever in that country. Carnage in three hotels, 56 dead. We're live with details on the investigation this morning. A similar scene overnight in Baghdad. One of the deadliest bombings there in months—34 killed at a crowded restaurant."[10]

There is, however, one positive consequence of days when lots is happening— on those occasions when there are multiple stories breaking that all relate to terrorism, an attack with few casualties can get coverage precisely because media will fold all the events into one larger story. For example, the fact that Paul Bremer gave a major speech on October 9, 2003 made it more rather than less likely that the several suicide bombings that same day would make the news agenda. However, the journalists' primary interest in Bremer's comments made it inevitable that the bombings would get second billing and also dictated that reporters would cover the bombings through the perspective of Bremer's remarks.

On those occasions when multiple attacks occur—such as Al Qaeda's bombing of the three hotels in Amman, Jordan, and its attack the next day on the Baghdad restaurant—media are more likely to cover both attacks more thoroughly then they might otherwise have done. In the case of the Amman/Baghdad bombings, the reporting began with the breaking news and then turned to stories about violence spreading in the region. More time in the news meant more types of news for both stories—from speculation about the Al Qaeda attackers to stories about the victims. Even the restaurant attack, which might not have gotten any real coverage had it occurred at another moment, had the TV networks doing immediate stories on the locals affected by the bombing. Victims were mentioned by name and their families interviewed. A shop owner gave an account of the chaos. Jordan received the bulk of the attention, however, with reporters pointing out that the attacks were literally Jordan's 9/11. (In the United States, dates are written month/day, so September 11 is 9/11. But in the rest of the world dates are written day/month, so the day of the attacks in Jordan, November 9, would be written 9/11, as well.)

Interestingly, in that 9/11 story two sets of actors could be seen struggling to frame their own narrative: the media that paired the Amman and Baghdad bombings and used the opportunity to tell about violence in the region, about civilian deaths, and about communities newly fearful, and the terrorists themselves—Al Qaeda—who manipulated the story of their strength and power by timing their attacks to come one after another. Like the two planes that struck the World Trade Center, where the first explosion ensured that the whole world would be watching when the second plane hit, the one-two punch of Jordan and Iraq also claimed more of the media's attention than would have been the case had only one incident occurred. Both terrorists and media want to keep their own message in the public view: Al Qaeda wants as much notice for its actions as possible; the media want to tell a compelling story that will keep their audiences tuned in. That doesn't make the media complicit in terrorism, but it does suggest both "groups" craft their messages to gain as much public attention as possible.

So what does Big Story coverage mean to the public watching and listening and reading at home? Well, it means wall-to-wall reporting of the event or issue. You know it's a Big Story when there is nothing else on the news. Big Stories occur when there's a critical mass of media coverage—where not just a couple of news outlets decide that the event or crisis or issue is worth covering, but where they all do. Big Stories are those where you see the same news no matter what TV station you turn on, which site you surf to, or what front page you look at. It's the Asian tsunami, Abu Ghraib, and the 2005 London bombing.

Saturation coverage often means that newscasters and reporters reprise the same sensational rumors over and over again—as in Fox News' reporting of the disappearance of Natalee Holloway in Aruba. And reporting that rises to Big Story coverage often packages the stories with sensational come-ons: "A New Threat to America?" "Britain under Threat," "The Bigger Threat." Either way, fear is an integral element in the Big Story coverage of terrorism.

Yet, at their best, Big Stories can give media the time and space to report in detail on the Who-What-Where-When-Why-How of an event, as well as the time and space to report from multiple perspectives: to look at the politics of an event and the human side of it, the economic repercussions and the cultural impact. When a terrorist attack does not receive multiple days of coverage (much less top-of-the-news coverage) the news audience usually doesn't learn much beyond the initial (and often incorrect) vital statistics about who was killed and who was injured. Questions such as who were the perpetrators, what was their agenda, were they caught, how is the community surviving remain unknowns.

tragedy and politics: what we hear, why we hear it

Truly extraordinary terrorist attacks make headlines for days—the Bali nightclub bombing of 2002, the Madrid bombing of 2004, the London bombing of 2005— as do extraordinary debates about terrorism—will UN inspectors (or US forces) find weapons of mass destruction in Iraq? Is Iran developing nuclear weapons?[11] More quotidian terrorism, especially in out-of-the-way places, doesn't command much coverage.

But no matter when terrorism does make the news—either with a big splash, or on the inside pages of newspapers and multiple clicks in on news sites—how is it talked about? It seems a no-brainer that of course the event—the deaths of civilians—takes precedence. The violence, the horror, the literal "terror" of a crisis is what is emphasized in news stories, right? Blown-up cars, destroyed homes and offices, crying children, keening mothers, frightened bystanders, medical personnel scrambling to tend to the wounded, security officers struggling to get control. That's what we see and hear. Right?

Not usually.

For all the visceral, magnetic, rubber-necking pull of tragedies, and for all that news media—especially television—do rush to cover the graphic aftermath of sudden violence, most of what the American and British media cover of terrorism relates to the impact of terrorism on governments and the body politic, not its impact on people and their very human bodies.

The International Center for Media and the Public Agenda, a center that I direct at the University of Maryland, conducted studies of the media's coverage of dozens of terrorist incidents over the years since September 11, 2001.[12] Over and over, time and again, my center's studies revealed that the victims of terrorism rarely appear in the stories about it. No matter which terrorist attacks we looked at, no matter what the context was, personal stories about named victims, the human repercussions of terrorism, the costs to local communities, the rending asunder of everyday life were all covered far less than the meaning of the terrorist event on the grand scale. It's not that the human topics weren't covered at all, but that they received only a fraction of the coverage of what a terrorist event was expected to mean for countries and political parties, for individual leaders and for alliances.

Media cover international affairs through the lens of their own country's foreign policy—especially as articulated by its leadership. Terrorism, it turns out, is no exception. So when President Bush framed his "War on Terror" as being about politics and ideology, American media looked at the political ramifications of terrorist incidents.[13]

According to Bush, terrorists want to "stop democracy . . . democracy stands for the exact opposite of their vision. Liberty is not their credo."[14] "The advance of democracy is the terrorists' greatest fear," he noted on another occasion. "That's an interesting question, isn't it—why would they fear democracy? What is it about freedom that frightens these killers? What is it about a liberty that causes these people to kill innocent women and children?"[15] As employed by the Bush White House, the term "democracy," like the words "family," "mother," and "child," became a political lever. "Democracy" became one of the chief rhetorical weapons employed by the administration in the aftermath of September 11: "the war on terror is a struggle between freedom and tyranny, and . . . the path to lasting security is to defeat the hateful vision the terrorists are spreading with the hope of freedom and democracy," argued Bush in a speech at The George Washington University in 2006.[16]

Here one sees President Bush characterizing democracy as less of a governmental structure than as a political weapon. Speaking to the Secretary General of NATO, in the Oval Office in October that same year, Bush noted that the Secretary General had "made NATO [into] a values-based organization that is capable of dealing with the true threats of the 21st century. . . . You know what I know, that the real challenge for the future is to help people of moderation and young democracies succeed in the face of threats and attacks by radicals and extremists who do not share our ideology, have kind of a dark vision of the world."[17] In his construction, "democracy" was the core political "value" that governments and security organizations such as NATO must use to counter the global extremist, terrorist agenda.

And most of the US media, whether they agreed with President Bush or not, bought into his framing of the global situation: the opposite of terrorism is democracy. Commentators argued as to whether democracy could be imposed or should be imposed, but few Americans tried to set up another equation, such as the opposite of terrorism is non-aggression, or the opposite of terrorism is physical safety. You can see the democracy frame at play in a lengthy 2006 *Washington Post* editorial titled "The Case for Democracy":

> The "democracy backlash" is in full swing, largely because of the carnage in Iraq and the electoral success of the terrorist organization Hamas in the Palestinian Authority. In the past week our op-ed writers from right to left have expressed doubts about, or opposition to, the Bush administration's project of encouraging democracy in the Middle East. . . . But even war planners far more diligent and serious than this administration's will get things wrong—an assumption that should be built into any prewar calculation. And even if President Bush had gotten a lot more right than he did, Iraq still might not be at peace today. . . . So it's fair to oppose democracy promotion, but only if you're honest about the alternative.[18]

It is downright un-American to be against democracy. The brilliance of Bush's framing of his tactics used to fight the "War on Terror" as the fostering of global democracies made it very difficult for the media to find fault with such an approach. Neither the short minute-thirty headline news packages favored by network and cable news programs nor the 700-word-long opinion pieces in newspapers and magazines allowed for the nuance necessary to overturn such an argument. And it occurred to few to even try to do so.

American media at least—and to a great extent British media as well—have generally forborne to frame terrorism as other non-Western media have done— as fundamentally about violence. Many Arab media outlets structure their terrorism stories around images of dead and wounded civilians. The images of violence against civilians that air on the Arab satellite channels make their political point that governments—especially the Israeli and US governments—typically act with impunity. But the effect of such a focus also serves to give some significance to the human costs of both the terrorist attacks in the region and the "War on Terror" that has opposed them.

Even by 2006, with the fighting in Iraq into its fourth bloody year, US military casualties climbing, and polls showing that a majority of Americans disapproved of the conflict, US media remained primarily focused on the politics of the war, rather than on the people caught in its maw. What did change, however, was that these news outlets began to offer an unremittingly skeptical portrait of the conflict, much as their British counterparts had already been doing. The deep cynicism of the UK public about the war had encouraged the British press to not pull their punches. In the UK, it is much more common for analysis to be larded in with hard news, so that cynicism and despair had permeated much of the print and online coverage of Iraq since at least 2004. But for Americans, 2006 was the turning point where the Iraq story became one of chaos with no end in sight. Debate over how to pull out led the opinion pages and network news analysis, rather than commentary over possible outcomes to the war or how a democratic Iraq should be built. The unremitting violence—so fierce that few Western journalists could even work outside the Green Zone in Baghdad—became a political argument. Individual suffering did began to appear out of an anonymous frieze of passing incidents, but images of death and destruction on nightly newscasts and in magazine photoessays and online slide shows tended to emphasize the frustrations, the futility, and the waste of the war writ large, rather than the problems of ordinary Iraqis.

In fact a survey conducted in the fall of 2007 of 111 journalists who had covered Iraq discovered that the journalists themselves—90 percent of whom were in Iraq at the time they took the survey—said that among the most over-reported stories from the war were stories on US military strategy and stories on statements or visits by elected officials. The top under-reported story—mentioned by 42 percent of the respondents, more than twice as often as any other topic? The impact of the war on Iraqi civilians.[19]

That's the coverage of Iraq. What of coverage of the rest of the "War on Terror"? Did the changes in the war in Iraq affect how media covered the terrorism story elsewhere? Not much. Even after it had become commonplace in the American press to state the formerly unmentionable—that the United States had likely advanced the cause of terrorism with its war in Iraq, rather than checked it—coverage of "terrorism" changed only marginally. Certainly there was greater alertness to the Bush administration's parsing of language, to the use of words such as "liberty" and "democracy," because they had been shown to have no real on-the-ground meaning in the conduct of the war. But still the US media's fundamental assumptions about "terrorism" didn't change: stories about the wider "War on Terror" remained framed as "us" against "them." The terms used to discuss terrorism remained political, not graphic, the debates remained focused on policy agendas, not human suffering, and the deaths of people in faraway places received relatively little attention.

But that still doesn't explain why the US media covered—and why they continue to cover—terrorist *attacks* through political lenses rather than through accounts of the casualties.

In some ways it's the terrorists' fault. Terrorists too have a political agenda and often plan their attacks to occur at significant moments. Timing, in other words, has something to do with the political focus. Take the Madrid bombing. It occurred on March 11, 2004, four days prior to the Spanish general election. Following the attack, political parties in Spain called off all remaining campaign events, although the elections occurred on schedule. While Elaine Sciolino's front-page *New York Times* story the day after the attack led with the number of dead and wounded, the context of the bombings dominated. In the first five sentences alone she mentioned World War II, the Basque separatist group ETA, Al Qaeda, an unnamed American counterterrorism official, the number of troops Spain currently had stationed in Iraq, the Spanish elections, and a statement from Prime Minister Aznar.[20] The grim details about the bomb blasts and injuries to the victims didn't come until the seventh paragraph.

Similarly, the London bombing on July 7, 2005, occurred on day 2 of the three-day G8 summit being held in Scotland, attended by the heads of state of the United Kingdom, the United States, France, Germany, Italy, Japan, Russia, and Canada. The day before the attack London received word that it had beat out Paris to host the 2012 Olympic Games. Said the editorial in the *Daily Telegraph* the day following the bombings: "London, a great and vibrant city, wins the 2012 Olympics. A day later it is paralysed by terrorist attacks on its transport system. Tony Blair temporarily abandons his colleagues at the G8 summit in Gleneagles to be briefed in the capital. The contrast between triumph and sudden vulnerability could hardly be greater."[21]

But even when there was no major political event looming, the larger political context for a terrorist attack remained the most common lead into the news. And for good reason. Media—both broadcast in its coverage of breaking news and print in its contextualizing of it (as Sciolino and the *Daily Telegraph* were doing)—would certainly be remiss *not* to reflect on the political ramifications of any terrorist attack. Those consequences are important and one can see in coverage of the suicide bombings in Iraq, for example, a constant reminder at the top of stories that each individual attack is part of a much larger reality.

- NBC Nightly News on October 9, 2003: "The eyes of the world were glued to TV screens exactly six months ago today when that statue of Saddam was toppled in the middle of Baghdad. It meant his regime had officially toppled as well. But as American soldiers and now some Iraqis themselves have learned, the danger didn't go away that day. Today, in fact, there was graphic proof to the contrary."[22]
- *Los Angeles Times*, October 6, 2005: "The blood bath came on a day when Iraqi politicians moved to quell sectarian tensions by reversing a controversial decision that would have made it harder for Iraq's draft constitution to be defeated in a national referendum."[23]
- *Christian Science Monitor*, January 6, 2006: "Post-election violence throughout Iraq over the past two days that killed more than 150 mostly Shiite civilians is straining talks intended to forge a new coalition government, say politicians close to the negotiations continuing between newly elected Shiite, Sunni Arab, and Kurdish politicians."[24]
- *BBC World* (video), April 14, 2007: "The aftermath of a lethal attack with potentially serious consequences. . . . Karbala was almost certainly targeted because it's one of the most important holy places for Shiite Muslims, the burial site of a grandson of the prophet Mohammed. The Sunni insurgents want to provoke a violent reaction, pushing Iraq down the road to civil war."[25]

But perhaps it's the logistics of coverage that best explains why the majority of time and space dedicated to terrorist attacks focuses on the politics and not the tragedy. Those attacks that are mentioned on the day they occur but that don't become Big Stories are not tracked further because the US and UK media judge that—for their audiences at least—the fact of a few more people dead in this faraway place doesn't rise to the level of ongoing concern. What matters about such an event, why it makes the news at all, is because it represents a larger threat to the Western audience; it itself is not a threat. The minimal coverage focuses on the macro issues that the American or British media believe are most important for their public: what the attack says about the power of the terrorists or the competence of the nation's political leaders or the need for outside governments to be involved, etc.

Media focus on what they think will hold our attention, what will keep us coming back to their channel, their news outlet. Those attacks that receive days and even weeks of attention (London, Madrid) receive that level of coverage because they are perceived as "mattering" in a range of ways. Over the span of time such an event is in the news it will be considered from an extraordinary number of perspectives. On the day after the London bombing, for example, the *Washington Post* ran 31 stories entirely on or with mention of the attacks on the Underground and the bus. Four stories appeared on the front page, there were two editorials, three op-eds, multiple letters to the editor gathered together, six stories in the business section, and still more scattered about the first and other sections. The lead story on the front page covered the breaking news details,[26] a second story on the page gave an analysis of the probable responsibility of Al Qaeda for the attack,[27] a third front-page story tracked the impact of the bombing on Washington's and other US cities' transportation systems,[28] and a fourth A1 story graphically told of the victims of the attack.[29]

The rest of the paper took up the similarities with the Madrid attacks, the "renewed bonds" between Prime Minister Blair and President Bush as a result of the event, the retreat of G8 protesters in the wake of the bombings, the probable effect of the attack on world financial markets and the travel industry, concerns about the safety of the 2012 Olympics, and on and on. While many stories took as their reference point the shock and horror of the events, in only a few was the actual destruction described, stories about victims and survivors told, people's names mentioned. Over the next several days there continued to be a notable number of stories in the *Post* about the human impact of the bombings, but they remained very much the minority of the coverage. And the *Washington Post* was itself notable for being one of the print news outlets to pay the most attention to the victims and survivors of the London and other terrorist attacks.

Stretched budgets, insistent deadlines, mechanical assumptions about what audiences want. These combine to create a virtual template for coverage of terrorism. But actually, we see the same process, the same habits, repeatedly occurring in other types of domestic and international news coverage. Take elections. In the year prior to the US presidential primaries and election, there are the who's-getting-in stories, the announcement stories, the fundraising stories, the gaffe stories, the poll stories. Then there's the period of the caucuses and primaries in which the poll stories and fundraising stories become even more prominent, but added to those are the who's-in-who's-out stories, the hometown advantage stories, the spoiler stories, the handler and the grassroots stories, the prominent issue stories. Then there's the lead-up to the convention stories: the VP nomination stories, the strategy stories, the stories about the effect of the relative state of the economy/housing/war. Finally there are the stories in the last weeks prior to the election: the debate stories, the distinctive platform stories, the poll stories, the accuracy-of-polls stories, the do-the-candidates-have-any-opinions-not-directed-by-poll stories. And then, take a breath, it's over. We all know this formula. Switch the names and the dates and we've seen it all before. It's an unusual news outlet that breaks out of the pack to cover topics outside the norm—or even to focus on the range of candidates running locally and at the state level. All the oxygen in the newsrooms is sucked up by the candidates for President.

So coverage of terrorism, like that of elections, focuses on politics and process. It features the horse race of it: Who's up? Who's down? President Bush or Osama bin Laden? So much is tediously familiar that at times one could be forgiven for thinking most media have a checklist of story types. What've we got? Story on how the attack was or was not anticipated? Check. What this means for the credibility and stability of the ruling government? Check. What the response is of Western officials? Check.[30]

Actually, the fact that the coverage of similar kinds of events follows a pattern is not really to be wondered at. Many of the angles of coverage are of genuine interest and concern. But a generic pattern of coverage is, however, to be remarked upon because if media do follow a pattern it means, first, that the coverage is rather predictable. And this is not entirely a good thing if media are trying to win an audience. There is value in predictability—you wouldn't want to *not* run the breaking news stories that bring the audience up to date on what is happening, for instance. But once those facts have been learned by the audience, what's to keep them tuned in? If the follow-on stories all sound familiar then there is little to be gained by watching, hearing, or reading them.

And second, patterns of coverage are to be remarked upon because typically following one pattern means that other ways of looking at an event are not being addressed. If the major lens through which media are looking at terrorism is the very lens held up by the government, one should ask whether that perspective is clear enough, independent enough for viewers to see all that they need to. Why did the Bush administration want its "War on Terror" message to be about democracy rather than death and destruction? How many reporters have even asked that question? At the end of the day the problem is not so much that US media look at terrorism and see the political necessity for democracy or that Arab media look at terrorism and see the human blight of carnage, as that there should be multiple lenses used to take in multiple views. Both the politics and the tragedy should be covered in due measure and with full recognition of governments', media's, and terrorists' stakes in telling the story in the way that they do.

 the voices of the powerful

Do stories like this one sound familiar?

BEGIN VIDEO CLIPS:
- **Jacqui Smith, British Home Secretary**: "We're currently facing the most serious and sustained threat to our security from international terrorism."
- **Peter Clarke, head of Scotland Yard's Anti-Terrorism Unit**: "Even at this stage, it is obvious that if the device had detonated there could have been significant injury or loss of life."
- **Gordon Brown, British Prime Minister**: "The first duty of a government is the security of the people."

BACK TO ANCHOR:
- **Becky Anderson, CNN international anchor**: "Stepped-up security and a call for public vigilance. Britain's new leadership is thrust into an emergency role after police defuse a potentially powerful car bomb. It's 5 p.m. here in London's Piccadilly."[31]

This was the opening to a special noon edition of CNN's signature program *Your World Today* on June 29, 2007, after two Mercedes cars containing petrol, gas cylinders, and nails failed to explode in central London. (The following day a burning car loaded with gas cylinders was driven at the main terminal building at Glasgow's international airport.) The attempted bombing in London came a week before the second anniversary of London's transit bombings and just two days into the new government of Prime Minister Gordon Brown.

Not just the story line should sound familiar, unfortunately—a terrorist attack on a heavily populated civilian area at a significant political moment—but the manner in which CNN began its story should too.

Who is telling us the news of a terrorist attack? Who are the sources in the media's coverage? We learned in the last section that most American and British media cover the politics of terrorism more than the human tragedy of it. So it should come as no surprise that the most frequent sources in the news stories are politicians and other government officials. The statements of presidents, foreign secretaries, the heads of security services, and military officers tell us the breaking bits of information and tell us what to think about it all. The voices of the everyday "man" on the street—even when he or she is a victim or other eyewitness—are

rarely heard, and, when used, their words are primarily included to add drama
and immediacy rather than hard information or context.

Political and military officials—frequently nameless—often provide us with the
basic facts of a story. How many people were killed? Said the lead in a CNN piece
from spring 2006: "An Iraqi Health Ministry official Saturday said the death toll
had risen to 81 people, with 160 wounded, in the attack on the Buratha mosque
in northern Baghdad."[32] What are the consequences of a recent attack? Said a lead
in a *New York Times* article from the fall of 2006: "Nearly all the tribes from Iraq's
volatile Sunni-dominated Anbar Province have agreed to join forces and fight Al
Qaeda insurgents and other foreign-backed 'terrorists,' an influential tribal leader
said Sunday. Iraqi government leaders encouraged the movement."[33]

Yet officials appear in reporters' stories as more than the spokespeople who confirm the details of an attack or breaking issue. Media are interested in giving us,
their audience, both the inside scoop on what just happened and some insights
about what will happen next. Who is most likely to know the answers? The government and the military. They have access to the intelligence and the security details,
and they have the power to take action. Even when politicians or other officials
are suspected to be speaking less than candidly about a breaking event or to be
telling a partial story rather than the whole truth, or to be spinning out only that
part of the news that advances their own agendas, media are still likely to feature
those official comments.

The whole dirty system as exploited by the Bush administration came out in a
front-page April 2008 article in the *New York Times*. Reporter David Barstow broke
the news that since 2002 the Pentagon had mounted a sophisticated information
operation, that in the words of some of those involved, was "an effort to dupe
the American public with propaganda dressed as independent military analysis."
Already in the months following 9/11, the White House and the Pentagon realized
that they needed to overcome American resistance for a possible invasion of Iraq.
Torie Clarke, the Assistant Secretary of Defense for Public Affairs and a former
public relations executive, had a idea about how the administration could achieve
"information dominance." As Barstow explained, "In a spin-saturated news culture,
she argued, opinion is swayed most by voices perceived as authoritative and
utterly independent." So Clarke gathered together "key influentials"—military
analysts, many of them decorated former officers, who in the weeks and months
following September 11 had been appearing on TV and radio, been quoted in
newspapers and magazines, and been publishing op-ed articles. Their real value
for the White House and the Defense Department? The analysts were not only being
asked to explain "the capabilities of Apache helicopters," they were also "framing
how viewers ought to interpret events."

The analysts were first curried to create public support for an invasion of Iraq
in 2002, then over the following years to counteract the "increasingly negative

view of the war" coming from journalists in Iraq, then in 2006 to marginalize war critics—including other officers—calling for Secretary of Defense Donald Rumsfeld's resignation. Over time the analysts were "wooed" in hundreds of private briefings with senior military leaders, given access to classified documents, and taken on behind-the-scenes tours of Iraq and Guantánamo Bay, Cuba.

Most had ties to military contractors, and several admitted to the *New York Times* that they used their extraordinary "access and information to identify opportunities for clients." There was, the *Times* noted, a cost to that access. If an analyst didn't toe the administration's line on air, "You'll lose all access," one said. As a result, some told the *Times*, they didn't share any misgivings for fear that "some four-star could call up and say, 'Kill that contract.' " That influence wasn't lost on the Pentagon, nor was that fact that there was a "financial relationship between the networks and their analysts," as many were paid each time they appeared as commentators.

"The Bush administration has used its control over access and information in an effort to transform the analysts," wrote Barstow, into "an instrument intended to shape terrorism coverage from inside the major TV and radio networks." And those broadcast outlets (as well as other news venues, including the *New York Times*— nine of the analysts wrote op-eds that appeared in the *Times*), did little vetting of the business ties of the analysts they used, even though most had "ties to military contractors vested in the very war policies they [were] asked to assess on air"—a clear breach of journalism ethics. The entire operation, which only ended because of the *Times*' publication of the story, reveals, noted Barstow drily, "a symbiotic relationship where the usual dividing lines between government and journalism have been obliterated." [34]

While Barstow's investigative piece dramatically documented the extent to which news can be intentionally spun by a calculating government, often no such efforts are needed in order for media to feature the messages of officials. Officials are typically the speakers who tell us why a certain threat or a specific attack matters. Political players are often quoted when they discuss the impact the attack might have on policy, and when they give their assessment of progress in a region in light, or in spite, of this most recent terrorist act. Media follow power. Statements of leading politicians on such topics are taken as bellwethers of policy. What tactics will President Bush, Israeli prime minister Ehud Olmert or Pakistan president Pervez Musharraf adopt in response to a specific attack or threat? Their public statements will give answers—or at least give clues.

- In October 2002, in the aftermath of the Bali nightclub bombing, the *New York Times* reported President Bush as saying: "I'm concerned about our homeland. . . . Obviously, if I knew of a specific piece of intelligence that would indicate a moment or a place in which the enemy would attack, we'd do a lot about it."[35] Why report this comment? Because although it seems to be stating the obvious, it also suggested that the White House was tying this event into its planning for US domestic security.

- In December 2006, at the height of concerns about Iran's nuclear program, the *Jerusalem Post* reported Prime Minister Olmert as saying: "I am anything but happy about it. I expect that significantly more dramatic steps be initiated . . . effective measures that are accepted by the international community to stop the Iranian danger." Why report this comment? Because it suggested that Olmert was considering a military response to Iran. As the paper also quoted him as saying: "I rule out nothing."[36]

- In September 2007, after a suicide attacker penetrated a Pakistan military base and killed 16 soldiers from an elite counterterrorism unit, MSNBC reported President Musharraf as saying: "The government will fight the menace of terrorism, extremism and militancy in all its forms and manifestations."[37] Why report this comment? Because although it appears to be pabulum, it suggested that Musharraf's government, which had been accused of turning a blind eye to terrorists harbored within its borders, would stand with the Bush adminis-tration in its "War on Terror."

Governments' responses to terrorism always get prime billing. It has often been noted that there is a symbiotic relationship between policymakers and the press. The studies we conducted suggested that this relationship is particularly strong when the subject involves terrorism. This seems to be the case for two reasons.

First, as mentioned, issues and events relating to terrorism involve questions of national security and intelligence, and often, if not always, occur in the complex realm of international affairs. Media naturally turn to the executive branch, the military, and the intelligence agencies for statements about the meaning of a terror attack. And when those authorities speak out about an attack or about a terrorist threat media prominently report their comments.

Second, terrorism has a compelling presence in the public's imagination: "terrorism" is violence that threatens civilians where they live. Media find it irresist-ible to report doomsayer threats and defense and security arguments verbatim. This has the unfortunate effect of enabling policymakers to use threats of terrorism as powerful tools of public persuasion and as forceful rationales for policy initiatives, as the Bush administration so clearly premeditated.

The nature of national security and intelligence crises is such that relatively few people other than those within government can speak with any authority. As a result, it is not unusual for coverage of a terrorist attack—even a major one— to be reported from the State Department, the Pentagon, or their international equivalents, rather than from the place of the attack itself. In part that is because news outlets, especially broadcast, often can't get their own people on site quickly enough to cover breaking news from where it happened. If they want to have their own reporters cover the story they need to do it close to home. (Although one way around the problem of not having a correspondent on site on the ground is to use footage from the region and have the news anchor or another reporter give a voiceover of what's being seen. There are problems with that approach, however, the most obvious being that viewers are not getting eyewitness information, but, at best, second-hand news.)

Having news reported from the State Department or the Pentagon also occurs because of that habit of media to turn to government officials to give the "inside" account of what is happening as well as background about what it all means. So, for example, much of CNN's breaking coverage of the 2005 hotel bombings in Jordan was reported by Jamie McIntyre, the network's senior Pentagon correspondent in Washington. His lead on the 6 p.m. news that first night of coverage focused on the scene in Amman—as translated through Pentagon-based counterterrorism officials. This is what he said, from his stand-up in front of the Pentagon: "As bodies were still being pulled from the hotels, suspicion began to center on Abu Musab al-Zarqawi as the possible mastermind behind the attacks. The pattern of attacks seems to fit the modus operandi of Zarqawi's network, similar to attacks in Iraq and other places around the world that were done by al Qaeda. The Jordanian-born militant is still believed to be in Iraq, at least as far as U.S. intelligence knows."[38]

Using official sources from one's own country is also a way to "nationalize" the event—if media interview their own, often what happens is that the event is tied back to domestic affairs and connections are made to domestic precedents. For example, in CNN's coverage of the Madrid bombings, US Secretary of Defense Donald Rumsfeld, White House Press Secretary Scott McClellan, former Homeland Security Secretary Tom Ridge, members of Congress, and other representatives from other American institutions all appeared or were quoted as commentators and sources. They all made multiple references to terrorist attacks on Americans—not those of September 11, but the bombing in Oklahoma City.

So officials of one kind or another give reporters the facts on a story, and their statements not only shape what we make of those facts, but refract those facts through "our" own national interests. And media not only put up with this, at times they abet it. Media are telling the story in the first place because they believe the news is of interest to their audiences—and showing that there's a connection back home is a powerful way to interest the public. Media also privilege what officials say because their statements appear to represent the "inside story."

Media have allowed themselves to be co-opted by government sources as a result, even when those voices are anonymous. What can emerge are stories with prominent figures on record in public statements, but with the analysis and critique of the threat or attack attributed to anonymous sources. But failing to name the names of sources—or even just negligence in sourcing—tends to buttress the government's agenda without allowing the media's audience a way to assess statements purporting to be facts. "Off-the-record" and "anonymous" have become the way business is done. It is extraordinarily difficult for journalists covering terrorism to defy these conventions and still retain their access to critical venues such as the White House, the Pentagon, the Home Office, and other government agencies.

This practice ultimately serves, however, to erode media independence and credibility. In 2003, for example, there was much coverage about the US concern over whether the Russian assistance in building an Iranian light-water reactor was a cover for assisting Iran in a weapons program. The secrecy of the program led to an extensive use of anonymous sourcing, with reporters using phrases such as "Washington believes" or "Washington suspects" or the "United States says" without any formal attribution of who was actually doing the believing or the suspecting, or even an identification of the general department affiliation of who was doing the "suspecting" or "believing" (a "senior Administration official," "a senior State Department official"). This *Los Angeles Times* story, reported from Moscow, was a case in point:

> Russia's cooperation with Iran in developing that country's nuclear power capabilities, which the *US fears* is in turn assisting a weapons program, was another key focus of Powell's talks. *The United States says* Iran is conducting a clandestine nuclear weapons program. "I think we have a better understanding of one another's concerns and we've come a little closer as to how we should deal with our concerns," he said. Russia has been helping Iran build a 1,000-megawatt light-water reactor in the western port of Bushehr and has considered more such projects. *Washington believes* that the Bushehr project, estimated to cost $800 million, is a cover for obtaining sensitive technologies to develop nuclear weapons. *It also suspects* that Russian scientists, without government approval, are helping Iran with a nuclear weapons program. (emphasis added)[39]

Who in the US "fears"? Who in the United States is "saying"? Who "believes"? Who "suspects"? We don't know.

And it's not just the US news outlets that rely heavily on anonymous sources when reporting on terrorism, intelligence issues and security policy. Consider the *Financial Times*, the London-based daily viewed by many as the world's top English-language newspaper for its in-depth coverage of global business, financial markets and politics (especially following Rupert Murdoch's 2007 purchase of the *Wall Street Journal*). Yet the *FT*, as it is called, which has won such prizes as Newspaper of the Year at the 2008 British Press Awards,[40] is among the worst offenders in its use of anonymous sources—even, or perhaps especially, on front-page stories.

An *FT* article on the security of Pakistan's nuclear weapons program following the resignation of President Pervez Musharraf in the summer of 2008, for example, only quoted one source by name—and that only 10 paragraphs into the article. Instead, the reporter attributed all other statements and analysis to "Pakistani and western officials," "a senior western diplomat," "analysts," "Western diplomats," "US officials," and "one senior US official" (quoted twice). In addition, entire paragraphs relayed information with no attribution at all, even anonymously.[41]

Editorials, too, rely on anonymous sources and passive voice attributions, such as a 2003 *Washington Post* editorial about Iran, which said that while Iran's "Islamic regime has been suspected of pursuing weapons of mass destruction for some time, powerful evidence has surfaced in recent months of a race by Tehran to acquire nuclear bombs."[42] In the instance of that editorial, it would have made a difference to readers to know if Iran was "suspected" of pursuing WMD by the CIA, by Russian intelligence, by the French government, by Mujaheddin-e Khalq (an exile opposition group)—or by all of these. It also would have helped to learn what that "powerful evidence" was—rather than having to take the editorial's word for the "power" of that evidence.

Vague sources leave readers with no understanding of who is advocating the positions cited. The situation is a Catch-22—lack of identifiable sources damages the credibility of journalists' stories, yet without those sources there would be far fewer stories.

An equally troubling problem is when major stories break—especially on the front pages—and the only sources who are quoted are those of the government or of like-minded others. This is particularly a problem in stories that cover terrorist threats, rather than terrorist attacks, such as those posed by chemical, biological, or nuclear weapons (often conflated under the single heading "weapons of mass destruction" or WMD).[43] The most infamous instance was a front-page article in the *Washington Post* that appeared during the hunt for weapons of mass destruction in Iraq. In the May 2003 story, headlined "Bush: 'We Found' Banned Weapons; President Cites Trailers in Iraq as Proof," no sources appeared other than members of the Bush administration or Prime Minister Tony Blair, the President's key ally. The complete tally of sources for the article was: President Bush, "US intelligence agencies," "Bush administration officials," Secretary of Defense Donald Rumsfeld, "US authorities," the CIA, Secretary of State Colin Powell, Blair (as reported by Reuters), and "a senior administration official." The lead to the article read: "President Bush, citing two trailers that US intelligence agencies have said were probably used as mobile biological weapons labs, said US forces in Iraq have 'found the weapons of mass destruction' that were the United States' primary justification for going to war."[44]

According to journalistic conventions, the *Post* editors' placing of the controversial allegation that American troops had "found" weapons of mass destruction in quotation marks in the headline and the reporter's direct quotation of President Bush in his charge, were sufficient to inform readers that the "finding" of WMD was not a fact, but an assertion. Yet casual readers of the *Post* could be forgiven if they came away from their skimming of the article's headline and lead with the impression that weapons of mass destruction had unequivocally been found. After all, the President said so—and the paper ran the story on the front page.

What problem does that article surface? That journalistic conventions need to be re-evaluated. Students of journalism are taught that basic news stories should lead with the most important piece of information. That often translates to what the most "important" player—the president or prime minister, for example—has to say. It's ironic. A venerable style of newswriting that students and journalists associate with impartial, "just the facts, ma'am" reporting, actually turns out to favor the powerful.

Why do journalists lead their stories with the powerful voices of politicians, rather than the compelling voices of eyewitnesses, for example? Because they have been taught to do so—for over 150 years. Journalists are taught to write breaking news in a style called the "inverted pyramid"—what most of the rest of us know as starting with the Who-What-Where-When of an event. The "inverted pyramid" style of news writing is a standard invented by the Associated Press wire service soon after its birth in 1848. Prior to 1848, reporters often wrote their articles as authors wrote their books: they'd start at the beginning and go on until the end. That makes good sense; the chronology of events is clear. But what it doesn't do is get quickly to the point: what matters most? If the report of a battle begins with the correspondent describing the dark and stormy night, it may be long column inches before readers learn who won and who lost. When time was not of the essence, that didn't much matter. But in 1848, time began to matter.

In 1848, a consortium of newspapers got together to take advantage of a new invention: the telegraph. Since no single paper could afford to pay the total freight, a number of New York papers came together in a cooperative to jointly pay for the use of the telegraph line to send news that had traveled across the ocean from the United Kingdom by boat. Once the ship made landfall in North America, if the news off the ship was telegraphed to New York rather than having to come down by steamship or over land, the papers that were part of the cooperative endeavor would have a "beat" on their competition—they could deliver the news faster to their audience.

But there were three problems for this new Associated Press wire service. First, it was expensive to send a telegraph—one had to pay by the word. Brevity counted. (In fact the telegraph led to the same kinds of stripped-down sentences as the text messaging of today that eschews adjectives, prepositions, and most punctuation. For example, the first successful powered flight by the Wright brothers on the North

Carolina coast in 1903 was announced via telegram. The message in its entirety read: "Success four flights Thursday morning.")

Second, one never knew when the telegraph line might be cut, by falling trees, lightning, or other misfortunes. Thus, better to transmit the most important information first and save the details for later. Third, not all the papers that were part of the Associated Press cooperative shared the same political perspective. So the "news" that came over the telegraph line had better be as "objective" as possible—free of overt analysis. Papers could add their own spin later.

So *voilà!* Out of necessity was born a style of newswriting still in place today for breaking news stories: a concise telling of the facts, leading with the most important information, all with a minimal amount of analysis. In other words, poor coverage can result less from intentional political bias on the part of journalists, editors, and producers than from routine adherence to tired journalistic conventions. The effect of such habits can be exacerbated by too few stories proffering alternative perspectives to the official line.

Okay, so whose voices do we hear most strongly when media cover terrorism? Those of officials. And whether media are covering terrorist attacks or terrorist threats, there are three results:

- Media over-rely on official (and former official) sources for both breaking information and analysis—and do too little vetting and public disclosure of their conflicts of interest.
- They present the officials' statements as fact, too rarely offering independent discussion or confirmation of those statements.
- They often let officials speak anonymously.

What's needed, therefore, is to get more perspectives higher up in breaking news stories—and to get more sources on the record. When time and space allow, an analysis or enterprise story that assesses the assertions made in the breaking story should be run in immediate and prominent juxtaposition to a basic, inverted-pyramid story.

 when caring about victims sells news

Are politicians *really* the only voices we hear in stories about terrorism? Of course not. Other people's voices slip in, and sometimes have a sizeable presence in a story. Who are these other people? Well, much of the time they are the victims: those who are injured, those who are killed, those who are the family and friends of those who are hurt, those who are eyewitnesses or those who are traumatized by the event. Do we learn a lot about these people? Do we learn who they are? When, actually, do we meet them?

How much is told about the victims of terror is a barometer for how much the media believe we care about the event at hand. We meet victims and survivors when media believe that their stories are compelling enough to grab our attention.

For Americans, linking the words "terrorism" and "victims" together still, years later, calls up memories of those who perished in the World Trade Center buildings on September 11, 2001.[45] It is not only the gut-wrenching, life-altering events of that day and the staggering number of those who died that calls those specific victims to mind, but it is how the media—print, broadcast, online—chose to commemorate them that allows those real people to live on in our imaginations.

To get a sense of the quality—not just the quantity—of attention the media paid to 9/11 and its aftermath, it is enough to consider that the attacks and their aftermath were the focus of eight of the 14 following year's Pulitzer Prizes for journalism. The *New York Times* won a record seven, including six for its news coverage of the terrorist attack of September 11, its victims, its causes and its consequences—"all transformative events in the modern history of the United States," as it mentioned. The *Times'* Pulitzers included the public service award for the section "A Nation Challenged," which closed every day with a full page titled "Portraits of Grief," consisting of 200-word biographical sketches of those who died at the World Trade Center.[46] The newspaper ran its "Portraits of Grief" stories daily through December 31, 2001; they and others that were written later remain archived on the *Times* website, and 1,910 of them (those published through February 3, 2002) were collected in a book. Some 140-plus reporters eventually contributed to the series. Some wrote only one. Others wrote many. And while writing obits is generally considered among the lowest-ranked jobs in the newspaper business (with the exception of page 1 obituaries of famous people), most of those who wrote a "Portrait of Grief" biography considered it an honor.

The "Portraits of Grief" began, wrote the *Times*, "as an imperfect answer to a journalistic problem, the absence of a definitive list of the dead in the days after the World Trade Center was attacked. But it evolved improbably in the weeks and months after Sept. 11 into a sort of national shrine. Three days after the attacks, reporters at *The New York Times*, armed with stacks of the homemade missing-persons fliers that were papering the city, began dialing the numbers on the fliers, interviewing friends and relatives of the missing and writing brief portraits, or sketches, of their lives."[47]

The "shorts" that made up the "Portraits of Grief" have been the focus of a tremendous amount of attention, not just because the *Times* ceded valuable real estate to hundreds of obituaries of ordinary cooks and firefighters and day traders, but because the "Grey Lady," the often stodgy *New York Times*, unbent enough to daily feature intentionally powerful, evocative, and emotional sketches of those who perished.[48] They formed a serial narrative of almost 2,000 chapters, each with its own compelling lead, specific details, quotations from family members, and poignant stories of hopes that would not be realized. "Leon Smith Jr.'s boots just might be impossible to fill. He wore the only size 15's in the Fire Department," was the opening of one profile.[49] Said another: "In 2000, Anna Ivantsov became a wife. In 2001, she became a widow. She was 20 years old. Fifteen months later, she spoke about her husband, Aleksandr Ivantsov . . . 'All I need to say is: He was my everything. That is very important to me to say.' "[50]

Hundreds of emails and letters were written to the *Times* editors about how turning to the short stories had become a daily ritual—and about how reading them prompted tears. It was both "good" journalism and journalism that "sells." In an article that appeared on the last day of the daily feature, several people were interviewed about their reactions to the series. "One felt, looking at those pages every day, that real lives were jumping out at you," said novelist Paul Auster. "We weren't mourning an anonymous mass of people, we were mourning thousands of individuals. And the more we knew about them, the more we could wrestle with our own grief." And Kenneth Jackson, a history professor at Columbia University, noted, "As you read those individual portraits about love affairs or kissing children goodbye or coaching soccer and buying a dream home, it's so obvious that every one of them was a person who deserved to live a full and successful and happy life. You see what was lost."[51]

"Mourning individuals." "We could wrestle with our own grief." "You could see what was lost." Those are the essential elements of why writing about victims matters. The Dart Center for Journalism and Trauma is a global network of journalists, academics, and health professionals dedicated to improving media coverage of trauma, conflict, and tragedy. Its mission, as expressed through its website and outreach, is in part to explain why reporting on victims and survivors matters—and how journalists can do so responsibly and responsively. "Producing an engaging, well-crafted and sensitive news story about crime victims, survivors and their loved ones is not only good for the reputation of the news organization and its employees, but it is also good for their communities," notes the website in its "Best Practices" section. "A civil society—people engaged in activities that improve and enhance the social welfare—can only be achieved if people are 'connected' with others in their community. One of the functions of the news media is to help people make this connection and to care—not only about those they know, but also about strangers who are in some way also a part of their lives."[52]

The *New York Times* stories of the victims of the 9/11 terrorist attacks helped their readers to make connections and to care. There were two indispensable elements in each of the brief 200-word profiles: names and details. That's what's

different in the 9/11 accounts from those of distant terrorist attacks. In coverage
of "distant" attacks, we don't usually learn names. Knowing them would make a
difference. In our studies of media coverage of terrorism, we were struck by how
few names we found of those who were killed. Sometimes, of course, names were
not known at the time that a story appeared—and in some cases the names of
victims may never be known. Bodies were atomized, family members able to
identify the victims were not found, continuing violence prevented such a civilized
closure to a life as identifying whose life was ended. But in other cases, those who
were killed were known, often immediately, or usually in short order. And even
in those cases, stories rarely mentioned names.

There were, of course, exceptions. Media are not monolithic. For the London
bombing in the summer of 2005, the *Washington Post* featured articles about
the American victims in London, the *Los Angeles Times* ran an obituary on a local
resident killed, and the BBC, taking a page from the *New York Times*, ran biographies
of everyone killed in the bombing.

But that was an exceptional case. Our studies also showed that in accounts of
the more geographically and psychologically distant terrorist attacks, the US and
UK media not only rarely mentioned names, but told few details about the victims
either. But those too have meaning. For some odd reason, it matters if we know
that a victim had size 15 feet, or left an achingly young widow.

Photos of victims are not enough. We need names—or if privacy forbids that,
at least tell us something that has personal meaning. *Newsweek*, for example, ran
an extraordinary photograph from Baghdad by Geert Van Kesteren across three
full pages—one page folded out—of three people: on the left a US MP crying out,
perhaps asking for further help; on the right, someone who looks like an Iraqi; and
in the center a UN worker in blue shirt and khaki vest, spattered with brilliant
blood, his head sheathed in a web of bandages around his crown and jaw. All that
can be see of his face is a nose and lip, still clearly dripping red. All we are told
about the picture is this: "Terror's Toll: An MP leads an injured U.N. worker to
safety after a truck bomb killed at least 20 and left others buried." He's a survivor
of the largest attack on the United Nations in the organization's history. The photo
is shocking. But we don't learn a single name. And without knowing more about
the image, about the people in it, we can't do anything with the shock we feel except
turn the page.[53]

One can only assume that the reason why we don't get additional information
is that, in the finite time and space of international news stories, the bean counters
make the judgment that a name or two or 20 would use up valuable room better
taken for analysis or some other facet of news. And details—well, no room for those
either. But few of us recognized any of the names or specifics mentioned in the
Times' "Portraits of Grief" section, and those turned out to have great resonance.
Numbers and statistics of the dead and wounded don't engage us. They may shock

us, they may allow constructive comparisons among events, but they don't make us care and they don't make us reflect emotionally, or oft-times intellectually, on a breaking event or its effects.

Exceptions to the rule of news outlets not giving out names or details are striking in their power.

- In May 2001—before 9/11—the highly regarded public radio programs NPR's *All Things Considered* and Public Radio International (PRI)'s *The World* reported on the death of two Israeli teenagers. Said the reporter for *The World* in his lead: "More than ever it seems that it's the children who are paying with their lives for the conflict between their Israeli and Palestinian parents. This time it was two 14-year-old boys, Yossi Ishran and Kobi Mandel, a US and Israeli citizen." Said the opening of *All Things Considered*'s story: "Kobi Mandel and Yossi Ishran decided to play hooky yesterday. They went to explore a cave just a few hundred yards from the Jewish settlement of Tekoa southwest of Bethlehem. Early this morning, the boys' bodies were found in the cave."[54]
- A story in the *Los Angeles Times* about the March 2002 bombing of the Park Hotel in Netanya, Israel, during the Seder meal for Passover, mentioned that one woman who was being identified was "a 67-year-old Holocaust survivor." Her brother, the article noted, "had hoped to identify his sister by her red fingernail polish but was told that DNA samples would be necessary."[55]
- The *Guardian* wrote a story about some of the victims of the 2004 bombing in Madrid: "The Jardin cemetery on the hillside at the edge of the commuter town of Alcala de Henares, 15 miles from Madrid, has eight rooms available for the traditional day of mourning around the coffin when people from the town die," explained the lead. "But the most tragic door of all contained the names of a father and son, Francisco and Jorge Fernandez, aged 52 and 22. 'They would have been sitting side-by-side as they always did,' said a close family friend, Jesus Laroda. 'They did the same every day, catching the 7.15 train together. Jorge would look at his study notes as they travelled. Francisco was a trade union official who worked in a banking organisation,' Mr Laroda said. 'The bomb must have been close to them, it would have been quick.' "[56]

These snippets of lives, scattered in among the facts about the events, the specula-tion about who was responsible, the reactions of those in authority, are arresting because they take the news out of the realm of politics. Those names, "Yossi and Kobi," that detail, "red fingernails," that description, "they were sitting side-by-side," cause us as listeners and readers to consider, if just for a moment, real human loss and grief. Feeling that, we perhaps are also prompted to reflect on our civic responsibility to "improve and enhance the social welfare" of our community, as the Dart Center has it—which must include the global community.

Those are the rare moments in coverage, however. Most of what we learn about the victims is at the top of stories, and amounts to hearing something like: a suicide bomber today killed at least 14 people, or at least 24, or at least 54, and injured more than 12 or 22 or 52. Period. Paragraph.

Personal identification with an event is critical to get people to care. When there's minimal coverage or when multiple attacks are folded into a single account, events blur together, the violence seems distant, and readers and listeners are hard pressed to identify a way to even think about the terrorism. Various terrorist attacks in Iraq in the first week of January 2006, for example—multiple bombings of a funeral at a Shiite shrine, attacks on police stations, and an American helicopter crash that weekend—were aggregated by many news outlets to be the "bloodiest" and "deadliest." A front-page *New York Times* article on January 5, 2006 stated: "Insurgents unleashed car bombs and suicide attacks throughout central Iraq on Wednesday, killing more than 50 people in the deadliest day since the national parliamentary elections three weeks ago." Broadcast outlets took the same approach. ABC noted the total number of Iraqi policemen killed in the past year. CNN's January 5 *Live from . . .* show began with "Second straight day of carnage in Iraq. At least 130 people are dead in one of the bloodiest days of the three-year insurgency." CBS called January 5 the "fourth deadliest day since Saddam Hussein's fall from power"; anchor Bob Schieffer led into the story with "Well here we go again in Iraq." Although assorted attacks were mentioned, from the coverage it was difficult to dissect the individual incidents and discern what had happened to whom. The coverage's minimal use of description for victims, perpetrators, and locations made the terrorism faceless and made it seem like the entire country was exploding. Were media to give more details about the people or the attacks, the events would have been more easily distinguished one from the other, and their causes, as well as possible ways to manage the violence, would have more easily emerged.

Most of what we learn of victims is statistics. The problem with using statistics is that they give the impression that there is an objective reality that can be reported upon, that will give an audience a bias-free evaluation of the events in the region. There is a presumption, with statistics, that they are self-evidently understandable. Often they are employed as a shorthand way to signal who has been victimized, what the aggressor has done. But statistics should only be used to supplement a narrative account; they should not be the substitution for it. The typical pitfall is for reporters to rely on numbers, such as death tolls, to relay a message. Numbers were the way that the Nixon administration and the Pentagon had gauged the vicissitudes of the Vietnam War—the daily body count, which was a new statistic for war, was only one figure in a lengthy list of numbers: of engagements, defections, hamlets lost, village "pacified," weapons captured, and people relocated. But as North Vietnamese premier Pham Van Dong told Harrison Salisbury at the end of 1966: "The problem does not lie in numbers." He then presciently identified the real problem: "one of relative morale and spirit between the United States forces and those opposing them in Vietnam."[57] The same is true of terrorism today—numbers, while not inconsequential, can obfuscate more than illuminate what is happening. Clarity rarely comes with statistics, despite most journalists' comfort level at reporting on "facts" that are clearly delineated: polling data, voting records, budget figures, insurance losses, civilians injured, soldiers killed.

The challenges involved in reporting in the aftermath of a terrorist attack or in a war zone are reason enough for media outlets to have to cursorily report on what's happening, to rely on statistics to make up a portrait of what happened. Those and deadline pressures are why the usual breaking news presentation of violence states just the basics. And those challenges and pressures become even greater when multiple events occur within the same news cycle. Without the ability to be in several places at once, reporters often roll the stories together, with general statistics covering all: "Two suicide bombers struck a popular restaurant in Baghdad and an army recruiting center north of the capital Thursday, killing at least 40 people and injuring three dozen more, police and witnesses said."[58]

It is often the case that further details about terrorism—especially when multiple attacks occur in the midst of a war—may be unknowable, at least at first, a fact that explains why different outlets could produce different sets of facts on the same story, especially in the same day's or the next day's coverage. So for example, the number of people murdered in Iraq on August 29, 2003 by a suicide car bomb was variously reported: the *Daily Telegraph* wrote 125 had been killed, the *Washington Post* claimed 95, and the *Guardian* said at least 80. Similarly, news outlets variously reported the number of casualties from the attacks in Iraq on December 14 and 15 that year: the *Guardian* said the attacks killed eight and injured 22, the *New York Times* said six Iraqi officers had been killed and 20 injured, while the *Washington Post* stated the attacks had killed 17 and wounded 33. ABC's nightly news broadcast said that seven people had been killed and another 30 wounded, and NPR's news program said only that several people had died and 20 others had been injured.

In effect the opening use of statistics is barely more than a rough benchmark—not to be taken as definitive, more as an indicator of scale. That's why, for example, some news outlets use loose constructions for death tolls such as "more than 30" or "at least 40" and fudge the number of wounded with a broad brush of round figures "three dozen more" or "20 others" rather than the precision of 37 or 46 injured. But it's not just breaking news where one needs to be wary of statistics. It's not just casualty figures that differ from one outlet to another. Statistics can change dramatically—not just over time, as in a changing civilian death toll following a terrorist attack—but from speaker to speaker, and about such "facts" as should stay static. For example, Paul Richter in the *Los Angeles Times* could write matter-of-factly about a nuclear debate in the US Senate:

> The bill would provide $15.5 million in funding for research on a large hydrogen
> bunker-buster bomb called the Robust Nuclear Earth Penetrator [RNEP]. Unlike the
> proposed low-yield bombs, which have an explosive force of no more than 5 kilotons—
> five thousand tons of TNT—this weapon would have yields in the range of tens of
> kilotons, to a megaton, making it at least six times more powerful than the bomb that
> was dropped on Hiroshima, Japan.[59]

Well, that seems straightforward enough. But 11 days later reporter Helen Dewar
of the *Washington Post* wrote in her article that the "high-yield 'bunker buster' bomb
would have a force 10 times that of the Hiroshima blast." And the next day, in a
story still following the same Congressional debate, Dewar noted that Senator Carl
Levin said that "the Robust Nuclear Earth Penetrator, or bunker-buster . . . could
explode with as much as 70 times the force of the Hiroshima bomb."[60]

Now that's confusing. In all three cases Hiroshima was evidently used to
signal to readers with only a casual understanding of the weapon system how
destructive the proposed "high-yield" bomb could be. But the first problem was
that the historical referent didn't adequately explain how powerful the Hiroshima
bomb was (it was about 15 kt). So was the new weapon six times more powerful
(i.e., 90 kt) than that dropped on Hiroshima, as Richter reported? Was it 10 times
more powerful (150 kt), as Dewar reported? Or was it 70 times more powerful
(1,050 kt), as Dewar reported Levin as saying? There were no explanations of the
discrepancies—and no corrections.

So we have three contradictory assessments of the power of a single nuclear
weapon—and one that is being built by the Americans, so presumably information
about the weapon is more readily accessible. But even aside from that exponential
difference in power, reporting this kind of data in isolation focuses attention on
one facet of a weapon: the "force" of the bomb. What about other concerns? In
none of the three stories, for example, was anything else said to explain what "more
powerful" than the Hiroshima bomb meant: More people—soldiers, civilians?—
killed? A greater area devastated? Greater fallout and longer-lasting radiation threats?
All of those? Or something else entirely?[61] When I think of Hiroshima I think of
people dying—but none of those three stories spoke about the potential victims of
this new weapon, or of the likely fate of its survivors. Such sins of omission are
often harder to detect by casual readers or listeners than factual inaccuracies, which,
generally speaking, are usually sooner or later corrected in the record.

Statistics have their clear limitations. Gotta have them. But by themselves they
are not enough. What else do we need to learn? We need details about attacks—
not just how many are dead, but who they are. Not just how they died, but what
happened afterwards. Not just what was the governments' response, but what it
all means—and not only for the "macro" country, but for the "micro" community
and for the individual families.

We often get some of that: the why it may matter, the what happened next. But we rarely get how the attack will affect a community and its families. We may get some sensational quick insights into what the attack looked like or felt like. Video footage of burning cars, running survivors, the blare of sirens. But when we just get voiceovers by anchors back in the studio or stand-ups by reporters on site but hours after it all, when the people we see on the footage or read about in print have no names attached, we are distanced from the horror, as if it were all just a made-for-TV horror movie: "In the dark and the screaming chaos, said one survivor today, it was sometimes hard to tell whether the man who appeared to be running toward him through the flames was alive or already dead," wrote the *New York Times* in the aftermath of the 2002 bombing in Bali.

When the coverage does introduce us to people identified by names and personal characteristics, the event becomes more accessible. We the readers and listeners and watchers can find points of intersection with those profiled. "Great chunks of freshly cut ice were piled inside the morgue at the Edhi Foundation, which provides medical help to the poor, where corpses from Thursday's bombing were stuffed into a cramped, chilly room," said the lead of a story in the *Guardian* following the suicide bomb attack in Karachi on the crowd celebrating Benazir Bhutto's return to Pakistan in late 2007. "Relatives filed through, pinching their noses against the stench. Noor Khan Burfat had come for his 21-year-old brother Amir, one of 50 security men killed as they tried to protect the armoured vehicle carrying Benazir Bhutto. The only compensation, he said, was that his brother's corpse was recognisable. Many of the others were charred or dismembered beyond recognition. 'Thank God,' he said, his eyes cold with grief."[62]

That's a powerful scene. We can visualize the pain Burfat expresses, understand his bitter gratitude for his brother's intact body, and also begin to comprehend that there are other families even less fortunate. Will we continue to follow Burfat— or those like him—in the days and months that follow? This *was* the deadliest terrorist attack in Pakistan's history, after all. Well, probably not. So our empathy is eventually squandered. We met him, we looked into his eyes, and then we looked away. But caring for just a little while, meeting him at that critical moment, does give some personal resonance to our understanding of what happened.

The American and British media are much more likely to follow any Westerners caught in distant terrorist attacks—to meet them in their hospital beds, to track them upon their return home, to briefly check in again on anniversary occasions. Such stories are considered to be more salient for American and British audiences. On November 10, 2005, the day after the bombing of the hotels in Amman, Jordan, Jim Lehrer led PBS's *NewsHour* with these words: "Al-Qaida in Iraq claimed today it was behind the suicide bombings in Amman, Jordan. The attacks last night struck three hotels yesterday. At least 59 people were killed, and close to 100 others wounded. Most were Jordanians, but the dead also included one American."[63]

Who are the journalists already keeping track of? The sole American. And Lehrer was not the only anchor to be tracking Americans in his coverage. So too did Wolf Blitzer on CNN and Rita Cosby on MSNBC: "We got this word that at least 67 people are dead . . . still no word if any Americans are among the dead."[64] Even the *Daily Telegraph* in London noted in its top mention of casualties: "Most of the victims were said to be Jordanians, but Americans were believed to be among the dozens of dead."[65]

What if there were no Americans? Who do we care about then? Perhaps the dead included women and children. The media might linger over them longer. *All Things Considered* reported on the Israeli–Palestinian conflict in May 2001 by saying, "In the predawn darkness, Israeli tanks and bulldozers charged into a Palestinian refugee camp in the Gaza Strip, tearing down 20 houses and sparking a four-hour gun battle that left a Palestinian teenager dead and 14 others, including three children, injured." In this instance one teen was killed and 14 were injured—only three of whom we learn anything about. Who were those other 11 who were hurt? Presumably they were neither children nor teenagers. Five months later, in October 2001, this time a terrorist attack on a church in Pakistan, an article in the *New York Times* counted: "Sixteen worshipers died, including seven women, three children and the Protestants' 45-year-old pastor." The headline also mentioned that the 16 dead were all "Christians."[66] So 16 Christians (i.e., not Muslims) were killed, including a clergy member, seven women and three children. Who were those other five? Presumably they fell into a class of people "we," the audience, care less about. Presumably they were adult men. Like Noor Khan Burfat's brother in Karachi.

Coverage of victims, the dead and the survivors, is not egalitarian. The habit of categorizing the dead, of creating a hierarchy of victims to care about, does not only occur in breaking stories where deadlines are pressured. A *Washington Post* article about state terrorism in North Korea led with the story about the horrific abuse of women in state-run prison camps and noted that the US State Department charged the government with four categories of abuse against its own people: "forced abortions, murders of babies in prisons, kidnappings, and experiments using chemical and biological weapons on inmates."[67] Two of the described abuses related to children, and those were the two mentioned first. And a *Washington Post* editorial on the "grisly" uncovering of Iraqi mass graves— evidence of state terrorism under Saddam Hussein—noted:

> Western journalists have described horrific and pitiful scenes . . . as Iraqis scrambled to dig up remains of lost relatives: tiny children found next to their mothers; pregnant women uncovered with their fetuses; and people still wearing blindfolds with holes in the backs of their skulls. Many in these mass graves are Shiites shot in groups after a 1991 uprising.[68]

The "fact" that "many" in the graves were killed after an uprising suggests that most of the victims were adult males, yet the first four categories of "people" mentioned as being dug up were children, mothers, pregnant women, and fetuses. Victims presumed to be of lesser interest are left entirely anonymous, folded into the larger number of those wounded or killed, or not even referred to at all. Injury to children appears to be a more heinous crime than injury to adults. To mention the abuse (especially the intentional abuse) of children is to make a moral statement. The reporting of such abuse is an attempt to irretrievably damage the reputation of those accused of the harm. And, not coincidentally, it grabs our attention.

As these examples suggest, the "most important" victims—the ones the news outlet believes its audience will care about—are identified by age or gender or other attributes ("mother," "son," etc).[69] Who are the victims who appear in the news? First, your own nationals, then other foreigners, then the natives of the country being attacked. And of those latter, those who matter first are infants, and then young children, pregnant women, elderly women, all other women, teenage boys, and all other men. There is, in effect, a hierarchy of innocence, a hierarchy of those we learn about. Consider the headline on the front page of the *Washington Post*: "Special Sorrow for the Young: Israelis Lament Number of Children Killed, Hurt in Bus Bombing," underneath a large photo of the shrouded bodies of a mother, Goldie Zarkowski, and her "infant son, Eli" during an ultra-Orthodox Jewish funeral. Or the large photograph on the front page of *USA Today* 13 months earlier of a Palestinian mourner holding up the body of a 2-month-old baby wrapped in a flag and a kaffiyeh, who was "killed in an Israeli air-strike."[70] Why infants and children? They are innocent. Their deaths are shocking.

One consequence of this hierarchy of innocence, this hierarchy of those we are presumed to care about, is that foreign media—such as the American and British press—cover poorly those attacks which kill only indigenous victims. In the 16 months or so after 9/11 there were a number of terrorist attacks that occurred in Pakistan, for example, that appeared to target American or Western people or institutions. In addition to the kidnapping and death of *Wall Street Journal* reporter Daniel Pearl, the incidents that made at least some news in the United States and Europe were an attack in March 2002 when the International Protestant Church in Islamabad was attacked and five people, including two Americans, were killed and 40 were injured; a suicide car bombing in Karachi in May that killed 15, including 11 French naval engineers; a suicide truck bombing outside the US Consulate in June in Karachi, that killed 11; and an attack on 13 mostly German and Austrian tourists in July who were visiting archeological sites in the north of the country. While these stories were treated as short-term crises, and rarely lasted as long as a week in the back pages of the news, despite the clear longer term reverberations they would have in the region, terrorist acts that only targeted Pakistanis received almost no international attention. So a

March 2002 attack on a procession of Shiites that killed 43 and wounded 160, or an August attack on a missionary hospital that killed three Pakistani nurses, one of the assailants, and wounded 20 others, or a September attack that killed seven Pakistani aid workers at the Institute for Peace and Justice in Karachi, barely received any mention. Those attacks didn't speak either to the Western media's concern over whether the "War on Terror" was expanding or to the safety of Westerners. There was certainly little ongoing, on-the-ground coverage of the trauma of those attacks, for example, or of how the survivors were coping, or of how the violence was affecting local infrastructure such as transportation, schools, and workplaces.

It was the attacks like the one on Bali—or the ones in London or Madrid—that had the American and British media most heavily covering the victims and using eyewitness reports most extensively. Their audiences' default interest in those attacks, which seemed to strike literally and virtually most close to home, was in part, of course, because they saw people like themselves as victims. CNN's coverage of the attacks on the hotels in Jordan in 2005, for instance, made note of the fact that the hotels had likely been targeted because all three—the Grand Hyatt Hotel, the Radisson SAS Hotel, and the Days Inn—had American ties and were frequented by Western diplomats, businesspeople, and military contractors. Highlighted also was the fact that a large wedding celebration for 900 guests had been occurring in the Radisson Hotel. CNN observed that although the wedding guests were Jordanians and Palestinians, the wedding had been in a Western style: the men wore suits, the bride had worn a white gown, her hair had been uncovered, she had been walked down the aisle by her father. CNN obtained wedding photos taken before the attack and used them on air to dramatically highlight the joyous crowd before the suicide bomber struck and the devastation afterwards, when 38 people were killed, including the bride's father and the groom's father.

Those were the images, sadly enough, that made that awful attack on the Jordanian hotels most memorable. It's not just the knowledge that a wedding celebration was brutally ravaged, it's the images that we saw, the ecstatic snapshots that dissolved into photographs of horror. And it's our access to what should have been a private moment reserved for family and friends that gave the coverage the power it had.

Media's ability to offer specific details on the victims of terrorism has been heightened by the erupting phenomenon of citizen journalism. Media don't have to go out and hunt for wedding photos. Increasingly, non-journalists know to post their own images and reactions to the internet, even from locales such as Iraq. The US military, for example, has struggled with how to manage the emails sent, photos posted, and blogs written by the men and women in uniform; the immediacy and candor of these soldier journalists has given new insights into war and terrorism that were previously unavailable. Online surfers can navigate to sites in which people like themselves are not just anonymous commentators

—a "soldier in Iraq"—or nameless victims—"a commuter in Madrid"—but are on-scene reporters. Cellphone images sent into the *Guardian* and the BBC websites in the minutes and hours following the London bombings, for instance, gave a powerful new voice to the formerly voiceless "man" in the street and readers of those sites became eyewitnesses by proxy, much as the tourist videos uploaded to the internet had given the world front-row seats to the tsunami-racked beaches of Thailand and Indonesia six months before. On sites such as Flickr and Moblog, freelance journalism has exploded, and mainstream media such as Reuters, and news aggregators such as Yahoo!, have not only ceded blogging space to people who happen to capture a news event live, but beg them to upload their images and their thoughts.[71]

In 2001, wives and husbands and mothers waited days and weeks for the *New York Times* to affirm their losses with a 200-word essay on their missing loved one lost in the implosion of the World Trade Center. By the London bombing in 2005, there didn't have to be a wait—families and friends could publish their own accounts of those who had died—and in many cases on a mainstream media site as elite as the one that had validated the deaths of the victims of 9/11.

Surely that shift, enabled by technology, has given audiences more opportunities to learn about victims, survivors, and their communities—immediately and in follow-up accounts. But the "formal" mainstream media coverage—the front page of the paper, the top of the TV show, the online homepage coverage—has not changed as much as it should have as a consequence of this new first-person-possible engagement with journalism. Mainstream media still prefer simple death tolls, questions about culpability, references to precedent, and discussions about political consequences over human interest features. While the amount of attention given to specific victims has increased as discussion of the politics of terrorism has become repetitive, statistical casualty counts remain the dominant way of reporting on the wounded and dead. Mainstream media continue to cover terrorism as power politics, above all. As the specific victims of terrorism are never the point of terrorism, those victims still don't loom very large, very long, in the reporting on terrorist attacks and threats.

 # parsing the difference between terrorism and war

Consider two Reuters stories that appeared on the same day on MSNBC's website, both picked up and published within 5 minutes of each other on October 12, 2007. One was titled "Bali bomb victims recalled on 5th anniversary," and the other "Iraq bomber kills child and wounds 13 in playground."

The first two sentences of each?

KUTA, Indonesia—Dozens of people placed flowers and pictures of their loved ones at a memorial on the site of a deadly bombing on Indonesia's Bali island on Friday, the fifth anniversary of the attack. Survivors and families hugged each other as they remembered the victims of the blasts that ripped through the Sari Club and Paddy's Pub in the heart of Kuta in 2002, killing 202 people.

KIRKUK, Iraq—A bomb killed a child and wounded 13 others in a playground as they celebrated the Islamic festival of Eid on Friday in the northern Iraqi town of Tuz Khurmato, police said. Police Colonel Abbas Mohammed said a would-be suicide bomber hid the explosives in a cart he was pushing that was filled with children's toys.[72]

The first is an update on an attack that received tremendous coverage for weeks from literally hundreds of news outlets at the time it occurred. It remained in the global memory five years later. The second is the breaking story of an attack that occurred the day the story appeared. While multiple online news outlets carried a version of this Reuters story, including MSNBC and ABC News (and NBC's *Today* show aired a 21-word story on it at 7 a.m.), the attack did not receive any follow-up coverage.[73]

Why the difference in coverage between these two events? Why did the chilling calculation of the second attack receive some very small global attention, but only for a moment? Asked another way: What's the difference in how media cover acts of terrorism (such as the suicide bombing in Bali), and terrorist acts during a war (such as the suicide bombing in Iraq)?

Do terrorist acts that take place during an ongoing conflict get covered differently than similar acts that occur in regions of no or only sporadic violence?

Yes, they do.

Day 1 stories for the kind of quotidian terrorism that erupts in Iraq are rarely stories entirely about a specific terrorist attack. While the breaking news—how many killed where—is typically reported at the top, news organizations adapt and use a given attack or series of attacks as an example of a larger point they are trying to make.

If there isn't much international news on day 2 and day 3, then there might be follow-up stories, but those also tend to focus on the general level of violence in Iraq and how this particular event relates to that trend. This is especially true for broadcasters with their small news hole. CBS stopped covering the suicide bombings that struck the Red Cross headquarters (also on the first day of Ramadan) the very next day after it occurred—October 28, 2003. Others continued to reference the bombings, but used them to talk about the decision of some aid agencies to withdraw their people from Baghdad and the fact that the death toll for the after-conflict had now surpassed that for the initial invasion. Others rolled the violence together with other attacks. NBC, for example, led its second day coverage not with an update on the Red Cross attack, but with other attacks, calling it "another deadly day." That is a common approach and one NBC used repeatedly, such as in its follow-up reports on the bombing of the Golden Mosque in February 2005: "It was another day of violence for Iraqis as well. At least 30 Iraqis killed in a string of bombings and shootings and the question tonight is whether the Iraqi government can keep the incidents of the past few days from spinning out of control."[74]

Let's walk through a couple of differences between terrorist attacks that occur in the midst of a war (but that target civilians) and terrorist attacks that occur outside of an ongoing conflict.

First, attacks that occur in the midst of an ongoing war—even those that are not only aimed at civilians but that seem geared to gaining publicity—are less likely to be called "terrorism." They are more likely to be discussed with very straight-forward descriptions: a suicide bombing, a kidnapping.

Second, there are differences related to whether the attack receives Big Story coverage: Big Stories linger in the news longer and are covered in a wider range of ways. Suicide bombings in Iraq receive less specific coverage than attacks in other countries not in the midst of a war. They are *much* less likely to be Big Stories. ABC News anchor Charles Gibson, for example, admits that he often cuts news items "on the latest small-scale bombing" in Iraq. "That becomes white noise and I really worry about that," he said. "I almost always take that out of there, and I feel guilty when I do take it out. You become inured to it. It washes over you and you don't really hear it."[75]

When a terrorist attack occurs in a non-war zone, as was the case in the attacks on mass transit in London, Madrid, and Mumbai, for example, the death toll is high, the impact on everyday life for an entire metropolitan area is great, and a sense of panic spreads through an entire country. But "ordinary" suicide bombings, especially in Iraq, tend to be more common and tend to affect fewer civilians.[76]

And third, there are differences related to when the story was in the news: today most generic, everyday-type terrorism—the suicide bomb attack somewhere in some distant country suffering from ongoing violence (Iraq, Afghanistan, Darfur, etc.)—is covered from the outset as a trend story, while in the first several years after 9/11 most terrorism was initially reported as a breaking news story. That played out in Iraq: our studies found that it was more common in 2003, soon after the conflict in Iraq began, for reporters to draft the trend story in the days following an attack. The first day of coverage would be breaking news. By two years later, reporters worked the trends and context into the initial day's coverage.[77] By five years after the March 2003 invasion, coverage of Iraq in the US media in general had dropped off precipitously and so too had coverage of the "events" of the war. Coverage of Iraq by major US news outlets during the first three months of 2008 was just 15 percent of what it had been during the same period the year before, allowing for even less time for coverage of specific events than there had been earlier.[78]

So one key difference in the coverage of "terrorism" in peacetime versus the coverage of "terrorism" in wartime is how long stories that are specifically about a given terrorist attack stay in the news.

When we conducted our studies we first wrestled with a very basic question: for any given terrorist attack, what's the time period we have to look at to ensure that we are going to be analyzing effectively all of the coverage of that event? Initially we decided we didn't know, so we picked long frames of time and simply tracked how many days after an attack media covered it. That's when we confirmed that there were no hard and fast rules for how long a specific story would stay in play—in large measure, as mentioned before, how long media cover an event depends on what the competing news is. If an important story breaks, then poof! smaller stories evaporate to make room for the next big thing. But in the case of the Bali anniversary story and the Iraq playground story that MSNBC ran the same day, there was no story in the news that day or the next several that was so large that there was literally no room for continued coverage. Yet still the playground bombing did not make the news in the US and UK media after the breaking account of the bombing.

We also confirmed that the same questions that are used to determine whether or not a story will be covered at all—a familiar location, a high death toll, a continuously available stream of images, a palpable risk to the media audience—also help establish how long that story remains in the news. In the case of the two MSNBC stories, there were significant differences between the two bombings. While both were "distinctive" horrors—a bombing of a nightclub, a bombing of a playground—the death toll from Bali was far higher than that from the attack in Iraq, and in Bali a significant number of white foreigners lost their lives. There was extensive still and video coverage of the devastation in Bali, while no still photos or video of the playground aftermath moved in the media (or at least none were carried by the UK and US media). And while the Bali attack made tourists the world over nervous about what might happen to them, the playground suicide bombing (or attempted suicide bombing—the bomber survived) seemed to threaten no one other than the parents of children in Iraq; it did not appear that foreigners were targeted or that people living outside of Iraq should be concerned about the same terrorist group attacking them where they lived.

As we conducted our studies, we also confirmed that media originating in different places—New York v. Washington, Los Angeles v. London, Paris v. Jerusalem—have different priorities and make different assessments of what's important. Of the almost 400 stories that appeared in major news outlets worldwide on the fifth anniversary of the bombing in Bali, for instance, the overwhelming majority appeared in Australian news outlets.[79] Why? Because Bali was Australia's 9/11. It was the worst slaughter of Australians since World War II: out of the 202 who were killed in Bali by the terrorist bombs, 88 were Australians. Hundreds of others were injured.

As we conducted our studies, we finally confirmed too that different media—newspapers, magazines, radio, network television, cable television, public television, online outlets—cover stories differently. In fact it's fair to say that many of those differences have to do with the observation that different kinds of media operate on a different "deadline" clock.

What does that mean? In the heated 24/7 online world, stories are posted within minutes of their occurrence, get rapidly picked up and linked and blogged and emailed, and then, unless there's some controversy that keeps them on top, they cycle down the list of the top stories in favor of a more recent story—often measured in minutes and certainly in hours. On the online news aggregators such as Google or Yahoo! News, events stay in the top ranks for less absolute time than they do in those other media which don't have as voracious a demand for news. It's a tradeoff. Online news aggregators can cycle more stories through than daily or weekly print or broadcast outlets. But the stories tend to be short breaking accounts, lacking background and context, although there is the ability to link to related stories.

On dedicated news sites that have their own staff-written stories—the *New York Times* or the *Guardian*, or the *Economist* or *Time* magazines, say—the most recent stories are also what are featured and come up first. Stories on those sites, which are often created for the longer format of print, include more detail and often analysis. They can be paired with related sidebar elements: a photo gallery, a video or audio clip, a graphic of some kind, and perhaps room for comments. But even these sites feel the pressure to continuously update their websites, so contextualized stories are not always what comes up if you are doing a search for news. For example, if you trawl over to the *New York Times* site, midday East Coast time in the United States, you are likely to see on its homepage, and on the front pages for the major sections, the stories written by the *Times*' staffers for the print edition for the paper. But if you go to the site and put a keyword—say "Iraq"—into its search engine, you will pull up pages and pages of articles, the first several pages being stories posted in the last 12 hours, most recent listed first. The first several pages are likely *not* to be the exclusive *New York Times*-written stories, but stories drafted by Associated Press (AP) and Reuters reporters. Several pages in, with posting times near midnight the night before—the deadline for the print edition—you'll finally find the *Times* stories. If you don't pay attention to the bylines of the reporters, but just skim the headlines of those search pages, you'll never realize that the stories are originating from outside the *Times*' stable of journalists.

On those mainstream media sites, however, coverage of war zones (Iraq, Afghanistan, Israel–Palestine, etc.) is extensive and archived. There are often multiple staff-written and wire or syndicated stories every day on what's happening in those conflicts. But the majority of those accounts are about the politics of the fighting and the implications of what has just happened. It's the minority of stories that focus on a specific act of violence. While the wars are extensively reported and the role of terrorism in the wars may be extensively discussed, any given terrorist act is just a blip in the coverage.

For news aggregators, such as Google and Yahoo! there isn't much of a historical memory on the sites—at least that is emphasized (although searches through archives are possible). The reason people head to Google News and other similar sites is because, as Google News asserts on the top of its page, they allow visitors to "Search and browse 4,500 news sources updated continuously." That power and timeliness is what is so seductive. If a visitor doesn't personalize that homepage, he or she can expect to see two or three stories in all categories listed on the page: a Top Stories category, then the World, the US (for American surfers), Business, Sci/Tech, Sports, Entertainment, and Health. Prominently next to each byline is the time the story was posted: 6 hours ago, 1 hour ago, etc.

The timeliness of the aggregators' list of top stories is critical, but the list also needs to be eclectic. That's where there are issues with ongoing coverage—the day 2, day 5, day 14 follow-up of an individual terrorist attack. The mantra of news sites is "keep it moving, keep it different," so follow-up stories are rarely displayed.

Interestingly, the media originator of the "keep it different" principle was actually not an online outlet but the newspaper *USA Today*. From its launch in 1982 as a national paper, *USA Today* was financially dependent on people picking up single copies on news stands—much more so than other papers which had metropolitan subscription bases. *USA Today* understood that above the fold on its front page there needed to be one of everything: a political story and a sports story, an entertainment story and a business story. Each potential buyer of the paper is interested in reading something different, so the paper wants to quickly make an appeal to as broad a range of people as possible.

Other news outlets increasingly have come to share *USA Today*'s approach. For those online surfers who do not create their own tailored homepages for the kind of information they want, most news sites put up a range of story types on their homepage. Even traditionally serious papers such as the *New York Times*, the *Wall Street Journal*, and the *Financial Times* break up both their websites and their print pages with "lighter" stories. The *Wall Street Journal*'s "middle column" on its front page has long carried an offbeat story that has nothing whatsoever to do with the breaking economic news of the day, but instead regales readers with news of such essential cultural milestones as toad-licking, the Miss Agriculture pageant, the search for a low-flatulence bean, and the trials of a professional fish-sniffer. Articles won't begin with the kind of been-there-done-that sentences that lead their top stories, such as "President Bush, saying many Americans have lost faith in their ability to compete in the global economy, vowed to revive the country's free-trade agenda," but instead with such irresistible opening lines as "First, pretend that you are a sheep."

Let's face it. People want to read about toad-licking and want, if just for a moment, to pretend that they are a sheep. And media get that. Online and in other media, the featured news on sites can run the gamut from "Al Gore, U.N. agency share 2007 Nobel Peace Prize" to "Iraq bomber kills child and wounds 13 in playground" to "Former psych patient accused of stalking Uma Thurman indicted." And the top story on Yahoo! homepage the same day as the Nobel Peace Prize announcement, the Iraqi playground deaths, and Uma Thurman's stalker? "World's oldest wall painting: Archaeologists have discovered an 11,000-year-old wall painting that resembles modern art," followed by links to a "List of the most expensive paintings" and to a story on "How to appreciate modern art."[80] As Harold Evans, the former editor of the *Times* of London, observed, "The problem that many media organizations face is not to stay in business, but to stay in journalism."[81]

Putting something on the page for everyone means that there is an extraordinarily small news hole for any given kind of story. In many outlets there's space for only one of anything. The space on the page for the war in Iraq, for instance, may not be given to an attack that has killed just a few people, but to a story that affects "more" people, such as one about the crisis on the Iraq–Turkey border. There may be additional space on the page for an article about terrorism, however, in which case the story "Iraq bomber kills child and wounds 13 in playground" may make it if there's not another more deadly attack that happened elsewhere. But you probably should forget seeing a account of more than a single terrorist attack on the same day—especially if that other attack didn't happen to kill children (in a playground, no less), or pregnant women, or a Holocaust survivor, or a lot of white foreigners going clubbing at a beach resort.

Assume then that you've got your single story out there in front of people, and it lasts, well it lasts until the next single story comes along. How long, actually, is that? Bali lasted for weeks, even years, if you count anniversary stories. The playground bombing lasted for less than a day.

Is there an average? Well, kind of.

It's more or less three days—initial breaking news, some analysis pieces, and then internalization of the event, making the coverage relevant for the local audience. That's how long the story on the deadliest terrorist attack in Pakistan's history stayed at or near the top of news in the US and UK media. The attempted assassination of Pakistani former prime minister Benazir Bhutto in late October 2007 that killed over 130 and injured at least 300 had a first day of breaking coverage—horrific photos from the streets of Karachi and from the hospitals, updates on the number of dead and wounded, and further details about what happened, such as this line from the *Guardian*'s top story: "TV stations showed graphic images of mutilated bodies lying on a street littered with debris, body parts and lumps of charred flesh."[82] Then the media on day 2 prominently featured the reaction stories: US Secretary of State Condoleezza Rice's call of condolence and the responses of other world leaders, the response of the Pakistani government and the Karachi police, the grief of the victims' families, and above all, stories on who Bhutto herself blamed for the attack: "Ahead of her arrival," reported the AP via

Yahoo! News, "she said she was warned suicide squads were dispatched to kill her. 'There was one suicide squad from the Taliban elements, one suicide squad from al-Qaida, one suicide squad from Pakistani Taliban and a fourth—a group—I believe from Karachi,' she said."[83] And then, on day 3, came the localization of coverage: why should we care about this, what does this mean for us? So, the UK and US media covered the Pakistani story from the American or British angle: "American influence over events in Pakistan may be ebbing fast," noted the story in the *New York Times*.[84] After that coverage became more sporadic—not on the homepages of websites any more, for example, but on the news sites crawls or the phrase-long teasers on the right-hand rails, especially when some specific new piece of information emerged or a particular news outlet got an exclusive—so NBC's *Today* show hyped its program four days after the attack by saying: "In her first American television interview since the assassination attempt against her, former Pakistani Prime Minister Benazir Bhutto sits down with NBC News' Ann Curry . . . to report on why Pakistan could become the most dangerous nation in the world."[85]

So "big" terrorism stories stay three days near the top of the news, and sometimes four or five days if the event occurs late in the week, in which case there may be stories on it (or on the trend that it represents) in the weekend wrap-up of news on television or in the Sunday papers, as was the case with the Pakistan attack. And sometimes it's four or five days if the event is very emblematic of a current trend and politicians or others in the news are picking up on the event as a way in to tell their own message. But sometimes the coverage lasts just a day if the story is horrible enough to make the news in the first place—an attack on a playground—but not significant enough in itself or sufficiently representative of a trend or a global risk to remain on the news agenda.

But all things being equal, stories of attacks not related to wars get more attention—*much* more attention—than those that are. Stories of attacks that are big enough to get into the news in the first place stay there for several days, but very quickly taper off into references in stories about politics. And stories suffer from the competition of other events. Those "other" events, don't even have to be about "terrorism," they just have to be perceived by the news outlet to be of interest to its audience. There's a lot of competition in the news business.

  ## co-opting the news / co-opting the public

"Terrorism" is to a great extent in the eye of the beholder. Not only is the definition of terrorism contested by those who have political differences, but many of the players have a vested interest in defining terrorism in a certain way.

Nearly everyone agrees that terrorism is an abhorrent moral wrong and that calling someone a terrorist tars that person as outside the pale of humanity. But simultaneously, nearly everyone disagrees on how to define and identify terrorism. That all suggests that media must be especially cautious about how they report on terrorism. Should reporters themselves make the judgment that someone is a terrorist or that a specific act of violence is terrorism? The first chapter of this book laid out the reluctance of many media organizations, especially in the last several years, to set themselves up as arbiters. Okay, then, should reporters in those outlets be allowed to quote sources who charge others with terrorism—name-calling, but one step removed?

Take a look at three news stories. Both quotations listed for each are from the same story; the first is the narrative voice of the reporter or newscaster, the second is a quote or soundbite from a source:

Washington Post, August 29, 2003

Journalist: "The blast—the third car bombing in Iraq in 23 days—blackened one wall of the shrine . . ."

Paul Bremer: "L. Paul Bremer, the civilian administrator of Iraq, blamed the attack on 'the evil face of terrorism.' "

NPR, *All Things Considered*, October 9, 2003

Anchor: "Dozens more Iraqi civilians were wounded in a suicide bombing outside a police station."

Paul Bremer: "The importance and urgency of this task is underscored for all of us today when terrorists car-bombed a police station . . ."

CBS Evening News, November 12, 2005

Anchor: "A remotely triggered car bomb turned this Saturday morning market into an inferno . . ."

Kofi Annan: "This behavior, this terrorism, this brutal behavior is absolutely unacceptable. It is murder. It is terrorism, pure and simple."

Some media are comfortable with quoting others who use the "terrorism" word, especially, when the person doing the name-calling is a prominent newsmaker—such as a high-level official, the Secretary General of the UN, the President. Other media are increasingly chary about even that.

When readers, listeners, and viewers hear the words "suicide bomber" do they automatically think "terrorism"? If they hear policymakers talk about the "evil face" or the "brutal behavior" of the actors responsible, do they think any differently about that event or do such remarks only validate what they already believe? Does it make a difference if the comments are only in the voices of the sources—not in the words of the reporters or anchors? Or is that a nicety that the public just doesn't notice?

Perhaps the question can be put more broadly. How does the language of coverage shape the public's understanding of terrorists and terrorism? And further, how do "we" understand terrorism when sometimes terrorism isn't even called terrorism and when sometimes what's called terrorism isn't terrorism and when sometimes some people call some things terrorism and other people don't? (Whew!)

Consider "The War of the Words" experiments conducted by psychologist Elizabeth Dunn in 2005 with two colleagues at the University of Virginia.[86] Dunn wanted to see whether the words reporters use to write about violence in Iraq influence readers' thinking about terrorism. The catch was Dunn wanted to know if reporters influenced their readers' thinking about terrorism even when they didn't use the word "terrorism" or its derivatives.

Dunn randomly selected a dozen newspapers from around the United States and searched for articles published between July 30, 2003 and January 30, 2004 that included the key words "soldier," "dead" and "Baghdad." She then handed off those articles to students, who in turn determined whether further specific words when used were used in reference to the United States and its allies or in reference to the Iraqis (or others) who were not American allies. Perhaps no surprise, the students found that when the words implying destruction, such as "explosion," "blast," and "threat," and those implying malicious motivation, such as "plot," were used, they typically described the actions of the "enemy." When more "benign" words, such as "forces," "campaign," and "strategy" were used, they described American and allied actions.

But then the study got interesting. As a psychologist, Dunn is interested in perception and memory. She wanted to know how the public understood those word choices. Would readers of articles about an act of violence make a judgment about who committed that act of violence if the only "identifying" elements were one or the other of those sets of words—the "benign" set or the "malicious, violent" set? She constructed an experiment in which a brief article of less than 100 words was drafted about the bombing of a building and given to two sets of respondents: students and shoppers at a mall. One version of the article included the benign set of words, the other version the malicious, violent set.

Lo and behold, when the description of the bombing included the benign descriptions of the violent acts, the participants thought that the United States or its allies had bombed the building and when the article included the words that signaled greater harm and destruction, the students and shoppers believed that terrorists were responsible. In other words, those few different words that were thrown into the article influenced the readers' assumptions about whether Americans or the enemy had committed the act of violence.

But Dunn also asked the participants in the experiment to respond to four additional statements: "This was a legitimate military action," "This bombing was necessary for national defense," "Terrorists were responsible for the described bombing," and "This bombing was an act of terrorism." In effect by responding to these questions, the shoppers and students were being asked to make a moral judgment about the bombing. And again there seemed to be significant differences: participants who read the "us" version of the article viewed the bombing as a necessary, legitimate act, and those who read the "them" article believed the bombing was an act of terrorism. (Dunn was savvy enough to consider whether the political beliefs of the participants might skew the results—perhaps liberals, for example, would be more likely, no matter the word choice, to see the bombing as wrong. But after controlling for political orientation she found that political beliefs did not affect how readers understood the articles.)

Then Dunn was ready for the really critical experiment. How accurately did the shoppers and students remember what they read? She had proved that a significant number of them made groundless assumptions about the information in the bombing article. But why did they make those assumptions? So the third part of her study was to give a new set of participants either the "us" or the "them" version of the bombing story. This time after the participants read the stories they were shown a list of 32 words and asked which of the words actually appeared in the version of the article they had read. Nine of the words had actually been used and 23 had not. In the list of words for the bombing article, seven of the fake words —the words that had not appeared—were associated with terrorism and another seven with patriotism. The seven fake terrorism words were: *extremists, maimed, suicide bomber, Islamic, destruction, terrorist, fear*. The seven fake patriotism words were: *patriotic, legitimate, Marines, official, soldiers, military, authorized*.[87]

You probably won't be surprised by this point to learn that those who had read the "us" version of the article reported greater belief that the "patriotic" words had actually appeared in the article and participants who had read the "them" article believed the "terrorist" words had been in the story. Seemingly minor variations in the wording of the bombing article—use of words such as "explosion," "blast," "threat," and "plot" versus words such as "forces," "campaign," and "strategy" —influenced memory for the description of the violent act.

Dunn's research strongly suggested that even minor tinkering with words can influence how news consumers understand the news. Dunn actually did yet one more experiment where the participants in the study read "us" and "them" articles that differed by only three words: *forces* ("us" version) vs. *attackers* ("them" version), *bombing* ("us" version) vs. *explosion* ("them" version), and *strategy* ("us" version) vs. *plot* ("them" version). Again, she found the same results.

What we've learned so far in this book suggests that what should have mattered to the study participants in judging whether an event was terrorism was what the event was—the tactics—and who and how many were killed or injured. But those details remained the same in the articles in the study experiment. Here are the two final versions of the articles in their entirety:

"Us" Version

Forces bombed a prominent building early this morning in an unanticipated offensive.
The *bombing* caused the building to collapse in thirty minutes.
Seventeen people died, 11 were seriously injured, and 9 were reported missing.
This event is apparently part of a *strategy* to . . . [*continued*]

"Them" Version

Attackers bombed a prominent building early this morning in an unanticipated offensive.
The *explosion* caused the building to collapse in thirty minutes.
Seventeen people died, 11 were seriously injured, and 9 were reported missing.
This event is apparently part of a *plot* to . . . [*continued*]

Dunn found these results to be quite troubling. As she noted, "The observed effects are likely to be magnified in real-world contexts, where people are exposed over a longer period of time to more information that is probably more extreme. Thus, simple linguistic differences in news reporting may influence the public's support for international policies." If media coverage triggers people to consider actors terrorists—even in the absence of a label of terrorism—then they are likely to condemn them, said Dunn, with the results that "moderate responses such as engaging in negotiation with the perpetrators may be seen as less acceptable."

Well, huh. *How* media cover an event can affect how people understand that event. An audience doesn't just pay attention to *what* is said to have happened. *How* media report the story apparently matters too. That was the contention anyway of Dunn's group of academic psychologists. Two polling organizations, the Program on International Policy (PIPA) at the University of Maryland and Knowledge Networks, decided to ask similar questions about the role the media might play in how Americans understand the news. In a series of polls conducted during the summer of 2003 of a nationwide sample of over 3,000 respondents, PIPA and Knowledge Networks tried to figure out what perceptions Americans had about the Iraq war, with a special eye to determining what role the press had in shaping those beliefs.

The polls discovered that almost two-thirds of those surveyed believed something that wasn't true. Half believed that the United States had found evidence that Iraq was working closely with Al Qaeda, over one-fifth believed that actual weapons of mass destruction had been found in Iraq, and almost a quarter believed that world public opinion favored the United States going to war with Iraq. How could that have happened? How could so many Americans think these statements were true when no evidence of links between Al Qaeda and Iraq had been found, no weapons of mass destruction had been located, and polls of world public opinion had found clear majority opposition to the United States' war in Iraq?

Like Dunn a year and a half later, the PIPA pollsters wondered if political orientation made a difference—were Republicans, who would be greater supporters of President Bush, more likely to hold these misperceptions? But when they controlled for all other variables, there was no difference between Republicans and Democrats. There was, however, a strong correlation between support for the war in Iraq and the likelihood that the respondent would believe one of the three false statements. 86 percent of those who believed all three of the false statements supported the war, more than 75 percent of those who believed two of them supported the war, and slightly over 50 percent of those who believed one of the statements supported the war. But of those who rightly knew that all the statements were false, less than 25 percent supported the war.

Because the pollsters had been interested in determining whether media might be influencing Americans' grasp of the facts, the respondents were asked about their primary sources of news. They were given a range of news outlets to select from: Print media (including newspapers and magazines), public broadcasting (PBS television and National Public Radio), and five different television news outlets: CNN, ABC, CBS, NBC, and Fox. It turned out that where the respondents got their news mattered tremendously. Only 23 percent of those who watched or listened to public broadcasting believed one or more of the false statements, but 80 percent of those who watched Fox News did. Of those who read newspapers or watched CNN or NBC roughly 50 percent believed one or more false statements. Of those who watched ABC, slightly over 60 percent believed one or more false statements, and 70 percent of those who watched CBS did.

How could that possibly have happened? Well, one explanation might be that those who watched the programming on Fox, CBS, and ABC were not paying as close attention to the news as some others, such as those who read the newspapers or got their news from public broadcasting. And indeed there did seem to be some correlation with those who got their news from print sources. Those who said they spent more time reading the news had fewer misperceptions about the war. But surprisingly the opposite seemed to be the case for those who primarily watched Fox News—those who paid more attention were more likely to believe one or more false statements.

How could watching *more* news have led some people to the wrong conclusions? Let Steven Kull, the director of PIPA, explain how:

> The first and most obvious reason is that the Bush administration made numerous statements that could easily be construed as asserting these falsehoods. On numerous occasions the administration made statements strongly implying it had intelligence saying that Iraq was closely involved with al-Qaeda and was even directly involved in the September 11th attacks. The administration also made statements that came extremely close to asserting that weapons of mass destruction were found in postwar Iraq. On May 30, 2003, President Bush made the statement: ". . . for those who say we haven't found the banned manufacturing devices or banned weapons, they're wrong. We found them."

> But the fact that misperceptions varied so greatly depending on their primary source of news strongly suggests that the way that the press reported the news played a role. This might be partly due to prominent reporting of official statements saying that it appeared that clear evidence of weapons of mass destruction had been found, while the later conclusions—refuting such assessments—were given little play. . . . For example, when President Bush made the assertion that weapons of mass destruction had been found, the May 31, 2003 edition of *The Washington Post* ran a front-page headline saying "Bush: 'We Found' Banned Weapons."[88]

Of the television outlets, Fox and CBS were especially pro-war in their reporting. Fox's coverage of the Iraq war was framed on air by its banner "War on Terrorism," implicitly confirming the Bush administration's association between Saddam Hussein and Al Qaeda. And anchors at both networks argued unapologetically for their pro-war stance. Said CBS Evening News anchor Dan Rather in an interview with Larry King following the fall of Baghdad in early April 2003: "Look, I'm an American. I never tried to kid anybody that I'm some internationalist or something. And when my country is at war, I want my country to win. . . . Now, I can't and don't argue that that is coverage without a prejudice. About that I am prejudiced." CNN's Aaron Brown admitted the same to those who accused him of being pro-war and pro-administration: "I think there is some truth in it." And Fox anchor Neil Cavuto, in response to criticism about Fox's gung-ho politics, defended himself by saying: "You say I wear my biases on my sleeve. Better that than pretend you have none, but show them clearly in your work."[89]

Dunn's experiments and PIPA's polling are strong evidence that audiences are influenced in what they think about terrorism by how media cover terrorism. They also suggest that those media that have firm guidelines in place about when it is appropriate to use the word "terrorism" are on the right track. Dunn and PIPA's data point up three key concerns.

1   Audiences can be directed what to think about terrorism. The word "terrorism" doesn't have to be used for consumers of a news story to be cued to think about terrorism and to make value judgments about what has occurred—and what should be done as a result. Other words and combinations of words can powerfully package a message about terrorism, even when it appears that the coverage is quite dispassionate.
2   Audiences can be influenced in their opinions by how news is delivered. Long, complex stories complete with background details, analysis, and multiple speakers from various perspectives—such are found on public broadcasting— do a good job of accurately informing their audiences about the news. Shorter newscasts, oriented toward headlines and especially toward more stenographic coverage of official policy and statements and less rigorous debate of that policy, are considerably less successful at giving their audiences accurate portrayals

of news and events, even leaving aside their ability to deliver depth, perspective, and context.

3   Audiences are less aware of the nuances of journalistic standards than are journalists themselves. The public makes assumptions about what is being said with little second guessing—if a statement appears in the media the public takes it on face value. This is where the issue of sourcing and attribution matters tremendously—but not necessarily in the ways that have usually been discussed. While journalists dither and worry (actually, entirely appropriately), about whether a piece of information included in a story is sourced anonymously or by reference to a specific person with an actual phrase or sentence that is put in quotes, the public reading the story or listening to the account is mostly just taking in the bit of information.

Take three examples from two elite, credible US news outlets. After US and allied forces took Baghdad in early April 2003, the hunt for Iraqi weapons of mass destruction began in earnest. As April ended, the month of May passed, and Iraqi WMD remained elusive, reporters became increasingly cynical about their existence. But even late in May few news reporters (as distinct from columnists or commentators) frontally challenged administration assertions about the existence of WMD or about the conduct of the search. However, by the simple expedient of juxtaposing contradictory statements, reporters tried to imply to readers that the administration's statements and conclusions were suspect. Judith Miller and William Broad did just that in a *New York Times* page 1 lead on May 21: "United States intelligence agencies have concluded that two mysterious trailers found in Iraq were mobile units to produce germs for weapons, but they have found neither biological agents nor evidence that the equipment was used to make such arms, according to senior administration officials." But what was the headline for the story laced with anonymously sourced doubts? "GERM WEAPONS: U.S. Analysts Link Iraq Labs to Germ Arms."[90] So to those who just scanned the front page of the *Times*, the overall impression made by Miller and Broad's article was that the trailers provided proof of Hussein's WMD program.

Similarly, as previously mentioned, the *Washington Post* was careful to put quotation marks around the "We Found" in its front-page headline saying "Bush: 'We Found' Banned Weapons." To a reporter those small marks were red flags that the statement was not a fact but an assertion. To most readers, however, those marks were invisible. Readers who scanned the headline could easily take away the impression that the President had announced that WMD had been found. The headline appeared to state a discovered fact, and the story's location on the front page (even if below the fold) only further confirmed the importance of the story. If the statement was only hearsay, what was it doing on the front page? In Kull's and others' estimation, such headlines lead readers astray.

A third example highlights the problem with using anonymous sources. In the *New York Times'* front-page analysis piece following the October 2007 Karachi bombing of former Pakistan prime minister Benazir Bhutto's convoy that killed over 130 people, all the sources in the first five paragraphs were anonymous, including the lead which set up the article's argument about a "nightmare scenario" that would emerge for the United States if Pakistan had a political meltdown.[91] That was credited to "one senior administration official." The next paragraph led with "White House officials" and the third paragraph led with "But other current and former officials" (of what? the article doesn't say). Deep into the story, after hearing from other unnamed officials and two named sources, we meet another "senior administration official," but this time we're told that that person "could not speak for attribution because of the delicacy of the issue." That official is quoted, not paraphrased. In those first paragraphs there are warring opinions put forward— on one side is the "senior administration official" and "White House officials" and on the other side are the "other current and former officials." Which side are we to believe? Will Musharraf be able to keep control of the country? Does the US retain any influence on his government? How can we tell? What is the value of even writing the story if there is no way for readers to evaluate the information given by being able to consider the credibility—or professional position—of the source?

As PIPA's polling suggests, stories that are sourced mainly by anonymous informants are not understood by news consumers much differently than those that are sourced by named ones. It is only in hindsight, when additional information surfaces that challenges the initial reports, that the problems of having information sourced anonymously emerge—such as in the stories in the lead-up to the Iraq war that quoted administration sources on weapons of mass destruction.

Words matter. If the PIPA poll evaluated media's influence at the macro level, Dunn looked at the micro level. Dunn's work clued us in to words' power, even words as seemingly impartial in their description of an event as "bombing" and "explosion." And what about the effect of other words too, less neutral on their face? What power do they have? Have reporters used them incautiously too? Typically such words only come to our attention when they themselves become the story. Take the word "madrassa," a new, post-9/11 vocabulary acquisition for many in the United States and Europe. Very few politicians or news outlets that use the word stop to define the term for their audiences. "Madrassa" literally means school in Arabic (and other regional languages, although Arabic is the root), but the inference the US public, for example, is supposed to make when it hears the word is that all madrassas are anti-American, anti-Western, pro-Taliban, pro-terrorist centers having less to do with teaching basic literacy and more to do with political indoctrination.

As the controversy early in 2007 over Democratic Senator Barack Obama's childhood schooling dramatically pointed up, the use of the word "madrassa" carries a loaded political meaning. The smear campaign against Obama began in *Insight Magazine* with an article that led with this opening line: "Are the American people ready for an elected president who was educated in a Madrassa as a young boy and has not been forthcoming about his Muslim heritage?"[92] The tale was spread on radio talkshows such as Rush Limbaugh's, and talkshow host Debbie Schlussel took up the cry: "His full name—as by now you have probably heard—is Barack Hussein Obama, Jr. Hussein is a Muslim name, which comes from the name of Ali's son—Hussein Ibn Ali."[93]

Newsweek columnist Jon Alter summarized the import of the attempt to "Swift-Boat" Obama, which had quickly moved to the public center stage on Fox News after the *Insight Magazine* debut:

> The subtext of the story was that Obama was some kind of Muslim Manchurian Candidate (or the Russian spy played by Kevin Costner in "No Way Out")—trained in an Indonesian religious school to be a jihadist who would do Al Qaeda's work from within. . . . Even after the story was debunked, the folks at Fox News Channel wouldn't apologize, and in one case kept pushing a line on the air they knew was false. . . . CNN dispatched a reporter to Obama's old school in Jakarta, where he revealed it to be a normal public school with religion classes only once a week and no indication of Wahhabism, the Saudi-inspired extremist philosophy. (Indonesian schools were even more secular 40 years ago than they are today.) The whole underlying tale was untrue.[94]

The *New York Times*, which had covered the Fox News controversy a week after it broke in *Insight*, ran a correction to its story. It too had run afoul of the politicization of the word "madrassa": "An article on Wednesday about a pointed exchange between CNN and Fox News over a Web site report that said Senator Barack Obama had attended an Islamic school or madrassa in Indonesia as a child referred imprecisely to madrassas. While some teach a radical version of Islam, most historically have not. (Mr. Obama's office has said the report is untrue.)"[95] Note too that even the *Times'* correction essentially used the phrase "a radical version of Islam" as code to mean "terrorism."

Six years previously, in the days and weeks and months immediately following September 11, stories, especially in American news outlets, tried to parse the answer to the question "Why do they hate us?" Madrassas became a convenient scapegoat: they hate us because madrassas train them to hate us. As the Americans and their British allies geared up for war in Afghanistan with the launch zone in Pakistan, stories repeatedly mentioned that Pakistan had thousands of madrassas across the country. The clear—and sometimes explicit—allegation was that the region was virtually awash with training camps for terrorists masquerading as schools for boys, as in this *Seattle Times* article from Sept. 16, 2001: "While most of Pakistan's 140 million people are devout but relatively moderate Muslims, there are several strong militant Islamic groups operating in the country and tens of thousands of religious schools that turn out young boys dedicated to jihad holy war."[96]

Madrassas were noted both as breeding grounds for terrorists and, not coincidentally, for discrimination against women. Boys who went to such schools were distanced from the softening "influence" of women:

*   *New York Times*, October 2, 2001: "Boys, raised without fathers, were sent to religious schools, or madrassas, taken away from daily village life and away from the influence of women."[97]
*   *Los Angeles Times*, November 4, 2001: "Hence, perhaps, the all-male madrassas in Pakistan, where boys as young as 6 are trained for jihad, far from the potentially softening influence of mothers and sisters."[98]
*   *Boston Globe*, February 24, 2002: "The religious schools that are springing up all over Pakistan create societies in which young boys are indoctrinated in a fundamentalist brand of Islam that teaches hatred of the West and of Jews. The schools are all-male societies in which the boys have no contact with girls or women—except maybe a mother or an aunt."[99]

Intellectuals as diverse as former Speaker of the House Newt Gingrich and *New York Times* columnist Thomas Friedman spoke harshly about the role the Islamic schools play in advocating hatred. Said Gingrich: "Some people really hate us. This is not a problem of communication. They understand what America is and what we stand for, and still they want to kill us. . . . The Wahhabi sect has become a worldwide movement of radical Islam perpetuated by madrassas that indoctrinate young males into this fanatical belief system, of which Al Qaeda is merely a symptom. Its goal is to create a world incompatible with our survival."[100] And Friedman noted: "50 years of failed democracy, military coups and imposed religiosity have produced 30,000 madrassahs—Islamic schools, which have replaced a collapsed public school system and churn out Pakistani youth who know only the Koran and hostility toward non-Muslims."[101]

Five years after Friedman and Gingrich's comments, following the October 2007 Karachi bombing of Bhutto's convoy, the *New York Times* reported that "Almost every major terror attack since 9/11 has been traced back to Pakistani territory, leading many who work in intelligence to believe that Pakistan, not Iraq, is the place Mr. Bush should consider the 'central front' in the battle against terrorism."[102] Friedman had the right of it. Poverty and a lack of state-funded public education had led to the growth of madrassas across Pakistan (and other Muslim countries, such as Indonesia)—there are an estimated 7,000–11,000 such schools, serving between 600,000 and 700,000 children, almost all boys. The desperate need for elementary schools, especially in the areas where Al Qaeda and the Taliban have thrived in the north and west of the country, in fact prompted the US State Department to launch a $750 million program to bring schools and economic development to those regions.[103]

But too often a broad brush was used in media stories. It's not as if there aren't "bad" madrassas out there, but conflating all Islamic schools together—as, for example, the *New York Times* was guilty of doing in the Barack Obama story— does not assist news consumers either in understanding the problem of why some madrassas are integral to the rise of Al Qaeda's and the Taliban's brand of terrorism or in understanding the range of possible solutions to the spread of terrorism.[104]

The most responsible coverage of madrassas comes when reporters tell their audiences why some of these most radical madrassas draw parents to send their sons. A page 1 *Washington Post* article six months after September 11 gave a more balanced account of the appeal of one of those:

> For anyone wishing better circumstances for their male children, the Darul Uloom Islamia madrassa in Karachi offers a number of benefits. The 10,000 boys there receive proper meals and medical care at a clinic staffed by doctors. The youngest boys—ages 5 to 7—mostly sleep at home, but older students stay in rooms that usually sleep three or four. Tuition and room and board are free.
>
> The teachers and scholars at the madrassa were held in high esteem by Afghanistan's Taliban leadership and by Osama bin Laden—so much so that bin Laden invited half a dozen members of its faculty to attend his son's wedding in February 2001. The madrassa is believed by Pakistani experts to be a breeding ground for terrorist organizations.[105]

These varied uses of the word "madrassa" serve as a case study to help us to follow the threads of language through a series of stories and detect how a word can carry significance beyond its specific definition. The various usages illuminate how those who are aware of the additional meanings of words can cannily use them to their own purposes. When is a madrassa a madrassa? When speakers, from all corners, have an agenda they want to pursue and mentioning madrassas, or blaming madrassas, serves that purpose. When is a madrassa not a madrassa? When it's just a school for boys.

To a tremendous degree, language shapes the terrorism issue—but our studies documented that most terms of the discussion go unexamined in the media.[106] Problematic words are too rarely flagged as being problematic. The choice of terms, the failure to define them, the conflation of disparate ideas, groups, events, places by the use of umbrella words and phrases such as "madrassa" and "weapons of mass destruction," are all ways that the coverage of terrorism can be distorted. The infinitely malleable nature of language makes it possible for a discussion to be skewed without any factual inaccuracies. We weren't lying, said a Bush spokesman to correspondent John Cochran of ABC's *Nightline*. "It was just a matter of emphasis."[107]

There is even a need for reporters to be clearer about the "who" of terrorism. As terrorist attacks became more frequent following 9/11[108] distinctions were not always made between different terrorist groups. Following September 11, Al Qaeda, for example, became a near-synonym to "terrorism." Its name and reach were invoked by both politicians and reporters—as was the generic threat of "Islamist terror"—especially in the coverage of regions where the indigenous terrorist groups were more or less unknown to audiences at home. In regions such as South Asia that have been historically more poorly covered in the United States than the Middle East, distinctive terrorists groups and their histories were often glossed over or blurred, such as in an editorial in 2002 by the *Philadelphia Inquirer*: "The United States has given insufficient attention to South Asia over the years. That changed after Sept. 11. Now, the U.S. interest in calming this region is clear. The militants that launched terrorist attacks into India—like the December assault on the Indian Parliament or the one last month on an Indian army camp—may even have links to al-Qaeda."[109] So, for example, reporters will not bring Al Qaeda into a story where Hamas is the perpetrator, but in accounts of terrorism in Asia and Africa, Al Qaeda often receives significant mention even when there are no explicit ties that are known between the group that claims responsibility for a bombing and Al Qaeda.

Then there are the frequent occasions when the perpetrators of specific acts are not identified at all or until late in the story—instead the term "terrorist" is used generically. That is both a consequence of officials not knowing what group (if any) is responsible for a given attack—say a suicide bombing in Iraq—but also a result of reporters not taking the time or space to discuss the specific background or agenda of a fringe terrorist group or of editors believing that leading a story with some unknown terrorist group will attract less of an audience than a story that leads with a discussion of "radical Islamic" "terrorism."[110] A classic case of that was a front-page, above-the-fold story by the *New York Times* titled "North Africa Feared as Staging Ground for Terror." The entire story focused on a single "Islamic terrorist organization," but failed to give the name of the organization until two columns and eight paragraphs into the story.[111] The problem with such approaches, of course, is that, by just referencing "terrorists" generically, all terrorism blurs into one huge—global even—scary and insoluble threat.

Journalists covering terrorism need to provide definitions. They need to tell their audiences about words or terms whose meanings are contested. They need to identify terrorist groups and distinguish one from another. And they need to do all that briefly in *every* article—*especially* in those front-page and top-of-the-TV news stories that people actually read and watch, not just in those that run in the back of the paper or air at the end of a newscast. The *Wall Street Journal* does essentially that in its articles that take a phrase to clarify ARM mortgages or how the commodities market relies on shipping. It can be done.

What else? Media shouldn't fall into the trap of adopting terms and phrases that are entirely constructed to provide spin. The first chapter of this book looked at the "spin" that the phrase "War on Terror" added to the post-9/11 foreign policy of the White House and Downing Street. But governments and militaries are always trying to put their best slant on a policy. Take WMD again. In covering weapons of mass destruction, reporters and editors do not cavil at using "cute" terms dreamed up by policymakers such as "mini-nukes" or "bunker-busters" (or quoting others using them), witness the *Washington Post* story with the headline, "Nuclear Weapons Development Tied to Hill Approval: Senate Democrats Fight Administration's Effort to Build 'Mini-Nukes' and 'Bunker-Busters.'" Such friendly characterizations are in a long history of military and administration officials using upbeat and accessible terms to refer to nasty weapons—whether the military hardware is officially named, such as the Patriot missile, or informally nicknamed, such as "Puff the Magic Dragon" or "Bouncing Betty." Employing such a term as "mini-nuke" conjures images of Austin Powers' "Mini-Me"—a wanna-be weapon not to be taken terribly seriously, although they are taken very, very seriously when non-aligned countries posit building them.

As writer Margaret Drabble wrote in the *Daily Telegraph*, "Long ago Voltaire told us that we invent words to conceal truths."[112] Journalists shouldn't be part of that conspiracy. They need to use words to unveil truths, not to help package the government's agenda.

 the stories that are told

We live by narratives, by the stories people tell. What we learned from Dunn's studies and PIPA's polls is that what matters is how an event is understood and how that narrative becomes the convention. "To a very large extent," observed writer Philip Gourevitch, "power consists in the ability to make others inhabit your story of their reality."[113] Those who tell the stories, map our understanding of our world. Those who manage our sense of "reality," control our interest in taking future action related to the story.

This process of shaping the news is called "framing." "Frames," which are just patterns used to explain events, operate by making a number of indirect points in ostensibly transparent stories. Each frame "organizes" an event or series of events in a particular way, perforce excluding other ways of considering that event.

Frames simplify, prioritize, and structure news events and issues. "Without knowing much, if anything, about the particular people, groups, issues or even places involved," Harvard professor Pippa Norris and others have noted, "the terrorist and the anti-terrorist frames allows us to quickly sort out, interpret, categorize and evaluate these conflicts."[114]

The framing of news is part of politicians' repertoire of "spin"—that marketing grab-bag of tricks government officials (and others) employ to put the best possible construction on a policy decision.[115] Governments "spin" their stories much like Rumpelstiltskin, trying to turn political hay into gold. Sometimes they spin information through careful choice of words. Sometimes they spin the news by co-opting sources—as in the Pentagon's military analyst operation. Sometimes they spin news stories by producing the stories themselves—for example, they disseminate news segments in the form of video news releases (VNRs) that when aired on local television stations seem to viewers to be reported by the stations' own staff but are in reality promo pieces reported by hirees of the administration. And sometimes governments spin the news through the outright buying of journalists—as when the Pentagon made covert payments to Iraqi newspapers to publish coalition propaganda, or when other Washington agencies paid American columnists to write favorably about the Bush White House.

And then there are the media, with their repetition of the government's spin or their own self-interested selection of which countries and events to cover and how to feature them. These actions too, are a kind of "spin," a "packaging" of the news, if you will.

Consider the example of the Cold War.

The frame of the Cold War made the world into an "us" versus "them" arena. Not only relations with the Soviet Union, but international affairs in Africa, Asia, and Central America were understood through the lens of communism. The fear of "losing" countries to the Soviets gave birth to the domino principle and the notion of proxy states—policies that prompted American engagement in countries such as Vietnam, Nicaragua, and Ethiopia.

The meaning of the Cold War frame went well beyond the James Bond stereotyping of who the good guys were and who the bad guys were. The Cold War defined who Americans could support and who they couldn't—anyone who was a friend of the USSR was no friend of the USA and vice versa. The "enemy of my enemy is my friend" logic made for some very uncomfortable bedfellows, but helped immensely in clarifying who Americans should care about and in defining who mattered.

Then the rattling of the Iron Curtain in the 1980s, which culminated in the tumbling of the Berlin Wall in 1989, changed not only the political landscape in Europe, but the perception of global politics. Entire regions fell off the political and media radar. Nasty conflicts in out-of-the-way places no longer mattered as proxy wars; brutal struggles for power were dismissed by both politicians and the press as internecine tribal or ethnic or religious conflicts without external ramifications.[116] There were few perceived overarching reasons as to why outsiders should care about sub-Saharan Africa, Southeast Asia, or even eastern Europe any more. No dominant vision—or even snappy moniker—appeared to unify what was happening, despite a call by many that "humanitarianism" compelled engagement. Indeed, there was a general retreat from international affairs on the part of both the Bush, Sr. and Clinton White Houses as well as of the media.

Then came September 11. "Every nation in every region now has a decision to make," said President Bush in his speech on September 20, 2001. "Either you are with us or you are with the terrorists."[117] Within weeks, Bush's new "War on Terror" frame became the default test used to discover who were Americans' global "friends" and "enemies." The "War on Terror" became the window through which all international events were viewed—a situation that emphasized places and events that had (or were purported to have) connections to "global terrorism," but that left others that didn't neatly fit the terrorism frame out of public view. Newsrooms scrambled to cover both domestic and foreign terrorist-related events—a scramble made all the more ungainly because all but a few media outlets were woefully understaffed with reporters expert in international affairs, a consequence of the past years' closing of overseas bureaus and cutbacks on time and space devoted to foreign news in order to save money and boost profits. Understaffing—and the prior undervaluing of international coverage—made it more difficult for news organizations to cover the assumptions behind the "War on Terror" frame, and parenthetically made it more difficult for them either to nimbly cover the changing terrorism story—from Osama bin Laden to anthrax to the Axis of Evil to weapons of mass destruction, and so on—or to cover foreign stories unrelated to the terrorism arc.

Now, truth be told, it is impossible *not* to frame coverage of events, issues, and people—the exercise of translating an event or situation into words and pictures inevitably results in choices being made. But media frames (and political frames) work by directing audiences to consider an event or situation in a particular way. The problems emerge in that while "framing" the news is inevitable, most frames are not only simplistic in their articulation of the causes and consequences of an event or the ramifications of an issue, they also—tacitly at least—enunciate a moral argument as the famous political frames have bluntly done: the "Cold War," the "War on Terror," the "Axis of Evil." Most frames ultimately place us into making rather binary moral decisions: support "us," not "them." "This" is the way to solve the problem, not "that." This yes-or-no, you're-either-with-us-or-against-us moral equation is a problem. The world is more complex than that.

At their most basic, "frames" are just one-dimensional stories that are constructed in rather formulaic ways. Just as we are conditioned to believe that fairytales that begin "Once upon a time" will end with "And they lived happily ever after," the news stories that are told of the terrorism in our world today also often follow certain conventions. If a story begins in a certain way, we can be conditioned to think that it will end in some predetermined manner. How do media make sense of terrorism? What's emphasized and what's downplayed or ignored? The news may focus on the arc of action, but frame that action in specific ways—either arguing that terrorism is an unstoppable force that we just have to learn to live with or that it is controllable if we find the right levers to pull. The news we hear may emphasize the mercilessness of the bad guys—assigning them demonic intentions—or focus on the righteousness of the good guys—making them seem heroic in their efforts. Some frames blame individuals or certain groups, other frames find social forces and political or religious agendas to be at fault.

To get an idea of the kind of frames in play and what their repercussions are, let's examine a few of the most prevalent that haven't already been mentioned.

1　The "Combative" or "Uncontrollable Cycle of Violence" Frame

Stories that follow this frame emphasize a laundry list of violent acts that seems to have no ending, and, at times, no point. Conflicts in Africa and the Middle East where terrorism has been ongoing are often represented in this manner—a manner that glosses over political distinctions and ignores or minimizes the influence of such socio-economic factors as demographic pressures, control of the water supply, and lack of educational and employment opportunities. The most notorious use of this kind of framing occurred during the media's coverage of the 100 days of the 1994 genocide in Rwanda. The *Los Angeles Times* wrote one month into that disaster that the killing taking place was just the "latest round of mass murder by the Hutu and Tutsi tribes," making it appear that the genocide was just another spree of tribal bloodletting with no larger agenda than the presumed tendency of the Hutus and Tutsis to frequently lapse into conflict.[118]

Coverage of an event framed in this way typically sets up a Hatfields-and-McCoys mindless cycle of violence—that side did this in response to the other side that did that, which was in retaliation for the first side doing this. Such a cataloging of events *appears* to give context to the most recent act, but when one traces back the causes mentioned all one has been told is of additional violence without any indication of why the violence began in the first place. NBC's breaking report of the bombing of the three Egyptian resorts in October 2004 followed such an outline. Said anchor Tom Brokaw:

It's another terrible night in the Middle East. This time, just inside Egypt, at three resorts popular with Israelis. A massive explosion tore the front off a Hilton Hotel. In all, more than three dozen people are believed to have been killed tonight. Two other resorts nearby were hit a short time later. This after the Israelis stepped up their attacks against Palestinian targets in the Gaza Strip in recent days as an answer to more attacks from within that embattled zone.[119]

Language can be a clue to this kind of framing of events. Using words such as "retaliation" or "aggression" may seem to speak to the issue of which side is culpable—which side is acting in self-defense against the offensive action of the other—but typically the cause given for the retaliation is some event just past rather than a larger explication of the context of the fighting. So, for example, in the coverage of the second Intifada in 2001, Noah Adams of NPR's *All Things Considered* could report:

Israeli troops battled Palestinian gunmen for about 90 minutes today in the Gaza Strip, jeopardizing efforts to arrange a cease-fire. Palestinian leader Yasser Arafat called for a truce over the weekend, following Friday night's suicide bombing in Tel Aviv that left 20 Israelis dead. Israel has not yet retaliated for that attack, saying it will give Arafat more time to implement a cease-fire. Today, each side blamed the other for starting today's gun battle.[120]

Here the explanation for the gun battle was presumably "Friday night's suicide bombing" (although Adams says that "Israel has not yet retaliated for that attack"), but the larger story of the fighting is not discussed or signaled. There may be a presumption on the part of reporters and editors that the public knows the background of long-running conflicts so that nods to context do not have to be made. But the implication of the stories, taken by themselves—and often in the aggregate— is that the violence has no proximate cause.

This kind of historical-ahistorical discussion of violence ironically most often surfaces when violence has become extreme, when stories become summaries of multiple attacks rather than discussions of single events, and when stories are rushed into print or put on air before much is known about the events that are reported. A front-page *New York Times* article from January 2006 that summarized multiple attacks across Iraq was such an example:

Attacks by suicide bombers killed as many as 130 people in Karbala and Ramadi on Thursday, rekindling fears of a return to mass sectarian killings after a relative lull and prompting Iraq's most powerful Shiite political faction to warn of retribution and indirectly blame the United States for the bloodshed. In a separate attack, a roadside bomb killed at least five American soldiers near Karbala, Iraqi and American officials said. At least two other Americans were reported killed in one of the suicide attacks.[121]

Who killed all these people? We don't learn. Why were they killed? We aren't told. Clearly the reporter doesn't know either, but the effect of hearing about the terrorism and the deaths without such information is that we have no way of making sense of it all other than by reference to such generic causes as "the United States" or by reference to statistics: how many killed, is the number of attacks increasing or decreasing, etc., etc. Neither the death tolls nor the United States raised up as the bête noir helps us either figure out what to make of it all or what to do.

On the other hand, although it may be unsatisfying not to have answers about who perpetrated an attack and why, it is far worse when media wander off into speculation about either—far better to admit that the details are currently unknown. Take as an example this exchange on CNN in the aftermath of a March 2004 bombing of the Mount Lebanon Hotel in Iraq. Anchor Carol Costello asked CNN security analyst J. Kelly McCann: "So who's to blame, do you think?" "Well, I think that everyone's in agreement that it is Islamist fundamentalists," responded McCann. "I think that trying to determine who, in fact, it is—because there's a loose affiliation. I mean you've got Zarqawi's affiliation with al Qaeda. You've got al Qaeda. You've got Ansar al-Islam. And although they're not linked at the arms, they do assist each other when it meets a common goal, which is basically to kill Westerners. So it'll be probably some time, unless someone claims responsibility and it's vetted, that we find out exactly who's responsible."[122]

Who should we fear? Well, we don't really know, but let's mention everyone who's out there and loosely tie them all together. Then for good measure let's say that actually the threat is as all-encompassing and as generic as "Islamic fundamentalists"—which of course *should* be a term that simply describes those who advocate a literal interpretation of the texts of Islam and of Sharia law, rather than be understood as a coded phrase that means "terrorists." (Interestingly, Wikipedia notes in its entry for "Fundamentalist Christianity" that after terrorist groups in Lebanon and elsewhere began to be referred to as "Islamic fundamentalists" after their capture of hostages in the 1980s and 1990s, the word "fundamentalist" began to be generally associated with "terrorism," and conservative Christians began to reject the term "Fundamentalist Christian" as pejorative in meaning, coming to prefer the term "Evangelical Christian.")

2   The "Blaming the Nation" Frame

Another frame that abdicates assigning clear responsibility for conflict is a frame that attributes actions generically either to a nation or a people—to the Iraqis, the Palestinians, the Sudanese, the North Koreans, etc. Discussing events in this fashion blurs together into one amorphous mass all actors and groups within a country.

It also is a bit akin to the passive voice—it begs the question of who actually is doing what. Who are the "Americans"—Democrats? Republicans? African Americans? People who live in Washington, DC? Who are the "Palestinians"? Followers of Hamas or Fatah or neither? And what about even larger blanket terms, such as "the West"? With Germany, France, and the United States as clear members of "the West," yet frequently at political loggerheads, how meaningful a term is that? And does "the West" refer to the new inductees of the EU such as Bulgaria and Romania? Does it include Turkey, which is not an EU member, but is part of NATO? When the *Daily Telegraph* in London says: "The West is stepping up pressure on Teheran over its continuing nuclear technology programme," which countries is it referring to? Who in which countries is actually pressuring "Teheran"?[123]

Take a look at how NPR and the *New York Times* spoke about the role of United States in the Iraq war in May 2003, following the march to Baghdad. Neal Conan, the host of NPR's *Talk of the Nation*, asked one of his guests about the length of time it was expected that American troops would stay in Iraq: "As you look ahead, does any kind of timetable present itself to you? I know that the United States has said, you know, 'As long as we're needed and not one day longer.' That's not a very concrete time proposal."[124] And a *New York Times* article on the regional repercussions of the Iraq war noted: "The United States has demanded Hezbollah's withdrawal from southern Lebanon and an end to Iranian and Syrian support for Hezbollah, which the Lebanese government embraces as a legitimate resistance force."[125]

Or consider how the issue of nuclear weapons in Iran has been discussed. A *Los Angeles Times* article said: "The United States, concerned that Iran may be running a nuclear weapons program, is pushing for the International Atomic Energy Agency to declare that Tehran has violated the Nuclear Nonproliferation Treaty, diplomats said Thursday."[126] And on another *Talk of the Nation* Conan simply observed: "the US has long believed that Iran is developing nuclear weapons; again, Tehran rejects the accusation."[127]

Now, on the face of it those statements seem ordinary and unexceptional, hardly rising to the level of comment. But once noticed, it becomes clear that we, the audience, don't actually know what is meant. Since the countries to which behavior is ascribed are clearly not entities that are themselves capable of action, is the audience to presume, in the case of the "United States," for example, that what was really meant is "the Bush administration"? But even if the audience does make that determination, who is the one acting in the Bush administration? The Department of State or that of Defense? The Secretary of State or the Secretary of Defense (and in 2003, there were clear distinctions between the holders of those two offices: Colin Powell and Donald Rumsfeld)? Or perhaps "the United States" refers to the Congress? Or American nuclear scientists? Without clearer attribution and sourcing, the audience has little way of assessing the credibility or authority of what the US has "said," has "demanded," is "pushing for," or has "believed."

As a result of such a national or regional frame, readers and listeners and viewers are encouraged to consider the country or region—"Iraq," "the West," "the Middle East"—to be monolithic. Such framing surreptitiously works to persuade us that "they," the members of that country or area, are all alike in their intentions and their interests, just as many rabid commentators in the blogosphere and on talk radio have tried to make Islam and terrorism synonymous in our minds. If we believe everyone within a country thinks and acts in a similar manner, there would appear to be little prospect of change, of diplomatic initiatives working, of important groups within a country being capable of engaging with others. Referring to countries and regions as the actors in global affairs may be nothing more than a lazy verbal shorthand, but it reflects a kind of sloppy thinking that can't apply any corrective force to facile political arguments and policies. If one is in the habit of thinking that "the West" always acts in concert, for example, then those occasions where there are serious and meaningful disagreements may get little attention—a factor that might partly explain how, in that PIPA poll taken in the summer of 2003, almost a quarter of Americans could believe that Europeans together with the rest of world favored the United States going to war with Iraq when, of course, they did not.

3   The "Individual Agency" Frame

The opposite problem adheres when politicians and reporters fall into ascribing to an individual actor greater power than can be realistically exercised. Since it is tempting to talk about the major political players who are recognizable to an audience—George Bush, Saddam Hussein, Vladimir Putin, Kim Jung-il, Pervez Musharraf, Mahmoud Ahmadinejad, etc.—it is also tempting to fall into the belief that these individuals—no matter that they are presidents or prime ministers or chairmen, or dictators—have complete control over their populations and factions. The implication of such attributions of power is that all politicians have to do is meet with and convince the opposing leadership to solve the outstanding problems. The dilemma of such a frame is that when the leaders fail to deliver—as fail they will—there is an obvious goat to blame.

As with all of these frames, there is some basis for their set-up. There is some basis for claims of great power—especially in the case of totalitarian states such as North Korea. But speaking of an individual as the representative of a country and implying that that individual is entirely responsible for the complex imple- mentation of all policy minimizes an audience's interest in any other indigenous authorities, experts, or bureaucrats, and lessens the pressure to solve the problem in any way short of dealing with (and often trying to remove) the figurehead.

Of course, these very political leaders abet this kind of extraordinary attribution, since they themselves often speak in such terms—claiming responsibility for events not entirely in their control, or blaming their counterparts for events gone wrong. When Bush was quoted as saying that Saddam Hussein is a "homicidal dictator who is addicted to weapons of mass destruction," the politics of such a statement needed to be discussed. Media can challenge that kind of simplistic causal thinking—but they too rarely do. The knee-jerk instinct to use the big quote should be joined by an effort to deconstruct that quote.

Especially in breaking stories, journalists matter-of-factly repeat politicians' comments verbatim—extreme quotes from major players make good soundbites, after all. Quotations from privileged individuals and prominent politicians, such as President Bush, Prime Minister Brown, or Cabinet officials, carry a weight beyond those from more "common" sources, and thus are more likely to be sought after and more likely to be used. For audiences, the authority of the speakers—or at least the prominence of the speakers—makes their words both memorable and powerful. But media repetition of the remarks by such sources helps to reinforce the sentiments expressed in the quotations. The *New York Times*, for example, quoted Richard Gephardt, the Democratic Minority Leader of the US House of Representatives, extensively in his floor speech during the October 2002 debate on the use of force against Iraq. Said Gephardt: "Once a madman like Saddam Hussein is able to deliver his arsenal, whether it's chemical, biological or nuclear weapons, there's no telling when an American city will be attacked at his direction or with his support. A nuclear-armed Iraq would soon become the world's largest safe haven and refuge for the world's terrorist organizations." And the day before, the *Los Angeles Times* quoted a House colleague who was making a similar case against Hussein. "Another Bush supporter, Rep. Cliff Stearns (R-Fla.), declared: 'Saddam Hussein is uniquely evil—the only ruler in power today and the first one since Hitler to commit chemical genocide.'"[128] Giving significant play to such sentiments lends tacit support to their arguments: that not only is it appropriate for US policy-makers to target and eliminate individual "evil" political actors, such as Saddam Hussein, but, by so doing, a crisis can be resolved.

Following politicians' lead, reporters' stories grant individual actors greater clout than they have, and often presume consequences that cannot be delivered if those individuals are to be eliminated from their political pinnacle. It may have been Hussein's decision to use chemical weapons against the Kurds in the Anfal of 1988, for example, but there were others in the country who made the weapons, who backed that targeting, and who launched the attack. It is unlikely that all operated under duress. More thought about other sources of power and potential power in Iraq—the Republican Guard, Baathists, religious leaders, tribal and religious divisions, etc.—would have helped the American public, and perhaps policy elites as well, understand the complexity of the power balance in that nation.

Finally, not to be forgotten are the flipsides of stories that are framed around an individual actor who is the evil influence—the Saddam Husseins and Osama bin Ladens of this world—and those are stories that represent an individual actor as the savior (or potential savior) in a situation. Such stories portray those leaders and candidates as the shining hope for their countries. Harry Smith, the morning anchor for CBS News, led into his October 2007 interview with Benazir Bhutto in this way: "Just a couple of minutes ago, I spoke with Benazir Bhutto. This is the brand-new, most recent interview with the former prime minister of Pakistan. She talked about last week's assassination attempt after her triumphant return to try to restore democracy in Pakistan. You will not want to miss this courageous leader's words. I asked her if she was willing to die for her country, and we'll have the answer to that question in just a bit." Her not surprising (and in hindsight poignant) answer? "I am ready to take the risk. The people of Pakistan are ready to take the risk."[129]

4 The "We Are the Ones Who Matter" Frame

News outlets cover their own. Australian media gave more coverage to the Bali bombing, which killed and injured so many Australian nationals, than any other foreign countries' media. Israeli media covered closely the bombings in Egypt and Kenya that targeted Israeli nationals. No matter how many of the indigenous country's people are killed, news outlets will remark on their own victims—and failing that, will mention those who are most like their own. So you get stories like the 2,000+-word article in the *Sunday Times* (London) that told about the "bravery" and "heroism" of a British soldier: "A Royal Marine in southern Afghanistan threw himself onto an exploding grenade to save the lives of his patrol. . . . Yesterday, fellow marines were reluctant to play up the incident. 'Such has been the ferocity of the fight 40 Commando has endured these past few months, this has been one remarkable incident among many,' said one senior Royal Marines officer as they prepared to hand over to the Parachute Regiment."[130]

And there are other ways that media signal to their readers, listeners, and viewers that "people like us" are the ones who matter. In coverage of many of the terrorist attacks in regions of the world of minimal political or economic interest to the United States (much of Asia and Africa for example), one can hear hints of a prevalent frame from the Cold War era: that terrorist attacks are, almost by default, proxy attacks on Americans and American (or "Western") values. In the coverage of the Mombassa, Kenya, attack in 2002 which killed three Israeli tourists and 10 Kenyans, for example, relatively little notice was paid to the indigenous effects of the violence; more prominent attention was paid to connecting the attacks to the United States. As a *New York Times* article noted the day after the account: "Once again, Kenyans have found themselves caught in the middle of a war that is not their own." Or as the *Los Angeles Times* headlined one article: "Kenyans Suffer Again in Anti-US Violence."

Most media find the chauvinistic angle on international news irresistible. The only international stories that get consistent coverage are those that intersect with the domestic interests of the media's audience. A perception of imminent risk (a security risk, an economic risk, etc.) to Americans or to the United States remains the best indicator of coverage in the US. What that means is that US media under-cover events that are perceived as not affecting Americans. As a result, for example, bilateral diplomacy between pairs of other countries (India–Pakistan, Russia–Iran, North Korea–Japan) or multilateral interactions where the US is not the dominant player receive little attention. How a situation affects Americans is what matters most: a *New York Times* story of Iranian President Mohammad Khatami's 2003 visit to Lebanon brought in the United States beginning in the third paragraph. (There are some outlets, however, such as the *Christian Science Monitor*, that more regularly feature bilateral or multilateral relations between or among other countries even when those relations don't primarily affect the United States—for example, a lengthy article on diplomatic talks between India and Pakistan only got around to mentioning US concerns 17 paragraphs into the story.)

5   The "Save the Innocents" or "Save the Children" Frame

Then there are frames that focus not on the politics of an attack or issue, but on the human side. When it may be controversial to chastise one side or the other on political and/or historical grounds, criticizing either or both of them on humanitarian grounds—where world opinion is coalesced against torture or harm to civilians in general, and children specifically—is relatively safer.

Focusing stories by framing them around those who are hurt can also be appealing because it offers a level of moral coherence to an otherwise messy series of events. But getting to that coherence is not always straightforward. Who gets mentioned—who's perceived to be "innocent" in a given situation—changes depending on the news outlet, and, in fact, has changed over time. The challenge with the notion of "innocence" is that, like "terrorism," its meaning is in the eye of the beholder. Post-9/11 President Bush and most Americans characterized those who perished on September 11 as "innocents" and those who killed them as "terrorists," for example. But pro-Al Qaeda and pro-Saddam forces familiar to viewers of Al Jazeera also described as "innocent civilians" those who died in Afghanistan or Iraq as a result of American bombing.

There has come to be a wider recognition that innocence is conferred, rather than inherent, that innocence needs to be asserted; it is not unequivocally self-apparent. During World War II, those who were killed in Nanking or in the Blitz or in the concentration camps were just called "civilians." Their innocence was implicit in their status as civilians. Saying "innocent civilians" would have been redundant. Today the innocence of the victims on each side of the war on terrorism is loudly proclaimed—just as it has been in the Israeli–Palestinian conflict. Affirming one's innocence may confer no protection, but it allows one to lay claim to the moral high ground.

As a result, descriptions of those killed or injured in an attack frequently lean hard on characterizations that frame the victims as not culpable in the violence. The *New York Times*' description of a suicide bomb attack in Iraq in January 2006, for example, not only gave a brief, gruesome account of the devastation, but led with the fact that the attack killed "pilgrims" and ended with the detail that an infant was among the dead:

> More than 60 Shiite pilgrims died just steps from the Imam Hussein shrine in Karbala, one of Shiite Islam's holiest sites, when a terrorist detonated an explosive vest just after 10 a.m., the Iraqi authorities said. Pools of blood and body parts were strewn about, and survivors shrieked and cried while people ripped benches from buildings to use as stretchers. The police chief in Karbala said the suicide vest had contained at least 15 pounds of high explosives and was studded with ball bearings that shot through the crowd to maximize the slaughter. Health officials said the dead included Iranian visitors and a 3-month-old baby, and that at least 63 people had been wounded.[131]

Children are always the most obviously innocent victims, and therefore have become a default way for journalists to capture the interest of their readers and listeners. If there is no American "hook" into a story, children work well as attention-grabbers. Children command our sympathies and our engagement. They keep our attention. Injury to them provokes our outrage. So using children to discuss terrorists threats or terrorist attacks is not only a "natural," but also one of the most powerful, tools of a journalist—or a politician.

President Bush recognized that power when he twice mentioned children and three times mentioned "the innocent" in his May 2003 "Victory in Iraq" speech: "In these 19 months that changed the world, our actions have been focused, and deliberate, and proportionate to the offense. We have not forgotten the victims of

September 11th—the last phone calls, the cold murder of children, the searches in the rubble." But it's not just US politicians who have employed the image of innocent children to defend or incite action. Others, including Osama bin Laden, have as well. In an audiotape released in early April 2003 as American forces were entering Baghdad, for example, bin Laden urged his followers to mount suicide attacks against the United States and Britain to "avenge the innocent children . . . assassinated in Iraq."

Katie Woodruff, Lori Dorfman, and Liana Winett observed in their 1995 paper "Frames on Children and Youth in US Newspapers" that the media's use of images of children reflects "a cynical" approach: "The innocence and vulnerability of children were used often to heighten irony, instill moral outrage, or intensify a call to action."[132] As the Bush administration's policies in Iraq came under increasing fire, the media referred to children increasingly often. Since children are the literal embodiment of a society's future, what they do is emblematic of what is happening in the whole of society. Children became ideal synecdoches for the contested Iraqi policy.

Scott Peterson, reporting for the *Christian Science Monitor*, used children to comment on US failures to protect Iraqi civilians from radioactive threats. On the outskirts of Baghdad, he wrote, is:

> a burnt-out Iraqi tank, destroyed by—and contaminated with—controversial American depleted-uranium (DU) bullets. Local children play "throughout the day" on the tank, Hamid says, and on another one across the road. . . . The children haven't been told not to play with the radioactive debris. They gather around as a Geiger counter carried by a visiting reporter starts singing when it nears a DU bullet fragment no bigger than a pencil eraser. It registers nearly 1,000 times normal background radiation levels on the digital readout.

Newsweek also underlined the failure of Americans to secure nuclear sites or to protect the population from radiation hazards by talking about the children:

> Last week American troops finally went back to secure the site. Al Tuwaitha's scientists still can't fully assess the damage; some areas are too badly contaminated to inspect. "I saw empty uranium-oxide barrels lying around, and children playing with them," says Fadil Mohsen Abed, head of the medical-isotopes department.[133]

Perpetual "live" coverage means little time for actual reporting and means that choices of what stories to cover and how to cover those stories are made on deadline and often on pragmatic grounds. Framing a story sets up a fast, knowable outline for coverage; reporting on a story from an "easy" feature angle or a known arresting one such as children—may be a way into a story for which there is little time and few resources to conduct an investigative report.[134]

Framing can also signal a political choice on the part of a reporter. Despite the near-deification of the principle of objectivity, increasingly journalists in the field—especially during crises such as Kosovo, Rwanda, and Bosnia—have argued that accurate reporting demands determining responsibility. "In certain situations, the classic definition of objectivity can mean neutrality," said CNN star Christiane Amanpour, "and neutrality can mean you are an accomplice to all sorts of evil. . . . An element of morality has to be woven into these kinds of stories."[135]

When journalists choose to take a stand, they can do so in several ways. They can churn out a passionate book. They can appear as talking heads (if their home institution will let them) to vent their perspective. They can pump out "news analysis" pieces instead of "just the facts ma'am" articles. They can simply select people to interview or quotes to use that support their own point of view. Or they can consciously or unconsciously frame stories in ways that are more likely to cast one side in a positive (or negative) light. That last often sneaks under the bar of scrutiny because of the inherent bias in the selection and ordering of information that goes into *any* story, even the most studiedly balanced one. Framing a story around innocence—and/or a child—is a below-the-radar way of taking sides. It is a way of packaging a terrorism story so that the reception of it is well-nigh assured. We all want to protect children.

 ## why some media do a better job

Stop for a moment and consider the media. "Media" is a plural noun for good reasons. The media are not some monolithic entity. They are a teeming mass of competitively driven, idiosyncratically motivated, technologically diverse schema for delivering information. Truth and accuracy are aspirations, not absolutes, valued more by some than others. (Many, actually, would dispute there is such as thing as "truth.") And news is variously understood to embrace the political as well as the embarrassing.

Different news outlets. Different agendas.

Even in this book, even among media that are serious enough to cover terrorism and credible enough to have substantial audiences, there are clear distinctions. There are clear distinctions among the British and American media and clear distinctions among online, broadcast, and print media. Every news outlet provides a slightly different kind and style of news. Some emphasize breaking news (CNN for example), others focus on news analysis (such as the *Economist*) and still others have lots of features (like the *Christian Science Monitor*). Some of the differences among the media are directly tied to the individual news organization's budget demands—some news organizations are owned by corporations that require annual profit margins of well over 15 percent, higher than the operating margins of the oil and drug industries. Other news organizations are family-owned and have different kinds of budget constraints and oversight. Some differences in reporting are due to the news outlets' interests in serving their distinct audiences: American or British, New Yorkers or Washingtonians, old or young, skewing male, skewing female, mainly white, trending heterogeneous. Different audience demographics compel particular styles of coverage and types of content. Other distinctions in news coverage reflect the fact that different outlets are up against different deadlines— hourly or daily or weekly. Online news sites and cable TV have deadlines every hour (and on occasion virtually every minute), the evening network news programs and newspapers have a daily deadline (at least in their broadcast and print incarnations), and news magazines have a relatively leisurely weekly deadline to hit. Some news organizations have an almost infinite news hole, especially when all their various news platforms (online, radio, TV, etc.) are considered. The BBC would be a case in point. Others have relatively tiny news holes, because they only really provide original news on one platform: Public Broadcasting's *Lehrer NewsHour* or PRI's *The World*, for instance.

Now lay on top of these factors other journalistic constraints that they all share but that result in each outlet making different news choices. Each organization, no matter how great or small its total news hole, has to decide what to highlight. What event will be on the cover, make the top of the news, be above the fold, land on the homepage? How will each handle a just-breaking story? Will the news outlet continue to give the current lead story prime placement or will it dump coverage of the older event in favor of the next big thing? And about that story —what's the best angle on it? Take Gitmo. The *Washington Post*, the hometown paper of the nation's capital, inclines toward reporting about the White House and Pentagon's defense of the legality of the detention camp at the US naval base in Guantánamo Bay, Cuba. For the *Miami Herald*, with its Cuban immigrant readership, Gitmo is a hometown story, as much about people as policy.

What about other tough stories, where access is difficult for reasons of safety— it's in the middle of a war zone—or of time—the event just happened and it's on the other side of the world—or because some government is preventing reporters from traveling there—the Burmese won't let journalists in? What do different news outlet do then? Some assign correspondents who are willing to brave the personal risks, others hire local stringers to cover dangerous assignments. Some dispatch their reporters on the next plane out to a faraway disaster, others report on a distant story from their home studio by having their anchors do a voiceover on top of some freelancer's video footage. Some news outlets decide to cover the forbidden story from as close to the censored zone as possible, perhaps interviewing via phone those who remain inside; others move on to another story, stymied by the difficulties in coverage.

Then what about those controversial stories where almost any kind of reporting is tantamount to taking sides? Which outlets ask the tough questions— and follow-up questions—of important administration and Pentagon sources, for example, and which decide that softball questions are the better part of valor, given that those same sources will be needed on other later stories?

In an ideal world, the role of media bears some similarity to that role that President Lincoln suggested for government: to consider events in proportion to their importance and to do so in a manner that considers "the better angels of our nature." To put that in journalistic terms: media should be fair, accurate, and balanced. They should seek to give citizens a greater understanding of local, national, and global events.

But in addition the media's role is to oversee the role of the government. The media should track whether government's proposed actions are strategically, legally, and even morally appropriate and proportional. In the famous words of Thomas Jefferson written to Edward Carrington, a delegate to the Continental Congress, in 1787: "The basis of our governments being the opinion of the people, the very first object should be to keep that right; and were it left to me to decide whether we should have a government without newspapers or newspapers without a government, I should not hesitate a moment to prefer the latter."[136]

Since 9/11, neither the heads of state of the United States and the United Kingdom nor the American and British media played anything like their ideal roles. What happened?

Let's go back and consider where we were prior to September 11, 2001. Less than a month before 9/11, on August 17, NPR's host Linda Wertheimer led into a story on the asymmetrical warfare in the Palestinian–Israeli conflict with an observation about the different terms used to discuss the fighting. "Throughout the decades of conflict between the Palestinians and the Israelis," she said, "it has been commonplace to describe the acts of the Palestinians, especially the suicide bombings that have become so frequent in recent months, as acts of terrorism. That word 'terrorism' has rarely been used to describe the actions or reactions of the militarily superior Israeli side. Now some experts on warfare are wondering whether different terms might not be more useful in understanding the nature of the conflict."

Three days later, in an unusually candid story on the same program, *All Things Considered*, Peter Kenyon began his report on the "war on words":

> Earlier this month, as Palestinians buried the victims of an Israeli rocket attack, including two young boys, tensions were running especially high, even by the standards of the West Bank. But when readers of the *Jerusalem Post* opened their morning papers,

they saw a front-page banner headline that read "Bad English Threatens Israel's Public Relations Effort." It seems a poorly translated press release had not only used the word "assassination" to describe the most recent killings, but referred to the West Bank and Gaza Strip as occupied territories. That may comport with international law, but it's anathema to the Israeli government. The soldier who did the translating was swiftly reassigned. Foreign Ministry spokeswoman Yaffa Ben-Ari says her department is constantly on alert for journalists and others who use terms that the government considers pro-Palestinian.

Then he continued,

This obsession with language permeates all aspects of the conflict. In fact, according to the government, there is no conflict with the Palestinians, only a situation. Suspected militants are never assassinated. They're intercepted while planning their next attack. That information is usually extracted through interrogation. But torture is never used, only moderate physical pressure. . . . The description of the land is as disputed as the soil itself. Some call it the West Bank, Palestinians and their supporters call it occupied territory, but those on the Israeli right wing, especially settlers, refer to Judea and Sumaria, ancient names suggesting past Jewish claims. By the way, they don't like to be called settlers. They think of themselves as residents, even though much of the world and a significant slice of the Israeli public considers the settlements illegitimate.[137]

There were not many news outlets nor individual journalists who were publicly challenging the terms the Israelis and the Palestinians—not to mention the Americans and other outsiders—were applying to that conflict. Doing so on NPR's part was not only clear-sighted, it was an act of courage, certain to infuriate everyone.

There were few if any similarly courageous mainstream American media voices a month and more later after 9/11. The Bush administration's phrase, the "War on Terror," became almost as familiar—and as standard—as the names "World War II" or "Vietnam War." After September 11, many media first sourced the terms of the "War on Terror" and "terrorist" to the President and other administration officials, then as the terms slipped into common usage they began applying them to the Bush foreign policy goals without attribution. The US media generally acquiesced in the deliberate terminology chosen by the administration, becoming as a result a virtual megaphone for the White House's messages.

Europeans were better at serving as critical filters rather than passive transmitters of information coming out of government. When reporters from non-American news outlets wrote about the Bush administration's "War on Terror," in the months following September 11, the words were typically placed in quotation marks and preceded by the phrase "US-led." That made it clear that the phrase "War on Terror" was part of the White House's political rhetoric and that the conflict was the idea of the United States. US journalists' omission of the caveat "US-led" and those little bits of punctuation was just one small indication of how most mainstream media in the United States reflexively covered the post-9/11 world. They covered the world by peering through the looking glass held up by the Bush administration.

Before, during, and after the Iraq war, British news outlets have been more willing than their US counterparts to challenge the White House's and Downing Street's interpretation of events. Now, to be fair, that has been in part because even early on there was vocal opposition in the UK to Prime Minister Blair's foreign policies that the media could call on for alternative perspectives. In the US the 9/11 attacks virtually ended Congressional opposition to the President's objectives. The opposition in the United Kingdom was not as constrained by circumstances, by the sense that the country was under direct attack and that it needed to rally around the prime minister.

Certainly by several years after 9/11 the British gloves were well off. As *Washington Post* media critic Howard Kurtz noted in a June 2003 column, "George W. Bush bloody well has it easy. He doesn't have to put up with the hour-by-hour pounding that the British press gives Tony Blair, with journalists calling him a liar and worse in a raging debate over whether Iraq really had weapons of mass destruction." Kurtz gave the details:

> The media assault on 10 Downing St. has been relentless. "Revealed: How Blair Used Discredited WMD 'Evidence,'" shouted the *Independent*. "No. 10 'Doctored' Iraq Dossier," bellowed the *Sunday Times*. When the prime minister denied that his government had misled anyone, the *Daily Mirror* ran a close-up shot of his perspiring forehead, with the banner: "Blair Feels the Heat." And the British press wasn't loath to critique the "tea-and-crumpets politeness" of their American counterparts: "*Guardian* columnist Gary Younge chided the U.S. press for 'at best a reluctance, and at worst a downright refusal, to engage with views and voices opposed to George Bush's foreign policy.'"[138]

Two years later, on May 1, 2005, a few days before the UK general election, the London *Sunday Times* published a leaked write-up of a secret July 2002 meeting in the UK among members of the Labor government and defense and intelligence officials. Called the "smoking-gun memo" by some, the minutes outlined the group's discussion of the military options and the political strategy for the war in Iraq.[139] The memo made direct reference to classified United States policy of the time:

> Bush wanted to remove Saddam, through military action, justified by the conjunction of terrorism and WMD. But the intelligence and facts were being fixed around the policy. The [National Security Council] had no patience with the UN route. . . . There was little discussion in Washington of the aftermath after military action . . .

It seemed clear that Bush had made up his mind to take military action, even if the timing was not yet decided. But the case was thin. Saddam was not threatening his neighbors, and his WMD capability was less than that of Libya, North Korea or Iran.[140]

The memo received major coverage in the UK press, but minimal attention in the US mainstream media.[141] Although US-based blogs such as the Daily Kos banged the drum daily on it, there were only a few major stories on it in the elite US press: the *New York Times* published a story on May 2, the Knight Ridder news service distributed a story on May 6, and the *Los Angeles Times* wrote a story on May 12. But these didn't make the front pages. There was so little coverage, in fact, that the ombudsmen for the two major US newspapers, the *New York Times* and the *Washington Post*, publicly scolded their papers for their poor handling of the story.[142] "I have to say I'm amazed that *The Post* took almost two weeks to follow up on the [London] *Times* report," wrote Michael Getler, the *Post*'s ombudsman in his column in the paper on May 15.

> The key line in the leaked memo, in my view, is the assessment by British intelligence, after a visit to Washington, that "the intelligence and facts were being fixed around the policy." That kind of assertion has been made by critics and commentators, but it has not been included in official post-invasion assessments here about how the country went to war under what turned out to be false premises about weapons of mass destruction and other matters. Investigating that assessment, coming from the key U.S. ally in the war, certainly seems journalistically mandatory. . . .
>
> *The Post* also failed to report that, on May 5, 90 Democrats in Congress sent a letter to President Bush about the "troubling revelations" in the London *Sunday Times* that the United States and Britain "had secretly agreed to attack Iraq . . . before you even sought congressional authority." [143]

Why? Why were the American media so little interested in the story that few major outlets—print or broadcast—covered it and the few that did tended to bury the news? On the *Lehrer NewsHour* on PBS, Daniel Okrent, the former public editor for the *New York Times*, bluntly tallied up what he believed the causes were for the American media's failures:

> I think the hunger for scoops, the sort of getting involved in the sound of the martial music, and the image I use is that you could almost sense certain editors spouting epaulettes on shoulders as they kind of become part of the war and not just looking like from a distance—and insufficient internal checking, too much reliance on questionable sources, and a variety of felonies and misdemeanors that would make a pretty good study in failed journalism.[144]

And there was one additional problem. In the consideration of terrorism, US media were long incapacitated by governments' co-option of the term—even when the

White House's use of it served a clear political agenda. In part the problem for media was that "normal" critical analysis of the administration's positions—say its stances on health care, education, or energy policy—was forestalled in the case of terrorism by reporters' concern that even a judicious investigation would paint the news organization as unpatriotic or at least contemptuous of national security policy. Until 2003 and the failure to find the weapons of mass destruction in Iraq, vociferous criticism of the "War on Terror" for most US news outlets was out of the question.

But even years later "terrorism" still retained its talismanic power. Politicians continued to have tremendous success in passing policies described as countering "terrorism." When in August 2007, for example, the US Senate passed a Republican plan that temporarily gave the federal government expanded power to eavesdrop on foreign suspects without a court order, civil liberty and privacy advocates were quick to criticize the Democrats. They "have a Pavlovian reaction: Whenever the president says the word 'terrorism,' they roll over and play dead," said Caroline Fredrickson, Washington legislative director of the American Civil Liberties Union.[145]

So those are some broad brush strokes about how American and British media have differently covered some aspects of terrorism post-9/11. Yet it is challenging to get much more granular than that because the differences among the media are not entirely consistent across time or types of events. It's a very different business to cover a presidential speech or a leaked memo than a terrorism attack that just occurred halfway around the globe. Of the many American and British news outlets, across platforms, that we've considered in our studies of media coverage of terrorism, it would be accurate to say that on most occasions each outlet appeared to make an effort to conscientiously follow recognizable standards of journalistic integrity. Especially in feature news coverage, in print and on radio, on TV and online, the reporters and hosts often attempted to consult with a range of sources, to use tempered language in their own commentary, and to introduce background historical and political factors to at least a minimal degree.

However, when the coverage was of breaking news, the reporters and hosts, anchors and editors struggled less successfully. Too often journalists resorted to what the trade calls "stenographic" coverage: writing down what the political or military officials say and not prominently signaling that there might be other perspectives or that the statements of officials might be tainted by self-interest. Some of the media's worst failings relate to inadequate or biased sourcing— under the pressure of deadline (or possibly because more neophyte journalists didn't recognize that there might be competing perspectives on the "facts" under discussion). Other problems occurred with the conflation of multiple events into single accounts and speaking of perpetrators and causes as if the agendas of all terrorists were the same—sometimes the perpetrators are unidentified except as "terrorists" even when the responsible group was known. But most lacking across the board was follow-up coverage after attacks—especially of the attacks themselves and their impact on local communities. The regional and at times global implications of an event were usually extensively covered—or at least covered more extensively than any other aspect. Poorly covered were the human and local implications of the attack. And follow-up coverage that has existed was often buried: as one reader of the *Washington Post* complained to the ombudsman,

> I understand that a lot of thought goes into determining which stories appear on page A1, but I can't understand how the follow-up about the London and Glasgow attacks winds up on A15. Instead, we have an analysis about the besieged President Bush, a worthy story, but not one that needs to be on the front page; similarly the horse race story about [Barack] Obama raising a lot of money. I don't quarrel about the [story on the] growing and shrinking of fat but Metro ambiance belongs in (of course) Metro, and at best the Google and dog show items should be in Style.[146]

Covering "terrorism" has included a tremendous range of stories—from unique attacks that have killed over 100 people and wounded exponentially more (such as Bali in 2002, Madrid in 2004, and Pakistan in 2007), to almost daily Iraqi suicide bombings with significant but lesser death tolls, to wars (declared and undeclared) in which terrorism plays an ongoing role (Darfur and Israel–Palestine, Sri Lanka and the Philippines), to political debates about national security and foreign policy, to rogue states' development of nuclear weapons. Given those, it is to be expected that some outlets would excel at covering policy, but do a poor job of covering breaking events, some outlets would take an internationalist approach to diplomatic efforts and others would cover politics entirely chauvinistically, and some would manage strong follow-up stories while others would punt on anything other than breaking news.

This suggests that certain outlets are uniquely suited to covering certain types of stories well—for one reason or another. Already mentioned is the *New York Times'* reporting on September 11. But other outlets such as the *Wall Street Journal*, the *Washington Post*, and WNYC (New York public radio), for example, had compelling coverage of 9/11—in large measure because they also "coherently and comprehensively covered the tragic events, profiled the victims, and tracked the developing story, locally and globally," as the Pulitzer Prize award noted in its recognition of the *Times*.[147] In other words, some outlets managed extensive, multi-faceted 9/11 coverage developed over a significant period of time.

In the years after 2001, Knight Ridder, with terrific reporters in its Washington, DC bureau such as Warren Strobel, Jonathan Landay, and John Walcott, stood out for its independence in coverage, especially on covering weapons of mass destruction. Until it was bought by the McClatchy Company in 2006, it was the second-largest newspaper publisher in the United States, with 32 daily newspapers, including the *Miami Herald* and the *San Jose Mercury News*. *Time* and *Newsweek* have distinguished themselves through their photoessays. *Nightline* during the Ted Koppel years, *Frontline/World* and *The World* produced by PRI, the BBC World Service, and WGBH have all done long-form broadcasts or series that provide "context, insight, and interesting interviews in a fascinating history lesson, told with impartiality and without sensationalism" "of the sort often missing from mainstream media," as the Overseas Press Club noted in its recognition of PRI's *The World*. There have been reporters both in the field and in home offices, such as Anthony Shadid in Iraq and Dana Priest and Walter Pincus back in Washington, all from the *Washington Post*, who have consistently turned in terrific reporting— even when their own news outlets haven't always given their work the space and the position it deserves. And that's just a once-over-lightly of organizations and journalists who have consistently worked to overcome the difficulties of reporting on dangerous or complex stories in the midst of budget pressures as well as pressures to reduce international coverage.

But the inadequacy of the above list in capturing what has been good suggests how difficult it is to chart simply how individual media differ in their coverage. Differences emerge in the content as well as the style of individual stories, in where or when stories are covered (front page or top of the news v. inside or later coverage), in how many stories are published or broadcast, and in what type of stories appear (breaking news, analysis, features, editorials, commentary). Over the past years there have been multiple occasions when individual news outlets have had consistently strong coverage of an event, and other occasions when that same news outlet has had one standout reporter but most of the rest of its coverage was formulaic, and still other occasions when that news outlet buried its best reporting and led with a mechanical, hackneyed, or even belligerent approach to the issue or event.

What else differs among media? It is worth noting that style and tone can vary dramatically from one news outlet to another. Consider the three most prestigious American metropolitian newspapers. Because of its pre-eminence as still, to some degree, the US "newspaper of record," the *New York Times'* articles are inclined to be more focused on a straight recapitulation of the breaking news than those of the *Washington Post* and the *Los Angeles Times*. Facts are related, numbers are cited, in all three papers, but *New York Times* stories are marginally longer and there are more of them, so especially in the aggregate the range tends to be broader. Stylistically, the *Washington Post* and the *Los Angeles Times* news stories are often more discursive. Oftentimes there is an overarching analysis, although it may come through in the ordering of a story or the selection of sources rather than in overt commentary. Hardly stream-of-consciousness gonzo journalism, the *Post* and the *Los Angeles Times* yet tell stories that are inspired less by the inverted pyramid than by feature writing.

Even when the "facts" that are reported are the same, an audience can come away with a very different impressions of an event when reading, listening to, or watching different media outlets. The tone of news stories is typically set by the opening sentences—different kinds of news stories demand different kinds of leads: a hard news breaking story will typically begin with a traditional Who-What-Where-When series of sentences, while a human interest feature story will often start with an anecdotal lead. However, different news outlets also have distinctive styles: a *New York Times* hard news lead will tend to be more "serious" and more comprehensively informative than the opening gambit to the same breaking story on MSNBC or CBS. Broadcast news outlets are often more dramatic than their print counterparts: "The religious fury that's descended on Iraq after the destruction of a sacred shrine yesterday accelerated today. The country is poised on the brink of an abyss," was how ABC Nightly News led into one story. "Panic, tears and body bags. Hopes that political progress in Iraq would temper insurgent activity seemed forlorn on Thursday," started one CNN news story. "Blood, chaos, body parts littering a pedestrian walkway that runs between the Imam Hussein and Imam Abba shrines."[148] Such an opening is less likely to be found in a front-page newspaper story.

But mentioning some of these differences doesn't mean that there are not times when one can talk about "most media" and feel comfortable doing so. Let's take two dissimilar kinds of stories as a way to look a bit more deeply at some of the similarities and differences among the media: first, the coverage of weapons of mass destruction and then the coverage of four major suicide bomb attacks in 2004 and 2005. How do different media cover an ongoing issue, such as the "War on Terrorism" and the role that weapons of mass destruction have played in the political debates and diplomacy? How do different media talk about breaking news—the suicide bombings in Madrid, London, Egypt, and Jordan?

Even when covering slow-moving trend stories—AIDS in Africa or climate change, for instance—the media's choice of what to cover falls roughly into two categories:

1 Cover what everyone else in your market is covering.
2 Cover something different.

Most media cover what everyone else covers. Some go more in-depth on stories. Some front the same story that others bury farther back. Some do follow-ups. Some just have better reporters, knowledgeable enough to ask better questions than their peers and to write it all up more clearly, to get it on the air more compellingly.

But what few news outlets do is cover different "stuff."

Over the past decade or more—since the nuclear testing in India and Pakistan in 1998—the media have covered breaking news about weapons of mass destruction better than might have been assumed, especially when one considers how restricted the access to WMD intelligence sources on Iraq, Iran, and North Korea, or at the White House for that matter, has been. The *New York Times*, the *Washington Post*, the *Los Angeles Times*, and NPR's *Morning Edition* and *All Things Considered* have all taken the panoply of WMD breaking news events seriously and covered them accordingly. They also deviate relatively little from each other in regards to what stories are covered and how they are prioritized, once questions of print vs. broadcast and regional demographics are taken into account. The *Guardian* and the *Daily Telegraph* also apply themselves to breaking news, typically spending less space on the same stories as their American counterparts, but not neglecting them either.

That is not to say, however, that there haven't been meaningful differences even between quite comparable outlets—the *Washington Post* and the *New York Times*, for example—often a factor of the interests of individual reporters or editors or of the specific geographic region of the news medium. A case in point: since 9/11 the *Washington Post* has put some of its most senior reporters on the national security beat, including Dana Priest, Karen DeYoung, Barton Gellman, Dana Milbank, and Walter Pincus, who, as Harry Jaffe, a media critic for *Washingtonian* magazine, noted, has been reporting on national security for the *Post* for a quarter-century and who has legions of sources in the Pentagon, the CIA, Congress, the State Department, the scientific community, and former UN inspector Hans Blix's office.

Through January and February 2003, during the lead-up to the war in Iraq, Pincus wrote 23 stories, nine of which landed on the front page—four in January having to do with Hans Blix, and the five in February relating to North Korea's nuclear plans or to Secretary of State Colin Powell's visit to the UN, and the questions raised in the aftermath of that visit. From February 5 to May 29, Pincus had only three front-page stories—out of 38 bylined pieces. In August 2003 Jaffe wrote: "According to reporters, editors continually underplayed Pincus's scoops and discounted their stories that ran counter to Bush's call to arms. . . . 'It was ridiculous. Many of the stories were buried,' says Priest, also a star on the national-security beat. 'Editors continually undervalued what he does.'"

But eventually, with pressure from famed Watergate reporter Bob Woodward and others (and with the indefatigable Seymour Hersh at the *New Yorker* and David Sanger and others at the *New York Times* also riding herd on the story), managing editor Steve Coll and others did begin to front Pincus's critical stories. From May 29 to August 10, Pincus had 30 bylined stories that related to WMD, 14 of which were fronted—including three in papers on Sunday. That's a record, wrote Jaffe, that put the *Washington Post* in the lead on the constellation of Iraqi WMD stories that has included the intelligence failures and the White House's exaggeration of intelligence claims into facts, the hunt for the "missing" weapons of mass destruction, and the spurious Niger nuclear transfer.

Others, too, noted that the *Post* out-reported the *Times*. Wrote Daniel Okrent, the "public editor" (ombudsman) for the *New York Times*:

> [A] story that ran in *The Washington Post* on Jan. 7 [2004], "Iraq's Arsenal Was Only on Paper," by Barton Gellman, was so stunning a piece of reporting that it led Bill Keller [the *New York Times* executive editor] to tell *The New York Observer* that it "caused everyone who competes with [Gellman] a serious case of indigestion followed by admiration." In a conversation in his office last week, Keller elaborated: Gellman's piece, he said, was "rich and subtle and deeply reported." I asked him why, if it was so good, it didn't merit a story in *The Times* recounting its main points, especially since *The Times*'s own reporting on Iraqi weapons programs last winter has continued to suffer a hurricane of criticism. Keller said that trying to do a summary of Gellman's work for *Times* readers ran the risk of oversimplification—that the nuances that made the piece so strong would not survive reduction to summary form. Gellman's piece, he said, was "easy to admire, hard to represent."[149]

Take another "serious" paper, the *Christian Science Monitor*. The *Monitor* is often the newspaper apart: in large measure because it is a daily newspaper that operates on a delayed deadline. Because the *Monitor* is mailed to subscribers, it has to operate on a different deadline than its ostensible peers; not only can't it "break" news, it "goes to bed" at midday, rather than in the late evening like most dailies—in effect putting its news almost a day and a half behind other city-based newspapers. It can't compete for breaking news with metro dailies. It can't compete on background analytical stories with the weekly news magazines. It has a small international news hole; it's a small paper with little real estate for any news. But repeatedly the paper has turned these limitations into advantages. Because it *can't* follow the pack, it is freed from pack journalism. It includes more news analysis, emphasizes trend stories, and tries to look at top stories through perspectives that others aren't likely to, such as giving an international perspective on a domestic story.

So, for instance, the *Monitor* was the only major news outlet in the country to run a story in May 2003 on the radiation hazards in Iraq left by American depleted uranium (DU) armor-piercing shells (although Science Friday on *Talk of the Nation* on NPR in April and the *Los Angeles Times* in June ran stories on DU). The *Monitor* article, by Scott Peterson, ran close to 3,000 words—almost four times the length of an average story.[150]

The *Monitor* tackles policy ideas, as the highlight for one article suggested: "Research on low-yield nuclear weapons underscores US shift from a strategy of deterrence to one of preemption."[151] And it explores new directions in science that others aren't investigating—such as a story about how scientists are genetically engineering certain plants to act as "'sentinels,' detecting harmful chemical and biological agents in the atmosphere," much as canaries used to be the sentinels for bad air in coalmines.[152]

So, there are differences among newspapers. What about similarities across media? Generally the news outlets—broadcast, online, and print, including the news weeklies—cover breaking news better than policy debates, and across the board there are relatively few investigative reports, although, when those occur, they tend to be extraordinary, such as Seymour Hersh's and George Packer's articles in the *New Yorker*, Michael Massing's series on WMD in the *New York Review of Books*, and a number of front-page series in the major papers.

Media cover breaking news better because events are easier to cover than ideas. "Ideas" tend to emerge in discussions of policy, and policy tends to be discussed when there is a news peg to hang it on—such as a David Sanger piece on ways the administration could counter North Korea's nuclear program that was pegged to a Crawford, Texas meeting between Bush and Australian prime minister John Howard. But there are a few exceptions to that rule, most regularly articles in the *New York Times* Week in Review section. It is there that the *Times* covers ideas and policy best.

Often the daily *New York Times* reporters, such as Sanger or William Broad, are given space to write incisive, analytical pieces on such topics as whether a quarantine would be effective in stopping North Korea from exporting plutonium or the historical limitations of intelligence in uncovering nuclear secrets. On other occasions, outside experts, such as Samuel Loewenberg or James Atlas, are brought in to speak to the value of Europe's precautionary principle in public policy and foreign affairs or the influence of Leo Straussian philosophy on the foreign policy of the White House. Occasionally, if the news peg is strong enough—and the article is sexy enough—that kind of analysis can be found elsewhere, such as a lengthy front-page article by Elisabeth Bumiller on the care and keeping of Bush's image. Another example was the 7,500-word tome in the *New York Times* Sunday Magazine by Bill Keller on the first and second "nuclear ages."[153]

Sadly, however, while some analytical stories are on the front page or at the top of the news, as a North Korea drug trade story was, most policy stories are buried where fewer people are going to discover them. NPR, for example, produced a long, excellent segment on containment strategies of nuclear weapons programs—a panel discussion among Linda Wertheimer, Ambassador Wendy Sherman, and Anthony Cordesman. Unfortunately, it ran on the *Saturday Weekend Edition*, when just a fraction of the weekday audience is listening.[154]

Looking at several specific stories in depth illuminates other issues. Consider two stories related to the "War on Terror" and weapons of mass destruction: the breaking story of President George W. Bush's "victory" speech, May 1, 2003, aboard USS *Abraham Lincoln* and the month-long story of the US Senate debate over whether to lift the 10-year-old ban on research and development of "low-yield" nuclear weapons that same month.[155]

In covering Bush's "Victory" speech, those news outlets, such as the *New York Times* and the *Washington Post*, which ran multiple stories on the speech, tended to run one lead story that was relatively "straight," repeating the President's words and describing the scene, eschewing verbs that put a qualitative spin on the subject, and then they ran one or more additional stories and editorials and opinion pieces that were quite pointed in their assessment of the address and content. Many of the broadcasters acted similarly. A number ran live coverage of the speech, then followed that with commentary. Most revisited the speech on the later evening news and on the morning news programs the next day. On the live broadcasts, anchors narrated the lead-up to the speech and then afterwards reporters recapped the main points made by the President and further described the drama of the locale. Then commentary followed. The reporters on NPR's *All Things Considered*, for example, detailed their observation that "whereas there had been a lot of talk about weapons of mass destruction as a reason for the invasion of Iraq, that theme had practically disappeared in his speech," and noted that the speech "couched that the reason for the invasion was the War on Terror, which is somewhat still controversial since they have not been able to prove very much connection between the two."

On the cable news stations, on the networks, and on radio, the immediacy of the video and audio clips of the jet landing, of President Bush deplaning in a jumpsuit, and of the cheering crowd acted to sweep audiences up in the Bush-orchestrated victory rush; but the immediate poking and prodding by the commentators acted to deflate that political bubble. Like that of the *New York Times* and the *Washington Post*, the cable news and public radio coverage was detailed and comprehensive, but the spin of the commentators left the impression that the news organizations were at best skeptical about both the timing and the context of the speech.

By contrast, those news outlets, such as the *Guardian*, the *Daily Telegraph*, and the *Christian Science Monitor*, which just ran one story on the speech, folded together "reporting" and "analysis." These papers, for example, clearly made choices about what to include or about how to describe the President and the scene that slanted the stories beyond a neutral recital of facts. The *Guardian*, for instance, started its story with a description of the "triumphal . . . gesture" of Bush's carrier landing, before reporting what Bush had to say—the opening lead emphasizing the meaning of the moment for the upcoming presidential campaign. The *Daily Telegraph* (with an article of less than 300 words) led with the most basic Who-What-Where-When lead, but by its selection of what to say in its short piece ("Bush Flies Jet to Carrier to Welcome Crew Home from War" was its head) made a decision to play down the claim of "victory" and emphasize the theatricality of the event. The *Christian Science Monitor* opened with the news of Bush declaring an "end to major combat operations," then moved to put that declaration into the historical context of the world wars.

The news weeklies were hampered by their deadlines, which meant that any coverage of the Thursday speech would have appeared on the stands almost a week after the event. The *Economist* omitted coverage of the speech, while *Newsweek*, its American counterpart, made do with briefly referencing the speech halfway through an article in its print edition about the challenges of nation-building. *Newsweek* did, however, post two stories specifically on the speech exclusively in its "web edition."

A different kind of story, about the Senate debate over whether to lift the 10-year-old ban on research and development of "low-yield" nuclear weapons, prompted a different kind of coverage. Different news organizations made different choices about when to cover the story, as, unlike the Bush speech, there was no single climatic moment. Because the news was, on its face, about a political debate, the characteristic story aligned along a he-said-she-said format, with much emphasis on the competing political perspectives on the issue. The inside-the-Beltway nature of the story and the complexity of the Congressional debate made it a natural for the US newspapers that cede space to cover political news and have reporters already on the Hill beat. Most focused on the familiar formula of partisan debate, and gave just a modicum of information on the arguments being made by all sides, although it was the *Washington Post* that did the best job at suggesting that the issue was more complex than a Democrat vs. Republican "Should we or shouldn't we have tactical nuclear weapons in our arsenal?" argument. But even the *Post* related very little of the larger meaning of the vote—for example, the budget implications for the military, for private contractors, or for the proponents of conventional weapons—or of the scientific and strategic debates over low-yield weapons, the effectiveness of "bunker-busters," the viability of nuclear weapons to "disarm" chemical or biological hazards, and so on.

The *Christian Science Monitor* wrote two stories quite different than the other papers, one from an international perspective: it used a reporter, based in Delhi, to cover the story. As the highlight said: "A plan to repeal a US ban on nuclear-weapons research could embolden India and Pakistan." Its second story also took a different tack than its counterparts—its thrust was less the political acrimony of the debate than the concerns raised by a military strategy that contemplates "nuclear attack options that vary in scale, scope and purpose." The article tracked the "US shift from a strategy of deterrence to one of pre-emption" and led with the "Strangelovian anachronism" of the US interest "in a new generation of nukes."

The Senate nuclear debates were an even more problematic story for other media that tend to avoid such inside-baseball stories. As a result, there was little coverage of the debates in the news weeklies, on TV, or in radio. Even NPR's *Morning Edition* and *All Things Considered*, news programs that originate in Washington, DC, within walking distance of Congress, only covered the arc of the story once after the Senate repeal of the 10-year ban on the development of "so-called mini-nukes." And, by and large, UK media failed to cover the debate despite the clear international repercussions. The *Economist*, however, was an exception. The magazine saw the final decision to lift the ban as a bellwether for the direction of US security policy and ran an article accordingly. As the editors wrote in the May 17 leader: "by treating nuclear weapons as just another explosive in the arsenal, rather than as a deterrent weapon of last resort, America would dangerously blur the line against nuclear use by anyone."

So coverage of the politics of the "War on Terror" has differed, at least to some degree, across media outlets. What about breaking stories? Are there any distinctions of note in how different media have covered those?

Well, many of the same comments as those made above could be repeated: there are differences among which news outlets are able to go live with audio and video, which are able to scramble significant resources quickly, which tend toward hard news coverage and which fold in analysis, which struggle with 24/7 deadlines, which are on air or online quickly, but at a sacrifice of thoughtful analysis and depth.

But there are additional differences among media not already discussed, that relatively consistently emerge—even in stories that on their face seem like they should provoke quite comparable coverage.

Let's take a brief look at how a few different media framed four attacks.

On March 11, 2004, a coordinated series of 10 explosions on four commuter trains coming into Madrid, Spain, during the morning rush hour killed 190 people and injured over 1,800. The Spanish government first charged the Basque separatist group ETA with the attacks, but later Al Qaeda claimed responsibility. Almost exactly seven months later, on October 7, a bombing at the Hilton Hotel in Taba, Egypt, killed 34 people, including Israelis tourists and Russians, and injured 105. Israel charged Al Qaeda with involvement, but a later inquiry by the Egyptian Interior Ministry into the bombings concluded that there was no Al Qaeda link.

Exactly nine months after that, on July 7, 2005, a series of four coordinated attacks in London, England, on three Underground trains and a bus killed 52, not including the four suicide bombers, and wounded around 700. A video statement from one of the suicide bombers was found that suggested a link between the bombers and Al Qaeda. Four months later, on November 9, another series of coordinated bombings, this time of three hotels in Amman, Jordan—the Grand Hyatt, the Radisson SAS, and the Days Inn—killed 60 and injured 115 others. Al Qaeda claimed responsibility.

All four of these attacks immediately riveted media around the world—although not equally. American and British media covered the attacks in London more extensively than those in Madrid, those in Madrid more than those in Jordan, and those in Jordan more than those in Egypt. Breaking news bulletins interrupted regular television programming in the case of London and Madrid, and online news sites in all four cases updated their stories almost minute to minute.

On the first day of the London and Madrid attacks the coverage was almost wall to wall, and both events remained the top stories for days and continued to get major coverage for several weeks. The *New York Times* carried 161 articles either entirely on the London bombing or that referenced it in the first two weeks following the attacks, the *Washington Post* ran 140, the *Guardian* 122, the *Daily Telegraph* 196, NBC 159,[156] CNN 193, and the news weeklies ran cover stories and inside articles in the double digits: the *Economist* had 29 stories, *Time* had 12, and *Newsweek* 18.[157]

There were considerably fewer stories on Madrid, but the coverage was still extensive: The *New York Times* carried 60 articles related to the bombing in the first two weeks, the *Washington Post* 49, the *Guardian* 79, the *Daily Telegraph* 63, NBC 23, CNN 145, and even the news weeklies had cover stories on it, with multiple inside articles.

The bombings in Egypt and Jordan received less attention than the two attacks in Europe, although Jordan garnered more attention in part because of its higher death toll and the drama of one of the attacks which targeted a wedding: the *New York Times* ran 12 articles on Egypt and 27 on Jordan, the *Washington Post* 5 and 22, the *Guardian* 9 and 15, the *Daily Telegraph* 6 and 14, NBC 9 and 24, CNN 37 and 78, and each of the news weeklies only ran two or three stories on each attack.

There are relatively straightforward explanations for the differences in coverage among the events and within each event among the news outlets. CNN, as a 24/7 breaking news channel, is of course going to repeatedly feature such a spectacular story as a major terrorist attack, especially since there was striking video footage from the scenes of all four (actually, the London attack had the least powerful images, a factor that elevated the importance of the citizen-taken cellphone videos). The power of the images helped propel the stories to top news on network programming, too. The news weeklies also emphasized images from the events; several ran what amounted to photoessays, which helps account for the extent of their coverage.

The importance of the locations, and the responsibility (or presumed responsibility) of Al Qaeda in each event, encouraged the media to give attention to the four events across the board, as did the high death tolls, the rush-hour attacks on public transportation systems (a fact that terrified commuters in every major city across the world), and the fact that the attacks in Jordan and Egypt targeted (among others) white tourists in American hotel chains. But the attacks in London and Madrid compelled more coverage because terrorism in those cities was perceived as more aberrant than terrorism in the Middle East. They also, for the US and UK media, were both actually and figuratively closer to home.

Given the literal and virtual proximity of the European attacks compared to the ones in the Middle East, it is intriguing to survey how the different news outlets described and explained the attacks. It would be natural to assume that, as all the attacks had a reasonably similar signature, they were equally characterized as terrorism and that Al Qaeda was more or less equally discussed as the perpetrator. But that wasn't the case. In a study that I directed, researchers searched the transcripts and articles for the two weeks following these four attacks for the news outlets' use of certain words. How many times did NBC use the word "terrorism" or "terrorist" or "terror" or any of its other derivatives? How often did CNN mention Al Qaeda? How frequently did the *New York Times* mention "Iraq" or the *Guardian* refer to the "IRA"? The results were quite suggestive—although the numbers that emerged must be taken only as indicative of the way that the news organizations translated these events to their audiences. For our study the researchers divided the total count for the number of times an outlet used derivations of the word "terror," for example, by the number of stories from that outlet, in order to arrive at a rough percentage of how frequently that news outlet referenced that word. Of course, the resulting number is a fiction, as there were occasions where words were used frequently early on, and then not referenced later (such as the early attribution of the Madrid attack to the Basque group ETA which prompted early use of the word "ETA" in the coverage), and other occasions where a word was used repeatedly in one article and rarely if at all in another. But again, the rough data remains suggestive of how the events were characterized. (Note, too, that some words, such as "terrorism," were searched for in the coverage of every attack, while other words, such as "ETA," "Israel," or "IRA," for example, were searched for only in certain attacks.)

Madrid was the story in which the media most lingered on the "terrorism" connection. The *Washington Post* used it on average (recall, however, that "average" is really a mythic idea) 7.4 times every article, the *New York Times* 6.8 times, and *USA Today* 7 times. By contrast the British papers used it slightly less: the *Daily Telegraph* 6 times and the *Guardian* 6.1 times per article. CNN mentioned "terrorism" or "terrorist" or some version thereof 8.4 times every story. That's a lot.

By contrast, specific perpetrators were mentioned less—ETA was mentioned by all the news organizations around three to four times per story (although if you consider that most of mentions were in the first few days of coverage, the numbers suggest that ETA was referenced perhaps as often in early articles as the more generic "terror." Overall, media mentioned Al Qaeda fewer times, around two times per story. That's surprising. We expected Al Qaeda to be frequently brought up—it is, after all the best-known terrorist group, responsible for the deaths on 9/11. To mention the group significantly less often than "terror" suggests how stunned all the media were by this terrorist attack—and that it was the "terror" of it, rather than the precise perpetrator, that was the most significant element to note. What we were surprised to find, however, was how frequently Iraq was mentioned—although a clear reason for its mention was that the pullout of Spanish forces in Iraq was both an issue in the upcoming general election and one of the demands made by the terrorists. CNN mentioned Iraq on average 6.7 times a story, the American papers between 3.6 and 4.8 times a story, and the British papers around 2 times a story. Why was Iraq mentioned more often in the American media? Because the commitment of Spain to the Bush administration's "War on Terror" loomed larger in the United States than in the United Kingdom.

In the media coverage of the London bombing over a year later, mention of "terrorism" dropped precipitously in all media, except CNN, where the number of times "terror" or "terrorism" or "terrorist" was mentioned per story almost doubled—to an astonishing 15.3 times per story. The usage of these terms dropped by half in the British press: the *Daily Telegraph* used versions of the word on average 2.1 times an article and the *Guardian* 2.8 times per article. The American press used the terms more frequently, but still less than they did when covering Madrid: the *New York Times* mentioned "terror" 4.7 times on average per article, the *Washington Post* 3.1 times. References to Al Qaeda and Iraq hovered around one time or less per story for all the news outlets, again except for CNN, which although it didn't reference Al Qaeda frequently, did reference Iraq 6.3 times on average per story. Interestingly, in the British media, there was a more frequent mention of the previous attacks of the IRA than there was of Al Qaeda. The *Daily Telegraph*, for instance, mentioned the IRA 0.7 times on average per article, twice as often as it mentioned Al Qaeda, and the *Guardian* mentioned the IRA 1.2 times on average an article, slightly over twice as often as it mentioned Al Qaeda.

In both the Egypt and the Jordan attacks, Al Qaeda was mentioned relatively rarely, but Iraq was referenced more frequently across the media than terrorism. The exception to that was the *New York Times* which only mentioned Iraq 3.3 times per story, but mentioned "terror" or its like 7.5 times, and the *Daily Telegraph*, which did not mention Iraq at all. The *Washington Post* referenced Iraq especially frequently in its coverage of Egypt, on average 8 times a story. CNN was another outlier, not because it chose to reference the stories differently than the others, but because it used the words so often. In its coverage of Jordan for example, it mentioned "terror" of some kind almost 10 times a story, but Iraq almost double that number of times. But the real surprise of the coverage of those two attacks was how often in the coverage of the bombing in Egypt the word "Israel" or its derivations were used—recall that Israeli vacationers were among the victims. While the *Daily Telegraph* mentioned "Israel" 6.3 times a story (more than three times its use of "terror"), the *Guardian* mentioned Israel 14.8 time a story (terror had been mentioned 4.2 times), the *New York Times* mentioned Israel 15 times an article, twice the rate at which it used "terror," and the *Washington Post* mentioned Israel a whopping 27 times a story, while mentioning "terror" or its like only 2.6 times.

Having waded through all those averages, what do we learn—understanding that such "averages" are only bellwethers for the connections the different media were making as they reported on the attacks and not "real" figures for how many times any given story used any given word?

Well, we learn that attacks are discussed by using the generic terms "terrorism" or "terrorist" more than by reference to a specific perpetrator, such as Al Qaeda. That Iraq is often drawn into discussions of terrorism, even when the specific attack does not specifically relate to the conflict there. That television uses "scary" words like "terrorism" more often than print media, even when the proportion of the weight that TV gives to various characterizations remains the same. (So, for example, in coverage of the Jordan bombings, both CNN and the *Los Angeles Times* mentioned Iraq roughly double the number of times they mentioned terror, but the CNN audience was hearing those terms repeated twice as often as the readers of the *Times* were. CNN mentioned terror 9.8 times a story while the *Los Angeles Times* mentioned it 3.7 times, and CNN referenced Iraq 18.6 times a story, while the *Times* referenced Iraq 7.3 times an article.)

What was the biggest news? That all media use certain "explanatory" terms over and over and over again: "Terror," "Iraq," "Israel." These words are not just used once or twice in a story. They are used repeatedly.

What's the problems with that? As Madison Avenue has long preached, repetition helps a message sink in. While we all have had the annoying experience of getting an advertising jingle stuck in our heads, research on consumer behavior has shown that it's actually true. Simple repetition of advertising claims increases belief in those claims—a phenomenon academics call the "truth effect."[158]

In a 1977 study, testers read subjects 60 plausible sentences every two weeks and asked them to rate the validity of the sentences. The trick in the experiments was that some of those 60 sentences were repeated—both true and false ones —week to week. The result? When the subjects were asked to judge whether a statement was true, what turned out to matter more than the actual truth or falsity of the statement was whether the subjects had previously heard it.[159] Fifteen years later, in another study of behavior, researchers found that it didn't even entirely matter where the previous information had come from. If a person had heard a statement before, he or she was likely to rate it as more truthful than new, unfamiliar statements. While it made some difference to the participants in this new study whether the statements had come from a "credible" as opposed to a "non-credible" source, the participants tended to rate previously heard sentences as more true even when the person initially giving the sentences had clearly stated that those sentences were false.[160]

Researchers Ann Roggeveen and Gita Johar discovered as well that the truth effect could be even more powerful "when multiple sources endorse the statement." The two discovered that the participants in their studies were more likely to rate as true claims that were provided multiple times, each time from a different source, then those claims that were repeated multiple times, but only from a single source.[161]

Why do people fall for the "truth effect"?

What matters is frequency, recognition, and familiarity. How many times do people hear the same statement? Do they recognize the statement is repeated? Do they grow to like it? Unlike the common cliché, "Familiarity breeds contempt," the opposite is actually true, found Roggeveen and Johar: "the more frequently a stimulus is encountered, the more people grow to like it."[162] In fact efforts to warn people about false information may have the opposite effect. As another set of researchers has noted: "the warning itself may enhance the information's familiarity."[163]

What that means is that whoever first states a claim is the one who has the most power in shaping public opinion—even if that claim later turns out to be entirely false. "If someone says, 'I did not harass her,' I associate the idea of harassment with this person," said Ruth Mayo, a cognitive social psychologist at the Hebrew University in Jerusalem. "Even if he is innocent, this is what is activated when I hear this person's name again."[164]

Hmmm. . . . this is beginning to sound like it has implications for how we the public understand terrorism.

Let's go back to our studies of how media cover terrorism and trace the through-line of the truth effect. First a suicide bombing is repeatedly described in the media—and by those they quote—using words and phrases such as "terrorism" and "Iraq" (frequency). Then, when we watch coverage of another attack, even if it is far removed in time and space from the first, we recognize that the same words are being used to describe it—"terrorism" and "Iraq" (recognition). Finally, when we read a story about the President's speech or a debate in Congress and the same word are used—"terrorism" and "Iraq"—we decide that we like the explanation (familiarity). The truth effect is made all the more plausible by the fact that we heard the same words as we listened to the breaking reports of the suicide bombings during our morning drive, read updates on various websites over lunch, and surfed past the latest news on a number of different television channels that night (multiple sources). And the fact that most of the sources we got the news from were brand names (BBC, newyorktimes.com, and CNN) further enhanced the truth effect on us (credible sources).

No wonder we buy into what we are told by politicians and the media about terrorism. Even when they are critical of each other's handling of issues or events, they are using the same terms to describe them. Even without the media stenographically covering government officials, even when the media question the government's message, it turns out that media and government are mutually reinforcing how we the public understand terrorism. In fact yet another study, this one conducted by Mayo, found that denying or contradicting a piece of information could, in the long run, actually work in people's minds to confirm exactly that which is being denied. As *Washington Post* reporter Shankar Vedantam reported Mayo's findings: "it is better to make a completely new assertion that makes no reference to the original myth" than "to deny a false claim. . . . Rather than say, as Senator Mary Landieu (D-La.) recently did during a marathon Congressional debate, that 'Saddam Hussein did not attack the United States; Osama bin Laden did,' Mayo said it would be better to say something like, 'Osama bin Laden was the only person responsible for the Sept. 11 attacks'—and not mention Hussein at all."[165] Or as anchor Bob Garfield of the radio program *On the Media* observed: "Now, if I understand . . . when people hear a statement involving a negative— let's say Saddam was not connected to 9/11—and they hear it often enough, somehow the 'not' disappears."[166]

Both media and government frame terrorism policy and terrorist attacks by using the same terms as the other one does. The larger packaging of terrorism is the same by both, even though the critique and the impetus may be different. Once a connection has been made—say between Iraq and terrorism, as media coverage of the four terrorist attacks repeatedly reinforced—once an idea has been implanted in people's minds, it can be difficult to dislodge.

Government officials frame the debate in ways they believe will keep them in control. It's about politics. Media—if not necessarily reporters—frame the news in ways that will keep their audiences watching, listening, reading. It's about profit. Packaging terrorism. Co-opting the news for politics and profit.

And what do politics and profit translate into? Ultimately, the packaging of terrorism by media or government—or even terrorists themselves—is all about power. Power over us.

ભ

True terror is a language and a vision. There is a deep narrative structure to terrorist acts and they infiltrate and alter consciousness in ways that writers used to aspire to.

Don DeLillo[167]

III

what are the images of terror?

 **the politics of images**

On February 5, 2003 Secretary of State Colin Powell traveled to the UN to make the Bush administration's case for going to war in Iraq. Following his address, Powell gave a press conference to a throng of reporters, photographers, and TV cameras just a few steps down the hall from the entrance to the Security Council chambers.

That's where hangs a tapestry copy of the twentieth century's most famous anti-war painting, *Guernica*—Pablo Picasso's commemoration of the victims of the 1937 German and Italian aerial destruction of the Basque town of the same name. For the press conference, UN officials used a large blue curtain to mask the huge artwork.

According to the conservative magazine *The Weekly Standard*, a British diplomat said the cover-up was at the request of television news crews who had complained that the Cubist masterpiece was too confusing a backdrop. "The Secretariat did it, to meet the visual requirements of the TV guys." *New York Times* columnist Maureen Dowd noted that diplomats had told her the backdrop provided "too much of a mixed message." As she put it, "Mr. Powell can't very well seduce the world into bombing Iraq surrounded on camera by shrieking and mutilated women, men, children, bulls and horses."[1]

Images are politically powerful—that's why they are so contested. From the opening salvos of the planes smashing into the World Trade Center towers in New York City, the "War on Terror" has been a war for public opinion—and one increasingly played out through media images.

Since September 11, 2001, images have been not just an indication to the world of what is happening on the real and virtual front lines, but a measure of who is winning the global battle for hearts and minds. Images are the way that the public and their leaders remember and "use" events. Consequently the management of them by all parties—Americans and Al Qaeda, Europeans and Arabs, governments and the media—has become a priority.

The management of images started with firefighters raising a flag over Ground Zero and Osama bin Laden on videotape from somewhere on the border between Afghanistan and Pakistan.

It continued. In 2003 we watched live as bombs burst over Baghdad and tanks got mired in red sandstorms. We saw the Iraqi TV footage of scared and battered American prisoners and a defiant Saddam Hussein. We saw the photo-op of a toppling, larger-than-life-size bronze statue and the unstaged trauma of the burned torso and bandaged knobs where arms used to be of a 12-year-old boy, Ali Ismaeel Abbas.

We've seen a lot more.

We've seen tape of cars in flames around the world—from Bali in 2002 to Glasgow in 2007.

We've seen hotels in ruins from Kenya in 2002 to Egypt in 2004 to Jordan in 2005.

We seen photos of commuters in shock and in bandages—in Madrid in 2004, in London in 2005, in Mumbai in 2006.

We've seen video of the Chechen siege at the Moscow theater in 2002 and two years later the video of rescuers running with the translucent bodies of children from the school siege in Beslan.

We've seen images from the assassination of Lebanese former prime minister Rafik Hariri in 2005 and the assassination of Pakistani former prime minister Benazir Bhutto in 2007.

We've seen the photos of the dead that never before would have been made public: morgue photos of victims so families could claim their own and close-ups of severed heads of suicide bombers so the public could help identify who was responsible.

We've seen footage of prisoners in orange jumpsuits praying behind bars and behind-the-scenes snapshots of other prisoners being tortured.

We've seen clips from videotaped snuff films made by terrorists interested in further terrorizing a global audience.

We've seen politicians standing tall, in front of flags and banners, telling us what they are doing; we've seen protesters on the streets calling for politicians to do something different.

We've seen victims and survivors crying in grief, pleading for peace.

Then there are the images we haven't seen—or don't remember.

Attention to one story can cancel out the possibility of another making the news.

On August 31, 2005, the same day that the flood waters of Hurricane Katrina were sweeping over New Orleans, up to 1 million Iraqis walking to a Shiite shrine in Baghdad stampeded when the rumor that there was a suicide bomber in their midst swept through the crowd. Almost a thousand people died and nearly 500 more were injured. That story was lost in the attention given to Katrina.

Other stories make us uncomfortable; they are hard to talk about:

The genocide in Darfur has displaced 1.2 million people and killed hundreds of thousands. Rape is used to terrorize, even though, as Nicholas Kristof has said: "In terms of rape, the official Sudanese position is that basically rape does not exist. . . . But, you know, you just go out and talk to these women, and they are incredibly bold and brave about acknowledging that they have been raped. I mean for all the shame that attaches to it. I wish we could be as bold in speaking out against it."[2]

And still other stories seem so beyond the pale that they are hard even to contemplate:

The war in the Democratic Republic of the Congo has killed 3.8 million. Up to a thousand people have been killed a day. Turkish lawyer Yakin Ertûrk, special rapporteur for the UN Human Rights Council on Violence against Women, wrote in a UN report released in June 2007 of "unimaginable brutality."

> Women are gang raped, often in front of their families and communities. In numerous cases, male relatives are forced at gun point to rape their own daughters, mothers or sisters. . . . After rape, many women were shot or stabbed in the genital area, and survivors [said] that while held as slaves by the gangs they had been forced to eat excrement or the flesh of their murdered relatives.[3]

What is the consequence of a lack of images? Here's just one example: Five months after the United Nations' appeal to world nations for crisis aid in November 2004, several country appeals had "zero" money pledged or committed, including Chad, home to all the Darfurian refugees.[4]

"The media is a huge factor in getting people to be generous," said Oxfam's funding manager, Orla Quinlan. "If they're visually engaged, that brings it home and makes it real to them."[5] The relief community knows well the direct connection between media attention and donations, especially for neglected crises. There is a phenomenon of "image multiplication." Pictures make all the difference. "The media is to political and public attention what other technological 'force multipliers' are to the military," noted Pamela von Gruber, publisher of Defense and Foreign Affairs publications.[6]

When Jan Egeland, the UN's Under-Secretary General for Humanitarian Affairs and Emergency Relief, appeared in December 2005 on the *Charlie Rose Show* for the first anniversary of the tsunami, he spoke about the role media play in getting people to pay attention: "We asked for $1 billion in the tsunami," he said.

> We got 90 percent in no time. . . . In northern Pakistan, we asked for only half of that, $550 million, and we have less than half of that three months into the effort. . . . If [the Pakistan earthquake] had happened in the middle of western Christmas and New Year's break, if the media had followed it as much, if we had had as many tourists there and as many video clips to run on CNN and BBC and so on around the clock, as we did at that time, we might have had the same kind of a response. But this happened in October. There are no images of how people died, how people struggled in the rubble. And we got much less.

The lack of media attention to the food crisis in Niger, Egeland argued, was also the cause for the lack of donor response there:

> We saw it was coming up as an emergency. My people on the ground appealed December of last year [2004] for money. We didn't get anything. We . . . appealed again in March [2005], in April. Then in May, it was really bad. And I told in big press conferences that now, soon, children will start dying. Still didn't get money. And then the BBC World Television did its images, and then suddenly we got more in 10 days than we had in the previous 10 months.

"Seeing suffering is a powerful incentive to give," agreed host Charlie Rose.[7]

For those reasons, Médecins Sans Frontières (MSF) publishes every year a list of the top 10 "Most Underreported Humanitarian Stories." According to Andrew Tyndall, publisher of *The Tyndall Report*, the 10 stories highlighted by MSF for 2005 accounted for just 22 minutes of the 14,529 minutes on the three major US television networks' nightly newscasts. 2005 had an unusually high amount of international coverage, but only six minutes of American weeknight network newscasts were devoted to war and horror in the Democratic Republic of the Congo and two minutes to the conflict and terrorism in Chechnya. The AIDS crisis received 14 minutes of coverage. The remaining stories highlighted by MSF's "Top 10"—conflict and terrorist attacks in Haiti, northeastern India, Colombia, northern Uganda, Ivory Coast, Somalia, and southern Sudan—were not covered at all.

So, how—and whether—the media cover stories matter. And pictures matter most. What do we do about the pictures that we see? Are we even aware that there are pictures and stories and events that we don't see?[8]

What images frame our world? How do media make the decisions about how to visually package their stories of the news—and how have politicians tried to control those images? Do we see the truth or only what government wants us to see? How independent are media in showing us what "really" happened?

What images are "necessary and sufficient" to tell a story is an imperative question. In covering terrorism, journalists have wrestled with such issues as:

- How to report on a terrorist attack unfolding live.
- How to cover the reaction to terrorist attacks—including the political photo-ops and grandstanding of politicians.
- How to cover the victims of terror—by definition civilians, and often children.
- How candid to be when covering terror, torture, and abuse.
- How and whether to use the videotapes of executions and other propaganda filmed by terrorists.
- How to balance what audiences can bear and what they need to be told.
- How to use images when they come from eyewitnesses—non-journalists who by design or happenstance are at the scene of a breaking event.
- How to use images to change minds and record history.

Different media have answered these questions in different ways. Their decisions about what to show—about how to present a story, how to package the news—had, at times, life and death consequences: consider what happened in the aftermath of the publishing of the Danish cartoons of Mohammed or the snapshots of torture from Abu Ghraib.

Images matter, in foreign policy, for diplomatic relations, for the way we all perceive the world.

when did pictures start to matter? some history

It's a temptation to think that it's only been in our brave new age of digital cameras and videophones, of 24/7 news channels and satellite uplinks, that images have mattered as much as they do. That because we can see more images, from literally anywhere, in real time, images somehow have gained in power relative to the humble word.

It's not true. Those in power have always been more concerned about pictures than copy. Images tell a more compelling story than do words. Napoleon III of France, during his mid-nineteenth-century reign, censored caricature more harshly than the written word—in a time of low literacy, political cartoons were intelligible to all. Famed photographer Jimmy Hare wrote about being stymied by the censors in World War I: "to so much as make a snapshot without official permission in writing means arrest." In 1965, CBS correspondent Morley Safer enraged the military and the Johnson administration by showing footage of US Marines using Zippo cigarette lighters to burn the thatched roofs of the village of Cam Ne in Vietnam. Although similar reports had been routinely documented in the print media, the visual effect of the television coverage so irritated LBJ that he is said to have woken up Frank Stanton, president of CBS News, with the demand "Are you trying to f—k me?" In June 1986, the South African government tightened already existing press restrictions with new guidelines cannily calculated to frustrate photographic coverage of disturbances throughout the country. Although reporters could still write about the violence in the townships and elsewhere, the apartheid story disappeared from the air when the only images available became file footage.[9]

Authorities across history have recognized that there are two ways to control images: one, don't allow them at all—which works for those who believe that no news is good news; and two, allow them with restrictions as tight as possible —a necessity for those who desire coverage but who want to spin it. Expedite reporting if it aids your effort and choke it off if its dissemination is problematic. Saddam Hussein tried both tactics: in late March 2003, he threw out CNN's reporters in Baghdad—since CNN is viewed throughout the world, its journalists offered an unwelcome competing perspective to his party line. And he put out his own images of the battlefield. The Iraqi video of battered prisoners and dead American soldiers which was met in the United States with such dismay was a propaganda triumph in the Middle East for giving weight to the notion that Hussein's forces could be a David to the American Goliath.

The Americans, too, played it both ways. On one hand, within two hours of the launch of cruise missiles at the "targets of opportunity" in Baghdad at the opening of the war that March, the Pentagon released dramatic tape showing one of the missiles shooting into the night. The real value the footage added to the story was negligible, but it was pretty to look at and contributed to the image of American might.

On the other hand, Defense Secretary Donald Rumsfeld and US Lieutenant General John Abizaid tried to intimidate US television networks from airing that Iraqi video of American POWs and dead soldiers by arguing that broadcasting the images would defy the Geneva convention governing the treatment of prisoners.

Facts and truth are enshrined in the cultural mythology of the Enlightenment: in court Americans "swear to tell the truth, the whole truth, and nothing but the truth." But the international events of the past years persuasively demonstrate that there is an ecology of truth. Truth is not an absolute. Institutions' interest in communicating truths is not a constant; indeed in the case of the government, truth is in the service of public opinion. Managing facts to create public support in wartime has long been understood as essential—it is simply the method of management that ever remains in question. "Correspondents have a job in war as essential as the military personnel," wrote General Dwight D. Eisenhower in a memorandum drafted in the worrisome days before the Normandy invasion. "Fundamentally, public opinion wins wars."[10] President George H. W. Bush's method for controlling and retaining public support during Gulf War I was to put a moratorium on journalists filing from the frontline and to filter the theater's information through official press conferences. President George W. Bush's method during Gulf War II was to invest journalists in the day-to-day operations of the US troops through the strategy of "embedding."

Twentieth-century war has offered a few models of what politicians, journalists, and the public have believed it appropriate to see from the frontline. During World War I the US media acquiesced in the military's censorship of photographs of injured and dead American troops for the reason that "such pictures" would cause "needless anxiety to those whose friends and relatives [are] at the front."

At the beginning of World War II, American newspapers, magazines, and newsreels could publish photographs of the enemy or even the Allied dead. But still not of American boys. Then, as the war wore on and began to demand significant sacrifices of the public, a problem emerged. One airman articulated the dilemma to novelist turned war correspondent John Steinbeck. "It seems to me," he said, "that the folks at home are fighting one war and we're fighting another one. They've got theirs nearly won and we've just got started on ours. I wish they'd get in the same war we're in. I wish they'd print the casualties and tell them what it's like." *Life* magazine, the premier photographic publication of the day, argued in an editorial that the men's sacrifice needed to be acknowledged. "Dead men have died in vain if live men refuse to look at them."

In September 1943, at the nadir of the war for the Allies, President Franklin Roosevelt approved the lifting of the censorship. He agreed. Americans needed to see what they were up against. Many media, however, were uncomfortably ambivalent about the new candor and showing photos of dead and injured American troops. Said the *Seattle Post-Intelligencer*, "[We want] no sugar coating of the war [nor] stomach-turning pictures."

But that first week after the graphic photos began to be released, *Life* ran one, full-page, opposite a new editorial. "Here lie three Americans," the editorial began,

> What shall we say of them? Shall we say that this is a noble sight? Shall we say that this is a fine thing, that they should give their lives for their country? Or shall we say that this is too horrible to look at? Why print this picture, anyway, of three American boys dead upon an alien shore? Is it to hurt people? To be morbid? Those are not the reasons. The reason is that words are never enough.

Exactly nine years later, in September 1952, *Life* magazine wrestled with the question of whether to publish a different kind of grim and disturbing picture. The occupation of Japan had ended and the press censorship had been lifted for the Far East. Photographs from the war that had languished unseen became available to journalists—including some from Hiroshima and Nagasaki taken on the ground in the hours after the atomic blasts. Should the images of the civilian victims be published? Yes, *Life* answered. "Dead men have indeed died in vain if live men refuse to look at them," the editors repeated.

In 1945, *Life* magazine had shown pictures of the bomb blasts from the air and had reported on the structural damage to Hiroshima and Nagasaki. At the time that satisfied the magazine's editorial conscience. Seven years and the Soviet Union's detonation of its own atomic bomb later, those sterile images were demonstrably no longer sufficient. "The motive for the first U.S. publication of the Hiroshima and Nagasaki collection is its terrible and vital pertinence to the age in which we live," the editors wrote. *Life*'s publication of the human photographs helped to answer questions not only about the totality of what had happened, but about such larger questions as who we thought the enemy was, who we thought we were, and how we could prevent ourselves from becoming the enemy.

Life published photographs of dazed and dying infants and toddlers in the aftermath of the blasts, of half-naked corpses hurled into a ditch, their shirts blown from their backs, and of clots of the "walking dead"—those who survived the blast, but who would not survive the experience. The grainy black-and-white images, from film washed in creeks, strongly conveyed the consequences of the deployment of a weapon of mass destruction. But *Life* noted in the final sentence of its essay how even those pictures did not do the event justice: "the people of the two cities warn that the long-suppressed photographs, terrible as they are, still fall far short of depicting the horror which only those who lived under the blast can know."

It made perfect sense that General Douglas McArthur's occupation administration had had no interest in publishing either in Japan or in the United States the Ground Zero eye-view of Hiroshima and Nagasaki. In the immediate days following the bombings in August 1945, Americans in the United States had seen photographs of the mushroom clouds—the scale of which gave credence to the bombs' seeming power to themselves bring the war to a close. But what end would the images of burned civilians in shredded clothes have served?

Despite the millions of civilians who were killed in World War II, few published photographs featured their plight; American periodicals focused on the trials of the soldiers. Pictures of desperate civilians are usually used to challenge the conduct of an enemy—the images from Hiroshima and Nagasaki challenged the conduct of Americans. During the war, public support was nurtured by the publication of such photographs as Joe Rosenthal's raising of the flag over Iwo Jima or Robert Capa's GIs struggling ashore on the beaches of Normandy—images of stolid American heroes persevering in the face of almost insurmountable obstacles. The moral crusade was for war—war against the evil of the Third Reich and the Imperial Japanese Empire—and such pictures identified the crusaders. It took seven more years, when the world had shifted on its axis, and the threat came from the prospect of nuclear annihilation, before the photographs from the atomic bomb sites could be published to serve the opposite goal: not to champion war, but to caution against it.

Even during the Vietnam War, which in memory seems to have been an era of unfettered publishing and broadcasting of images, the media struggled over whether to show photos of injured and dying civilians. The photographs which are now synonymous with that conflict were not then published to universal approval—and in some cases were not published at all.

The famous image of the burning monk, taken in 1963, was not published by the *New York Times* nor many other US newspapers, "on the grounds that it was not fit fare for the breakfast table," remembered the photographer (and later *New York Times* editor) Malcolm Browne. And while Nick Ut's photograph of the little naked girl running down the road after a napalm attack, taken in 1972, did appear on the front pages of newspapers around the world, virtually every newspaper that published it—and every television station that aired the image or the simultaneous footage of the scene taken by the ITN news cameraman Alan Downes—received outraged letters deploring the publishing of the graphic scene.

"The love of peace has no meaning or no stamina unless it is based on a knowledge of war's terrors," noted *Life*'s 1952 editorial. That was true in World War II with Hiroshima; it remains true today. Those at home need to know what has been done in their name. If the public doesn't know what is specifically happening—or how the actions of its government and military are being understood by different audiences—then policymakers are freed to make their decisions based on other goals and other standards of conduct. And those policymakers are freed to represent their intentions and their actions in whatever moral cloak they design.

"it's no time to be squeamish": the "jumpers" at the world trade center

Life magazine belatedly published the images from Ground Zero in Japan, having come to believe that the images were essential to Americans' understanding "war's terrors"—specifically the terror wreaked by atomic weapons.

What was covered of the American Ground Zero?

The moment the second plane hit the North Tower it became obvious that it was terrorists—not some incompetent pilot—who had struck the World Trade Center. It was that second fireball, then, that made the greatest impact.

Executive producer Shelley Ross of ABC's *Good Morning America* remembered, in an article by Lori Robertson for the *American Journalism Review* (*AJR*), that ABC's control room was flummoxed by the first plane crash. "The first person who uttered anything out loud . . . said, 'Maybe air traffic control has gone haywire?'" Ross said. "The second [plane] came in, and I knew . . . that was no accident. . . . It was pretty stunning."

As bits of information and news streamed into the television networks and print newsrooms in those first minutes, it became clear that the country was in the midst of a terrorist attack: planes had been hijacked, the White House was being evacuated, other planes were in the air but unaccounted for. Said Ross, "Then, as it unfolded, we're gathering information, and what you're really doing is bringing people live pictures." But "the real stunner" came when news came of the plane crashing into the Pentagon. "And then it felt like Pearl Harbor."[11]

Most photographic icons throughout history have gained their force from their visible human element: the soldiers slogging ashore on D-Day, the lone man standing against the tanks in Tiananmen Square. But in the iconic images of 9/11 of the second plane hitting the tower, of both towers enveloped in flames, and of the towers imploding, the humanity has to be intuited. There is a certain parallel between those pictures and the photographs of the mushroom clouds over Hiroshima and Nagasaki. They both only intimate the loss of life. But both sets of photographs are insufficient by themselves—the telling of both events is not complete without other images showing the personal tragedy of those trapped, the emotional strain on those who watched. Media struggled with what to show of the human toll.

On September 11, it was difficult to know what to show—not just because of the scale of the 9/11 attack, but because it unfolded live in front of television cameras. Many TV news packages on stories are, say, 120 seconds long. Into those two minutes can be crammed 350 words, 30 different pictures, three or four sound bites, and who knows what else. That day, television went live with the story round the clock, essentially for days. Without commercials.

Network television, for once, was widely praised for guiding Americans through the opening day. On CBS's *The Early Show*, the first news came from anchor Bryant Gumbel: "It's 8:52 here in New York. We understand that there has been a plane crash on the southern tip of Manhattan. You're looking at the World Trade Center. We understand that a plane has crashed into the World Trade Center. We don't know anything more than that."[12] In the next hour all three network morning shows had upended their programming. By 10 o'clock, Peter Jennings had made it to the office to take over from Diane Sawyer. Co-host Charles Gibson had left the studio and was unsuccessfully trying to get downtown to the site. *The Early Show* passed the coverage off to Dan Rather, while NBC's top-rated *Today* anchors Katie Couric and Matt Lauer remained on a while longer. Jennings stayed at the anchor desk for 17 straight hours, an effort described as "Herculean" by television critics.[13] At one point, Jennings broke his composure after receiving phone calls from his children. "We do not very often make recommendations for people's behavior from this chair," he said, "but . . . if you're a parent, you've got a kid in some other part of the country, call them up. Exchange observations." Said *Washington Post* columnist Marc Fisher, "We watched Peter Jennings' beard grow, and we were somehow reassured that he did not shave, that through morning, afternoon, evening and on into the night, he did not leave the desk, that he confided in us his uncertainties, that he shared the confusions of each hour. He grew more pale and more vulnerable, as if he knew that we needed him to be human, so that we could be together."[14]

According to a Pew survey of Americans released four days after the attack, 81 percent of respondents said that they got most of their news of the attack from TV, 11 percent said they relied on radio, 2 percent said they got their breaking news from the Internet, and only 1 percent said newspapers. But that said, all news outlets were inundated with people wanting the latest information.

Newspapers sold out their runs, even after they had doubled them. At moments on NYTimes.com there were so many people coming to the site that the system couldn't record them all. To help, it suspended its registration system, allowing users to go directly to stories without signing in. Some news outlets tapped servers that had been dedicated to other functions. CNN.com utilized CNNsi.com and CNNfn.com; ABCNews.com tripled its capacity by using ESPN.com and ABC.com servers. The news sites also stripped nonessential content from their front pages—images, navigation, and even advertisements—in order to reduce the file size of each page; CNN.com's homepage went from about 255 kilobytes of data to about 20 kilobytes.

Some sites converted email news alerts into full news delivery services. At 8:52 a.m. Tuesday, just as Bryant Gumbel was breaking the news to the *Today* show audience, CNN.com sent out its first bulletin: "World Trade Center damaged; unconfirmed reports say a plane has crashed into tower. Details to come." As the story developed, CNN.com began sending full stories to its e-news subscribers. Between Tuesday afternoon and Wednesday morning, all the major news sites launched special pages resembling the special sections the newspapers were putting out, with subsections labeled by such topics as: "The Attacks," "The Human Cost," "The Economic Impact."[15]

Those in charge in the newsrooms faced new ethical challenges. Should they show the moments of death—the mass murder of the planes' impact on the buildings, the individual suicides of people jumping out of the towers, the deaths of thousands of people when the buildings subsequently collapsed?

As the hours passed, the media agonized—what to say and what to continue to show. Papers around the world ran a photo by Reuters photographer Jeff Christensen. Christensen, who had been aiming his telephoto lens at the towers, took about 80 photos and then raced uptown to Reuters office to move them on the wire in time to make the 1 p.m. European deadlines of Reuters' clients. Only then did one of the papers notice some people in a corner of one of the shots and called Reuters. The service cropped the image—to about a tenth of the original frame. In clear view were people hanging out of the windows of the burning North Tower with no way to escape. "I didn't really realize I had that, to be perfectly honest," Christensen told *AJR*. "It was one of those things." The photo was taken about 20 minutes before the tower collapsed. A police helicopter had approached the flaming tower shortly before he took the shot. "I'm sure those people were hoping there was going to be some type of rooftop rescue, but it didn't happen," Christensen said. "I'm pretty sure that those people didn't make it."[16]

Other news outlets, hundreds of newspapers all over the country, all over the world published another photo—the one of a person freefalling out of one of the towers. The image was out of a sequence of about a dozen of the man's plummet taken by Associated Press photographer Richard Drew.[17] Drew captured the man's head-first perfect-seeming dive at 15 seconds after 9:41 a.m. The other photos in the sequence all show the same man tumbling, turning, less graceful, less in control. Drew shot six or eight or more of the jumpers through his 80–200mm lens as he stood where the ambulances were gathering near West Street. Each time the policeman or EMT next to him cried "Oh my gosh, look at that!" he looked up with his camera and photographed the falling body. "We were watching one guy, who is in one of my photographs that has been published a lot," remembered Drew, "some guy was actually clinging to the outside of the building, outside on the girders. He had a white shirt on. We were watching him for the longest time while all these other people were falling, and I alternated between that and this other stuff."[18] The *New York Times* published the singular image of the perfect-seeming dive on page 7. *Newsday* editor Tony Marro said to *AJR* that similar photos were coming in all day. At least 200 people either fell or jumped to their deaths.[19] "Half of all the stories were people saying how horrifying it was to see people jump or be thrown out," Marro said. "We decided to run this because it was small enough and the person was unidentifiable."[20]

They were called jumpers, although the New York Medical Examiner's Office emphasizes "They didn't jump. Nobody jumped. They were forced out, or blown out." The news stations wrestled for a seemingly endless period of time over whether to show the scene: the jumpers jumped for more than an hour and a half, usually one by one, starting not long after the first plane hit the North Tower. One photograph froze a tableau of three people in mid-air, evenly spaced, as though they went out as a team of sorts: first you, then you, then me. Some tried to hold on to makeshift parachutes of tablecloths and curtains. The fabric tore away in their hands, like the jackets off their backs in the 10 seconds it took them to fall, as they accelerated up to 150 mph. One of the jumpers hit a firefighter on the ground and killed him; the fireman's body was anointed by New York Fire Department (FDNY) chaplain Father Mychal Judge. Shortly thereafter, Father Mychal himself died after giving the last rites to a fireman. As a group of firefighters carried his pale, slumped body from the rubble, a photographer snapped the image. That image too made its way around the world.

On television, European and Mexican channels showed footage of more jumpers than did their American counterparts. ABC and MSNBC did not show the jumpers. NBC, CBS, and Fox did for a time and then stopped. At CNN, footage of the jumpers was shown live, then, as *Esquire* magazine related, after Walter Isaacson, chairman of the network's news bureau, had "'agonized discussions' with the 'standards guy,' video of jumpers was shown only if people in it were blurred and unidentifiable; then it was not shown at all." French documentary filmmakers, brothers Jules and Gedeon Naudet, who just happened to be already shooting a film about the FDNY that day, and who went to the Twin Towers when the calls came in, decided not to get videotape of the jumpers smashing into the pavement. But in their film *9/11* that later aired on CBS there is audio of "the booming, rattling explosions the jumpers made upon impact," although the two men "edited out the most disturbing thing about the sounds: the sheer frequency with which they occurred."[21]

Said Jonathan Munro, deputy editor for ITN News in London: "It was a massive challenge to try and understand the motives and the reasons and the cause that had led the hijackers to do what they did. . . . Unless we found the right bar in that context all we were doing was being voyeuristic about these amazing pictures without explaining what on earth had precipitated such a change in the world."[22] The papers and newscasts that ran images of the human tragedy fielded complaints from readers and viewers that they were exploiting the tragedy, invading the privacy of those in their last moments, being unnecessarily graphic. Many argued that those in the photos would be known to their loved ones. But oddly enough, despite earnest, lengthy attempts to identify the falling man in the most famous shot of all—that taken by Drew—he remained unidentified. Despite those who believe that possibly he just might be one of those 29 people who died from the Windows on the World restaurant or one of another 21 who died working for Forte Food, a catering service for Cantor Fitzgerald, no one is really sure. Said Tom Junod at the end of his article on the photograph in *Esquire* magazine: "One of the most famous photographs in human history became an unmarked grave, and the man buried inside its frame—the Falling Man—became the Unknown Soldier in a war whose end we have not yet seen."[23]

Five days after 9/11, relatives had blanketed New York City with photos of loved ones missing since the collapse of the towers. A wall outside Bellevue Hospital papered with photocopies of those missing became a testament to hope and a space for commemoration. Perhaps one of those missing posters was for the falling man. The *New York Times* instituted in its "A Nation Challenged" section a daily "Portraits of Grief" back page that through photographs and homely descriptions gave recognition to how enormous the impact of 9/11 had been. Perhaps one of those obituaries was of the falling man.

In the end, despite the fact that some media showed some of the horror of the day, they did not broadcast or publish images that could compare in the level of explicitness to the *Life* magazine photographs of Ground Zero in Japan. "Pictures of body parts from the 9/11 attacks" noted *Newsweek* director of photography Sarah Harbutt, didn't make it into publications, "not because of censorship, per se, but because editors found it hard to deal with such a harsh reality." Editors, she observed, are susceptible to their own emotions and sensitivities when choosing images. The sole exception: a photograph of a severed hand in the *New York Daily News*. It looked like a yellow rubber glove abandoned, by itself, on a patch of grey pavement. A *Daily News* editor commented, "You can't do the story without doing the story. It's no time to be squeamish."[24]

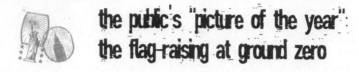

the public's "picture of the year": the flag-raising at ground zero

On September 11 Americans desperately wanted to know what had happened.

But on the day after September 11—and for days and weeks and months to come—what the public also wanted was news of what Americans were doing about the attacks.

On the morning of September 11, throughout the New York and New Jersey area, photographers grabbed their equipment and rushed to frame the World Trade Center debacle. Famed war photographers Jim Nachtwey and Susan Meiselas happened to be in New York. They ran to Ground Zero. The gritty, dun-colored images they took looked like photographs from war zones more distant: San Salvador, Baidoa, Gaza, Groszny.

New York Daily News photographer David Handschuh, president of the Newspaper Press Photographers Association, was on his way to teach a photo-journalism class at New York University when the police radio in his car announced that one of the Twin Towers had been hit. He sped to the scene, following a fire truck going against traffic. Recognizing him, the fire fighters waved him to follow. None of those men survived the day. When they all got to the towers, Handschuh looked up in time to take a picture of the exact moment the second plane hit the South Tower. With two digital cameras he shot closer and closer. Although he started to flee with the collapse of the first building, he got caught in the debris cloud that first threw him, then trapped him under the glass, steel, and cement that rained down. Dug out by several rescue workers, with a shattered leg, two damaged knees, and burns from the hot cement, he handed off his cameras to a *Daily News* colleague.

Then there was Bill Biggart. Biggart also had rushed to Ground Zero, taking shot after shot on both his SLR and digital cameras. When the second tower imploded he was crushed and killed; days later his cameras were dug out of the debris. His SLRs had been smashed, but the flash card on his digital camera was intact and showed that he continued taking pictures even in his last seconds. In the 150 or so photos recorded on the card one can see that Biggart "is going closer and closer," said Chip East, the photographer who rescued the images. "As you go through, you see people's reaction, and you see how people are handling all this . . . every one of Bill's pictures are about people and how they are reacting to this story. We need to remind ourselves this story isn't about buildings, but about how people are affected by the loss of these structures."[25]

Those photographers who weren't on Manhattan took pictures from where they stood. Steve Ludlum of the *New York Times* captured the image of the South

Tower exploding behind the Brooklyn Bridge—one of the series of images from the *Times* that would go on to win the Pulitzer Prize that year. And dozens of photographers trapped on the New Jersey waterfront took pictures across the Hudson River of the burning towers, and documented the shocked victims being offloaded by rescue boats.

Photographer Thomas Franklin, of New Jersey's Bergen County paper *The Record*, joined those on the Jersey side.[26] Like others around him he took image after image on his digital camera of the fire and smoke on the other side. Then he ran afoul of the police. One officer patrolled the side streets, trying to keep those with cameras away from the waterfront. He put a strong hand on Franklin's shoulder and propelled him away. In the encounter, somehow, Franklin recalled, his camera slammed against a lamppost. All the images he had shot that morning, including those of the South Tower collapsing, were erased. John O'Boyle, a photographer for the Newark *Star-Ledger*, who was there, recalled saying, "Tom, Tom, Tom. There's nothing you can do now. You have to keep going. Put in a new disk and start again. Just keep going."

Franklin put another disk into his camera and resumed prowling the waterfront, taking pictures of the injured. He stumbled on another Jersey photographer, John Wheeler, a freelancer, who had managed to convince a police captain to let him get on a tugboat going across to Manhattan. Both men got on board, and once across the Hudson they wandered about, taking photographs of the city that had turned the color of dust. As the day wore on the two split up. Franklin began to worry about making his deadline. With 30 pictures left on his disk he thought it was time to get back to New Jersey. He turned onto Liberty Street, heading home.

A hundred feet ahead of him three firefighters had an American flag wrapped around its pole. The men were part of a group which had been digging in the rubble for survivors for six hours when the call came to evacuate the area. One of them, Dan McWilliams from Ladder 157 in Brooklyn, peeled off from his retreating crew when he spotted a flag still flying from its 10-foot mast on a yacht docked at the World Financial Center marina. McWilliams liberated the flag, carefully furling it around its pole so that it wouldn't touch the ground. As he made his way back to the evacuation area, he passed his fellow 157 firefighter George Johnson. "Gimme a hand, will ya, George?"[27] Another friend, Billy Eisengrein, of Brooklyn fire company Rescue 2, joined in: "You need a hand?"

First thinking to just plant the flag in the ground on its own pole, the men then saw a construction trailer on Liberty Street with a partially damaged, tilted, yet much larger flagpole with a green flag still clinging on it. The men took the green flag off and patched the frayed cord with electrical tape. It took a minute or two until the American flag was clipped on and hoisted up. Then the job done, the three men walked away. McWilliams remembered that "a few guys yelled out 'good job' and 'way to go.'" "Every pair of eyes that saw that flag got a little brighter," said

McWilliams about his fellow firefighters. But he didn't notice that the flag had attracted the attention of others too.

It wasn't only Tom Franklin who happened to be watching the scene on Liberty Street. Through a second-story window two photographers noticed the scene. The magazine photographer hung up on her editor in mid-sentence to snap the shot out a broken window. The newspaper photographer rushed to take some pictures over the magazine photographer's head. A paramedic down on the street whipped out his camera and recorded the event. So too did a video crew from the New York Police Department.

Franklin lifted his camera and framed the three men wrestling with the flag. From over 30 yards away he zoomed in to get close-ups of the men, then zoomed out to capture more of the surrounding scene of Ground Zero. He struggled to get all three faces in the shot and to capture the flag fluttering, rather than hanging limply. By his twelfth frame, the men were hoisting the flag up the pole, but one of the men's faces was obscured. Then at 1/640th of a second he shot frame 13. All three firefighters looked up at the flag; the men, the flag, and the pole formed a perfect triangle. It was 5:01 p.m., not quite eight hours after the attacks. "The shot immediately felt important to me," Franklin said. "It said something to me about the strength of the American people and about the courage of all the firefighters who, in the face of this horrible disaster, had a job to do in battling the unimaginable."[28]

"Out of that uncertainty, there arose a symbol of hope," said Governor George Pataki, in describing the photograph almost a year later, "a symbol of the confidence that we as New Yorkers and as Americans have always shown when confronted with evil."[29] In fact, on September 11, 2001, Wal-Mart sold 88,000 US flags. It was a day that brought out the patriotic instinct in every American. Especially those at Ground Zero in New York City.

Franklin left Liberty Street and headed back across the river to make his deadline. Faced with gridlock on the roads he headed into a hotel to sort through his photographs on his laptop. Borrowing a phone he sent 40 pictures back to his photo editor, Rich Gigli. At 8:35 p.m., as photographer Danielle Richards monitored Franklin's transmission, she shouted, "Oh, my God!"

Deadline was 9 p.m. The editors had 25 minutes to figure out whether to run Franklin's picture. As *Record* reporter Adam Lisberg recorded in his first anniversary account of that day, the editors had a lot to weigh: "The flag picture was unlike anything else they'd seen, but it told a story of reaction, not the news of the day. Other pictures showed rubble and devastation, but without as much visual impact. Wire-service photos captured unimaginable explosions, but they didn't showcase *The Record*'s own staff."[30]

They decided to run on page 1 an AP photograph of the South Tower exploding as the second plane erupted in a fireball. Franklin's photograph was prepped to run large and in color on page 32, the back page of the news section. As

The Record went to press, photo editor Gigli decided to pass Franklin's photograph on to AP in New York. At 12:08 p.m., after deadline for most East Coast papers, he sent it in.

Minutes after receiving the Franklin picture, the New York office of AP sent the image on to its members. At least a dozen papers in the Midwest and West, from Ann Arbor to Topeka to Walla Walla, received it before deadline and ran with it the next day on their front pages.

The following day, September 13, the *New York Post* ran a full-page black-and-white version of the picture. *Newsweek* put the photograph on its cover with the headline: "God Bless America." Franklin appeared on the *Today* show.

Then it began to get crazy.

In October, US forces newly deployed in Afghanistan raided a Taliban compound and left as their calling cards black-and-white copies of Franklin's picture with the words "Freedom endures" emblazoned across it. When news of the raid and the cards leaked out, reporters hounded Franklin for his reaction. He changed his home phone number.

Then the Fire Department received $180,000 to create an 18-foot bronze statue of the flag-raising for a memorial outside the department's Brooklyn head-quarters. In December 2001, former New York Mayor Rudolph Giuliani unveiled the clay model of the statue by sculptor Ira Schwartz—which revealed that the Department had decided to change the scene a little: the three white firefighters had become one white firefighter, one black firefighter, and one Hispanic fire-fighter. Faced with a firestorm of protest, the department abandoned its plans for a politically correct statue.

The urge to reproduce the photograph in 3-D remained. A year after September 11, the New York branch of Madame Tussaud's Waxworks celebrated the completion of its life-size depiction of the three firefighters raising the flag on a plat-form of reproduced rubble. The exhibit, entitled "Hope: Humanity, and Heroism," had taken over 70 craftspeople several months to create. The firefighters had had to travel to London to be photographed and measured in 250 dimensions. Firefighter George Johnson remarked, "I think a display like this is good to show Americans and show the whole world that anybody can be blindsided by a cowardly sneak attack, but you know that you are never going to knock us down."[31]

Franklin's image was also even reproduced on a US postage stamp—the first time ever that the US Postal Service converted an unretouched photograph into a stamp and only the second time in history that the Postal Service had created a "semipostal" stamp, where customers pay more for the stamp than is needed for first-class postage. The difference in price went to the Federal Emergency Management Agency (FEMA) to support survivors of the attack and the families of those killed. Creating the stamp required an Act of Congress to allow the three firefighters to appear— usually US stamps commemorate the dead. In 2002, Christie's auction house in

New York sold the only existing original print of the image for $89,625, an amount vastly exceeding its estimated selling price of between $3,000 and $5,000.

Franklin's photograph won a plethora of awards, including Photo of the Year in the Sigma Delta Chi Awards by the Society of Professional Journalists. To the surprise of many, however, it did not win the Pulitzer Prize, although it was one of three Pulitzer finalists in the breaking news photograph category. "I thought Franklin's image was a good news of the day photo of the aftermath," said John Glenn, one of the Pulitzer judges. "We were determined we would be fair and would not penalize the image because of its exposure. But the truth is, it was not the most dynamic work in the contest."[32]

Nor did Franklin's photographs place in the top three of the Pictures of the Year International competition, although the judges submitted it to MSNBC, which conducts the Public's Picture of the Year contest. It overwhelmingly won that award with more than three times the votes of the runner-up. Reporters Mark Edelson and Sarah Franquet of the *Palm Beach Post* asked David Rees, the director of the POYi contest, to explain why the photograph had been shut out of many of the top professional awards even though it had become the ubiquitous icon of 9/11. "I think," Rees said, "that the POYi judges were trying to pick what they believed were the photographs that held the most journalistic value. Perhaps the success of this photograph shows that there can sometimes be different value systems at work—that the public may not be looking for 'the best' in term of composition, lighting, technical merit or even journalistic relevance—but are instead looking for a picture that connects with their hearts and mind."[33]

Why was the photograph so embraced by the public, but not equally lauded by professional journalists? Capturing the likeness of pivotal moments is the role of news photographers. The best photojournalists have an ability to distill a crisis into a visual synecdoche—an icon that represents that moment and no other. Each new icon—consider the video (and the still photograph taken from it) of the man standing in front of the line of tanks in Tiananmen Square—immediately adds a new image to our visual vocabulary.

In years past, the Pulitzer Prizes have recognized the incisive power of iconic pictures to freeze a pivotal moment in time. Think of the photographs that captured Jack Ruby's murder of Lee Harvey Oswald, the assassin of President John Kennedy; the point-blank Saigon street-corner execution during the 1968 Tet offensive during the Vietnam War; the keening of a bystander over the body of a young man killed by the Ohio National Guard during the protests at Kent State University; the naked Vietnamese girl running down the road after a napalm bombing; a mob of Somalis dragging the body of a US soldier down a street in Mogadishu, Somalia; a firefighter cradling the body of a 1-year-old killed in the Oklahoma City bombing. The power of each of these Pulitzer-winning images resides in the revolutionary moment revealed by an arresting aesthetic. The public at home had never before seen the expression on the face of an accused assassin as he is shot, or been witness to a child screaming in agony after being napalmed, or watched as those who they had thought to rescue desecrated the body of an American soldier. These icons referenced no other news images; they added new ones to the canon.

By contrast, much of the force of Franklin's picture of the Ground Zero flag-raising derived from its implicit allusion to a previous iconic image: Joe Rosenthal's photograph for AP of the flag-raising on Iwo Jima. Those who saw the Ground Zero picture immediately recalled its World War II precursor and found comfort in the resonance. Both images tell of men, in the midst of cataclysm, together planting a symbol of American freedom on contested ground. The war in the Pacific and the Bush administration's "War on Terror" do have a few elements in common: one of those few may well be the reaction of Americans to an external threat. In both cases the impulse existed to band together, to hoist up the flag, to make heroes of those on the frontline.

But conflating the assault on Mount Suribachi with the assault on the Twin Towers did service to neither event. The political freight of the Pacific photograph—its tale of a war, already hard fought, against a known enemy—anachronistically weighed down the Ground Zero picture. For all the passion of the September 11 flag-raising, for all that the photographer framed a moment of patriotic audacity, what cleaved history in two that day was not the realization that Americans could be indomitable in the face of crisis. That had been demonstrated repeatedly in the past. The alteration in history occurred because Americans discovered that they were supremely vulnerable—not just to a powerful state but to a handful of rogue terrorists. Along with the World Trade Center, September 11 exploded the myth that a Fortress America could exist given a large enough arsenal stocked with the most futuristic weaponry.

The photograph summarized well the ethos of defiance and patriotism that unified the country in the hours and days after the World Trade Center's collapse. Yet the fame the photograph achieved told more about Americans' reaction to the terrorist attack than about the attack itself.

"is american blood more precious than iraqi blood?" ali ismail abbas and pfc. jessica lynch

How are the civilian victims of the "War on Terror" pictured?

Governments and their hometown media are generally interested in distancing their own citizens and audiences from the negative human consequences of their nations' own policies—and equally interested in emphasizing the human costs of their enemies' strategies. For instance, Americans at home didn't see the death and destruction that the march to Baghdad in 2003 caused—but most of the rest of the world did. The 35 million viewers who watched Al Jazeera saw images of injured Iraqi civilians, scared US POWs, and dead Americans—and so did those viewers who watched the BBC and ITN, or LC1 TV in France or ZDF News in Germany.

Al Jazeera's TV coverage of the 2003 fighting in Iraq, for example, noted Mohammed el-Nawawy, co-author of *Al Jazeera: How the Free Arab News Network Scooped the World and Changed the Middle East*, focused "on the casualties. They show[ed] very gruesome images of civilian casualties that we [didn't] see on America media." But according to el-Nawawy, that's a problem for Americans. "While there have been many more deaths and injuries of Iraqis, coverage of them [by US television] is far outweighed by coverage of US casualties and POWs. The question that strikes Arabs in this context is: Is American blood more precious than Iraqi blood?"[34] Seeing those civilians—as the rest of the world saw them— was critical, many believed, to understanding the reality on the ground in Iraq and elsewhere and was certainly critical to understanding the emotions in the region and across the globe. Such images were the way by which the world formed its opinions of the "War on Terror," the war in Iraq, and American foreign policy in general. If Americans don't see the same images as the rest of the world, they can't understand the reactions of others.

But for all that many commentators argue that Americans have a civic obligation to look at the effects of their foreign policies, it has been a hard sell. Consider the story of one 12-year-old boy: Ali Ismail Abbas.

Ali's public story began in the early morning of Sunday, March 30, 2003 when a US missile struck four houses in a cluster of eight cottages in the district of Zaafraniyeh, a dozen miles south of Baghdad.[35] The Zaafraniyeh district is an area of both farmland and industry, a zone that was of interest to Americans because of its ties to Saddam Hussein's purported WMD arsenal. Ali's house was surrounded by farmland that Ali's father and uncle tended. But two nearby factories in Zaafraniyeh had been visited in December 2002 by UN weapons inspectors because of suspicions that they had the capability of processing not only consumer goods, but biological agents. Another nearby factory was suspected of manufacturing missiles, and the 23,000-acre Al-Tuwaitha nuclear research center was only several miles away. In addtion, the Iraqi army had put antiaircraft artillery in the civilian neighborhood a half a block away.

Around 6 in the morning, a bomb struck Ali's house, killing his pregnant mother, his father, and his younger brother. His mother's face was sliced open. Fire charred his father black, curling his arms into a frozen embrace. His brother's body was intact, but his head from the nose up was chopped off. Eight other relatives of Ali perished in another one of the homes that had been hit. In all, 16 died in the attack.

A neighbor pulled Ali out of the rubble. He wasn't expected to survive—one hand and arm was a charred claw, the other hand and forearm were missing, crumbled off like charcoal at the elbow, only two long white bones sticking out. Ali's torso was grossly burnt and his lungs were damaged by smoke inhalation. But he and the other members of the family were rushed to Al-Kindi hospital, one of Baghdad's principal hospitals. Ali was taken to the emergency room, the rest of his family to the morgue.

On Monday, the last day of March, *New Yorker* reporter Jon Lee Anderson visited Al-Kindi hospital and Dr. Osama Saleh, an orthopedic surgeon and the head of medical services. One of the doctor's assistants pulled up images of Ali on a computer in his office. The doctor said Ali was still conscious, Anderson recalled in an article in the *New Yorker*. " 'I don't think he will survive, though,' he said in a flat tone. 'These burned people have complications after three or four days; in the first week they usually get septicemia.' " Putting on a green smock, face mask, gauzy hair net and shoe coverings, Anderson and the doctor then walked to the burn unit. "Dr. Saleh," wrote Anderson, "carefully pulled back a coarse gray blanket, and I saw Ali's naked chest, his bandaged stumps, and his face. His large eyes were hazel, flecked with green. He had long eyelashes and wavy brown hair. I didn't know what to say."

On Tuesday, April Fool's Day, Yuri Kozyrev, an award-winning Russian photographer on contract for *Time* magazine visited the hospital. He had gone to Iraq in 2002, after covering conflicts in Yugoslavia, Kosovo, Chechnya, and Afghanistan. He too walked down the corridor to the burn unit. He took a picture of Ali lying in the hospital bed, his aunt's hand on his head. Ali's face was turned toward the camera, a patient suffering could be read on it. His arms were gone, both amputated, with only white bandages covering the knobs that remained. His torso could be seen through an iron cage that held a blanket over him, but his abdomen was hardly recognizable as such—white antiseptic cream was smeared over his blackened body. The religious simplicity of the photograph—the greyed green walls, the deep red of the hospital sheet, the black robe and head covering of the aunt, the white punctuation of the bandages and painted iron frame—lent not only a dignity to the scene, but a demand for an almost biblical honor and respect from viewers. This is how the martyred saints must have looked.

Kozyrev sent the photograph to *Time*. Managing editor James Kelly decided to run the image and two others of Kozyrev's in its next issue, dated April 14, but on the stands Monday, April 7. Before running it Kelly "polled every other editor on the magazine, especially those who had children, and they all said 'You have to run this picture. It's so important as a part of the story of the civilian casualties that we're responsible for.' "[36] The debate went on for six hours. *Time* magazine's choice to include the photograph of Ali, together with its selection of other images for its photoessay,[37] was so extraordinary that the *New York Times* ran a lengthy story featuring the "terrible and beautiful" image of Ali and exploring how Kelly selected the 10 photographs that made up the magazine's photo coverage that week.[38] That article too appeared on Monday, April 7.

Meanwhile, other reporters and photographers made the trek to Al-Kindi hospital. On Sunday, April 6, Reuters Persian Gulf bureau chief, Samia Nakhoul, a Lebanese national and a Reuters photographer, Faleh Kheiber, an Iraqi national —both Arabic-speaking—came to Al-Kindi as part of their daily monitoring of Baghdad hospitals. "What's the worst case you have received?" Nakhoul asked one of the nurses. "She told me, 'Well, there's this boy, he's been burned.' So I asked if I could see him. I wanted to know what 'the worst case' meant." Nakhoul and photographer Kheiber donned gowns and masks and were shown to Ali's room. She spent an hour talking to the boy and his aunt. Finally the two journalists left, the photographer already in tears. "I have covered the Lebanon war, but I had never seen anything like that," said Nakhoul in an interview with the *Guardian*. "I was very, very shocked and I was trying to hold myself together and not break down in front of him. . . . When I came out I started sobbing like I have never sobbed in my life. I couldn't file the story for hours, I just sat and cried."[39]

The next day, Monday, April 7, several Canadian papers ran Nakhoul's article and Feleh Kheiber's close-up of Ali, still with bandaged stumps and a blackened torso, his head now bandaged, and a hand with a pad of gauze swabbing his face.[40] The *Calgary Sun* ran the story and image of Ali on page A21 and the *Toronto Globe and Mail* ran Kheiber's photograph on page A6 accompanying a story that made no mention of Ali, focusing instead on the clashes between US and Iraqi forces. *USA Today* folded Nakhoul's story and Kheiber's picture of Ali into their own larger front-page story on the battle for Baghdad. *Time* magazine hit news stands with Kozyrev's photograph, and the almost full-page *New York Times* article on how US media were covering the war in images also came out.

By Tuesday, April 8, Ali was in all the London papers: the *Daily Telegraph*, the *Evening Standard*, the *Express*, the *Independent*, the *Mirror*, and the *Times*. MSNBC ran a segment on him, with John Draper from ITN News reporting that so many people in Britain had called to donate money for him that the charity the Limbless Association had already set up a trust fund to bring him to England to have new arms fitted. John Draper also appeared in another video package on CNN with Wolf Blitzer. The brief noon segment was less than 300 words long, but Draper closed with these thoughts:

> Ali's aunt is by his bedside, wiping his tears, telling him his parents are in heaven.
>   The sight of youngsters like Ali and the other civilians injured as the fighting in Baghdad has intensified, is causing much bitterness among Iraqis and makes harder the American aim of persuading them they're being liberated, not conquered.

The Red Cross is delivering drugs and anaesthetics, which some hospitals have already run out. It's hard to imagine the pain and sheer misery this boy is going through.

Ali says if he can't get artificial arms, he wants to die.

John Draper, ITN News

Every day the newspaper coverage in England, Canada, and Australia grew exponentially. But there was silence in the American press until the following Monday in the next issue of *Time*. Managing editor Kelly wrote a note "To Our Readers," that gave more details about the injuries that Ali suffered and the loss of most of his family in the missile attack. "Events as vast and unwieldy as the war in Iraq often hit home hardest when seen through the experience of a single person," Kelly wrote in his lead acknowledging the "photo that drew such attention." Kelly ended his résumé of Ali's immediate situation with these sentences: "Ali's doctor says the boy is in danger of dying within weeks. It's hard to imagine something more emblematic of Iraq's humanitarian needs than a young boy simply running out of time."[41]

Clearly *Time* magazine readers had responded to Kozyrev's photograph, but other US news outlets didn't pick up his image or that of Reuters photographer Kheiber. It wasn't the Americans who made Ali the poster child for the war—it was the British. Not only the Limbless Association, but other British relief charities used photographs of Ali to launch a series of fundraising appeals, including a joint campaign by the British Red Cross and the London *Evening Standard* that raised over £300,000. The charities were inundated with offers to help the photogenic child. "We were involved in a media group that covered his return to Britain where he was fitted with prosthetic limbs," recalled Jonathan Munro. "We did a lot of coverage of humanitarian suffering in Baghdad. . . . It's plainly more emotive to see a child in the state that Ali Abbas was, than it would have been to see someone who was a middle-aged man. Why? Because of human nature. We are, as adults, protective towards children. That's how we're built. That's how we're made to be."[42]

Two weeks after Ali's story first made news in the US, the New York paper *Newsday* noted: "The story of 12-year-old Ali Ismaeel Abbas has saturated Europe, the Middle East and Canada, having been splashed across the front pages of newspapers and highlighted on television programs for more than two weeks. In many countries, he has become a symbol of the war." *Newsday* reporter James Madore quoted Simon O'Hagan, an editor/readers' advocate for the *Independent on Sunday*, based in London, as observing that Ali " 'has become the single most memorable image of the war for British newspaper readers . . . This boy is building up to be like the napalm girl in the Vietnam War,' he said, referring to the now-famous 1972 photo of a naked girl running down a road after being burned by a bomb."[43]

The greater public opposition to the war in Britain and on the Continent prompted news outlets there to focus more on how the conflict was affecting civilians. The story of Ali, mused Channel 4 reporter Lindsey Hilsum:

> played hugely here [in Britain] because he was a child, and partly because in a strange way, I think in Europe we identify with the victims in these wars . . . the issue of Iraqi victims is big here. It does matter. Many people here identify just as much with the Iraqis as with the Americans. I really think that now. I think that's even truer elsewhere in Europe—even people who support the war, who thought the war was necessary or thought the war on violence was a good idea or all the rest of it. There is such an anti-war feeling in Europe because of our experience of war and the absolute disastrousness of it.[44]

Perhaps for those reasons, the British were not hesitant about making Ali into a poster child in campaigns aimed at the young. BBC's *Newsround*, for example, an extremely popular children's television program, created a special section devoted to news about Ali and to messages sent in by children.[45]

Yet in the United States there was a hesitancy about showing Ali's picture at all, much less on occasions where American youngsters could see it. CNN and MSNBC lightly followed Ali's story, but few American newspapers took up the images—especially the stark original one. "In the United States," *Newsday*'s Madore noted several weeks after Ali's plight became public, "people knew little of the boy until last week when U.S. forces responded to international pressure and flew him from a Baghdad hospital to a treatment center in Kuwait . . . the bulk of feature stories told by US media outlets, journalism experts said, have concentrated on Americans, such as Army Pvt. Jessica Lynch and the other prisoners of war." The US media have concentrated on "stories about acts of heroism and quick military victory," he wrote, unlike the media in Britain, "America's staunchest ally."[46]

The rescue of Pfc. Jessica Lynch occurred the same day that Yuri Kozyrev traveled to Al-Kindi hospital and took Ali's photograph. It was a difficult moment in the war; attention had been drawn to a series of grim incidents—several groups of American soldiers had been captured, US troops had shot and killed seven women and children in a van that failed to stop at a checkpoint, a suicide bomber had killed four American troops near Najaf. And beyond those incidents was the key focus of the conflict—the fate of the US forces moving up to Baghdad, poised for a ground assault on the city.

But on April 1, in Central Command's media center in Doha, Qatar—the city where Al Jazeera is headquartered—public information officers briefed reporters on the news that Special Operations had staged a raid on the hospital where Jessica Lynch was being treated and that she had been rescued. The team had even filmed their own assault, in the green glow of night-vision photography. As reporters from across the world sat expecting news from Baghdad, CentCom news management detailed a minute-by-minute account of the saga of Jessica Lynch. Many journalists grumbled (in scenes captured live by the documentary film *Control Room*), but the Lynch story went out on air.

Natasha Walter recalled the story for the *Guardian* newspaper later in the month:

> the unforgettable image was the one taken as she was being rescued, lying on a stretcher, with her pale features so fragile yet so gritted, her teeth clenched and her eyebrows lifted. Perhaps the most telling thing about this image was that we saw it at all; that a cameraman had been there to record her rescue. This feeling that we had been invited right inside the covert operation added to the way this real event had such an artificial feel—it was almost too photogenic, almost too perfectly plotted. Journalists said that her story would surely be turned into a film, but it already was a film, recorded at the time and played out to an international audience.
>
> Its impact relied on our understanding that this soldier was not a run-of-the-mill combatant, but rather more vulnerable and more precious. Until the time that Lynch was captured, all the images of American soldiers had communicated an alienating invulnerability, as they charged through the desert in their steel cages. Next to those brutal pictures, America embraced an image that suggested a gentler side to their soldiers. Who could accuse Lynch, that fragile flower, of brutality?[47]

In the midst of the drive to Baghdad, the US media, especially television, emphasized the push of US forces advancing across the desert, the skirmishes for ground, the battles on urban streets, the troops' acts of bravery in the face of fire. Promos for MSNBC, for instance, montaged patriotic scenes of American might— US soldiers under a setting sun, helicopters in flight, the American flag waving in the breeze—set to stirring martial music. Promos for Al Jazeera montaged scenes of the *effect* of American might—President Bush's warnings to Saddam Hussein, a wounded and crying Iraqi child, burning oil fields, missiles dropping on buildings —set to stirring plaintive music.[48]

For American television, the war's mission was defining—the "regime change," the bringing of "freedom," the defeat of "terrorism." Al Jazeera, together with other Arab satellite channels—Abu Dhabi, Al Arabiya, and Al Hayat-LBC News Report —adopted a Tarantino-esque perspective on the war: violence was the defining element of the conflict. Not only did Al Jazeera and the others not flinch from showing wailing mothers and close-ups of wounded children, but the aesthetics of the telling, the shots that lingered on the injured and dead, were essential to the story they unfolded.

On April 8, 2003, el-Nawawy wrote in an op-ed in the *Christian Science Monitor* that he had examined news coverage between Al Jazeera and MSNBC "headline for headline" the previous week. El-Nawawy noted a distinct difference in the reporting. "While the American media showcase US military power and the high morale of the American troops in what is described as a 'war of liberation,'" he noted, "the Arab media focus on Iraqi civilian casualties and damage to Iraqi cities in a 'war of occupation.'" And he observed specific distinctions between the two networks:

> The headlines on Al Jazeera were: More Iraqi civilian casualties result from the US and British troops' bombing of civilian targets in Baghdad and Basra; Iraqi information minister announces the destruction of US tanks by Iraqi resistance; and 120,000 additional US soldiers are sent to the Persian Gulf.
> MSNBC's headlines during the same news cycle were: Giant explosion from an Iraqi missile rocks Kuwait City; Iraqi guns halt civilian flight from Basra; and more casualties reported from US bombing on Baghdad.[49]

That difference suggests how the Al Jazeera effect came into being. What was the Al Jazeera effect? It was the reviling of the United States and especially the Bush administration by the Arab world—even by those who hated Saddam Hussein—because of the high civilian death toll of the war. Americans didn't fall afoul of it, because, as John MacArthur noted in the *Washington Post*, "American television viewers, unlike those in France, Canada and Egypt, almost never saw" civilian casualties. CBS Evening News correspondent Jim Axelrod, embedded with the Third Infantry Division, said he tried, but "a lot of killing was done out of camera range." On the one occasion when he did see "maybe a dozen, fifteen bodies in the streets and on a bridge" in an Iraqi village, he "referenced" them in a script and his cameraman shot the corpses. But the New York office edited the piece with the result there were no clearly visible corpses in what aired.[50]

The sense that many casual observers had that American television did not show the human costs of the war was borne out by a team of researchers led by professors Sean Aday and Steven Livingston at George Washington University's School of Media and Public Affairs. The researchers analyzed 600 hours of coverage on CNN, Fox News Channel, and ABC from the start of the war on March 20 to the fall of Baghdad on April 9—two days after the images of Ali Abbas appeared in *Time* and in the British press. They examined both the morning shows and afternoon and evening coverage, but, as they noted, "Instead of including every story they ran during that time (which would make percentages of casualty stories look artificially low because many stories weren't about fighting) we only examined stories that included images of battles (including artillery firing and bombs falling on Baghdad), casualties of any sort, or both."

Of the 1,710 stories the team analyzed, only 13.5 percent included any shots of dead or wounded coalition soldiers, Iraqi soldiers, or civilians. "And even when the dead were shown," wrote one of the lead researchers, "they were more likely to be hidden inside a coffin, under a sheet, or represented by some surrogate image such as a shoe." "In truth," the researcher noted, "rather than showing viewers 'the price' of the Iraq war, television instead transformed a war with hundreds of coalition and tens of thousands of Iraqi casualties into something closer to a defense contractor's training video: a lot of action, but no consequences, as if shells simply disappeared into the air and an invisible enemy magically ceased to exist."[51]

The temptation for the US media to default to the heroic was not confined to network and cable television. It was major newspapers, pre-eminently the *Washington Post*, that helped to propagate the legend of Pfc. Jessica Lynch. They repeated the morale-boosting fantasy of Lynch as the sweet girl next door who under duress had become a desperate fighter who had gone down shooting when her convoy made a wrong turn and come under attack. Suffering from gunfire and stab wounds, she was saved, the *Post* reported, by daring Delta Forces in a bold night-time raid. The *Post*, in the words of Jeff Stein, a former US Army intelligence case officer (writing a review of *The Jessica Lynch Story* for the *Post*'s "Book World"), "midwifed the Lynch myth from the Army to the front page without double-checking the initial reports to see if they were true."[52] Early on in the war, said Michel duCille, picture editor at the *Washington Post*, "I think all the media, including the *Washington Post*, we went with the wave of trying to tell the story, but we weren't going against the American authorities."[53]

The more pedestrian truth soon emerged (and was also printed on the *Washington Post*'s front page)—that Lynch had not fired at her attackers, that her gun had jammed, that she did not kill any Iraqis, that she had not been slapped or tortured, that she had been well treated by the Iraqi doctors (they had even tried to deliver her in an ambulance to US forces and but had been shot at) and that the Special Forces commandos had encountered no resistance during her rescue. As Lynch herself later volunteered, she was not "a hero."

Yet the Lynch story was one that the American public wanted to hear. Eight months later, the inevitable made-for-TV movie appeared, and 15 million Americans watched it. The premise of the war as a battle to save the world from Saddam Hussein's weapons of mass destruction had been shown to be fiction, but the larger fiction of Americans in Iraq as reluctant fighters, there only to bring democracy, freedom, and peace was one that the US public at home still wanted to believe.

It was, in short, a brilliant piece of "emotional porn," those "moments suffused with feeling but almost empty of content," as Charles McGrath, editor of the *New York Times Book Review*, has defined them. "I saw them most often," he said,

> on the "Today" show, but I'm sure they were on other programs as well. The way it works is this: Katie Couric, her eyes narrowed with concern and sincerity, interviews some recent war widow or bereft grandmother, say, sitting in a living room halfway across the country. How did you feel, Katie asks, when your son or your husband was killed in action? What was he like? What will you say to your children or grandchildren? Eventually, of course, the mother or grandmother will start to cry, and we'll mist up, too. How could we not? Such valor, such sadness and poignancy. "Thank you," Katie says, gravely. "Thank you for talking to us." Then a quick wipe of the eye, and it's time for Al and the weather.[54]

There has been no made-for-TV movie of Ali Abbas in the United States. But there has been a book about Ali, *The Ali Abbas Story*—in the United Kingdom. HarperCollins published it on the first anniversary of the start of the war. Written with the cooperation of the Limbless Association, all royalties go toward a fund for Ali. HarperCollins has no plans to launch the book in the United States.

"Children are the great innocents of the world, aren't they?" observed Jonathan Munro at ITN. "They don't go and wage war. So if they are the victims of war, that is always a very telling statement on how humanity has degraded itself into a situation where noncombatants are being affected."[55]

terrorists want an audience, too: daniel pearl, nicholas berg, and beyond

If the controversies over whether or not to show the images of the Falling Man and Ali Abbas were heated, they were nothing to the debates that erupted over whether news outlets should show stills or clips taken from the videotape of the execution of Daniel Pearl.[56]

The first post-9/11 hostage seizure that came to the world's attention was that of *Wall Street Journal* reporter Daniel Pearl who was kidnapped on January 23, 2002 in Karachi, Pakistan. Khalid Sheikh Mohammed, an Al Qaeda operative reported to be third in command under Osama Bin Laden, later claimed responsibility. A month after Pearl's kidnapping, on February 21, the US State Department confirmed that Pearl had been beheaded. On the 26th, CBS aired a 30-second portion of the videotape of his execution on the evening news, in which he could be seen being forced to declare: "My father's Jewish. My mother's Jewish. I'm Jewish." Anchor Dan Rather explained: "the video illustrates how far an enemy will go to spread its message of hate for the United States."

The three-and-a half minute video of Pearl shows him first speaking, then his throat being cut (he appears to be already either unconscious or dead), and his severed head held aloft (his decapitation is not seen). Those three edited sections are interspersed, music video-style, with clips of scenes from Palestine, Chechnya, Kashmir, and Bosnia and with a voiceover of a radical harangue against the "enemies of Islam."[57] The video was made available to the BBC, but a decision was taken not to use it. In an article on the BBC's website, the BBC noted that "The corporation's guidelines state that: 'There are almost no circumstances in which it is justified to show executions or other scenes in which people are being killed.' "[58] For most other news outlets it was also an easy call: mention that the video existed—even describe what it depicted—but refrain from showing any stills or clips from the tape. So for example, the *Guardian* explained: "In a gruesome few minutes of video footage the kidnappers are shown talking to Pearl before one of his captors suddenly lunges forward and cuts his throat with a knife."

CBS was pilloried by most US media, by the White House, and by Pearl's family, which said that the network had aided the "terrorists in spreading their message of hate and murder." "Danny believed that journalism was a tool to report the truth and foster understanding, not perpetuate propaganda and sensationalise tragedy."[59] Both right and left criticized the decision. The conservative magazine the *National Review* asked a group of Middle East and media experts their opinion and excerpted their answers. "This very wrong decision is only more evidence that our elite media does not have a clue about the deadly and depraved nature of our enemies, and the seriousness of the war we are in—or the need in such troubled times to respect rules of common decency and concern for the feelings of the bereaved family," said Victor Davis Hanson, a senior fellow at the Hoover Institution. "While all journalists should be sensitive to the free-speech issues here," said author William McGowan, ". . . airing the video was first and foremost a violation of basic journalistic taste and a violation of Daniel Pearl's basic human dignity." James Phillips of the Heritage Foundation said, "The tape may help CBS boost its viewer ratings, but it had little news value. The details of Pearl's death were already widely known. But by broadcasting the grisly tape, CBS has helped Pearl's killers to disseminate a recruiting poster for their bloodthirsty movement." And columnist Daniel Pipes said, "It is outrageous that CBS would go against the Pearl family's wishes and broadcast the tape—but it's also oh-so-typical of the major media. That said, broadcasting the tape is probably salutary, for it brings graphically home just who the barbarians are that killed this fine young journalist and who threaten all of us Americans."[60]

Then Peter Kadzis, the editor of the *Boston Phoenix*, and Stephen Mindich, the publisher, decided that Americans needed to see the entire video. They put a link to it on the *Phoenix*'s website with a cautionary—and explanatory—note above. "This is the single most gruesome, horrible, despicable, and horrifying thing I've ever seen," Mindich wrote. "The outrage I feel as an American and a Jew is almost indescribable. That our government and others throughout the world, who have had this tape for some time, have remained silent is nothing less than an act of shame." A week later, the *Phoenix* published two small black-and-white photos grabbed from the video on its print editorial page—one was of Pearl talking, the other was of his severed head.

Judea Pearl, Daniel Pearl's father, wrote an impassioned op-ed piece for the *New York Times*: "To preserve the dignity of our champions, we should remove all terrorist-produced murder scenes from our Web sites and agree to suppress such scenes in the future."[61] *Wired* magazine wrote a story about the FBI's attempts to limit the spread of the uncensored version of the video of Pearl's death. Several sites were contacted and ended up removing the video. The Poynter Institute, which usually is liberal-leaning, published a column by its ethics writer Bob Steele which led with "I see no legitimate journalistic purpose in the decision by *The Boston Phoenix*." Then Steele continued, "*The Phoenix* and publisher Mindich lost sight of that principle—to minimize harm—in publishing these images of Daniel Pearl's death. Any journalistic purpose in publishing the photos of his death is considerably outweighed by the emotional harm to Pearl's widow and family. At the least, publishing these photos is insensitive and disrespectful. It may be cruel."[62]

Yet there were many, especially among journalists, who believed that the decisions made by CBS and the *Phoenix* were the right ones. Dan Kennedy, the former media critic for the *Phoenix*, first disagreed with the decision and then changed his mind: "I concluded that the reason for publishing the photographs—to witness the evil with which we must contend—outweighed the reasons for not publishing." And he charged that the argument that the images caused pain to the family was flawed. "There are few businesses less sensitive to family considerations than the media. News is often about bad things happening to good people, and families frequently object to the way loved ones are portrayed. Just ask any photographer who's been assigned to cover the funeral of a teenager who died while drinking behind the wheel."[63] Another journalist, David Poland, observed,

> I believe that by protecting "our public" from the truth that only eyewitness or camera-witness can offer, we are doing them a huge disservice. . . . Truth is not always pretty. And it sure isn't selective. Showing this tape is not sensitive. But it is truth. Not showing a tape of a body hitting the ground at the World Trade Center is editorial judgment. But not ever showing images of bodies falling—that's censorship. The image of a body falling says everything that needs to be said. The Pearl tape is different. His beheading is the story here. The list of demands is the story. The choices that the editors of the tape made is the story. There is no avoiding it.[64]

Kidnappings, noted Bruce Hoffman, a Rand terrorism expert, are "the apotheosis of terrorist theater," with the terrorists themselves often creating a play of sorts. In the digital world of do-it-yourself media, the terrorists are able to produce a video which announces the abduction, makes demands, sets deadlines, shows the hostage pleading, and then sometimes shows the terrorists executing the hostage. The theatrical performance is often astonishingly successful at helping terrorists achieve their goals. "Taking hostages brings them attention. It makes them appear to be potent players. It brings them recruits. It dismays their foes and makes their foes' lives untenable. And it creates political crises at home," said Brian Jenkins, another expert. "If we were cold-blooded analysts, we'd have to concede that it is in their view a good return on their investment."[65]

Two years later, in May 2004, CBS, NBC, ABC, and Fox, together with Arab networks Al Jazeera and Al Arabiya, all broadcast edited footage of the kidnapped

American contractor Nick Berg up to the moments of his execution. "The news story itself is strong enough," explained Jihad Ballout, spokesman for Al Jazeera. "To show the actual beheading is out of the realm of decency." Most news outlets opted to use the footage of Berg kneeling in front of his captors before his death. But Phil Griffin, vice president of MSNBC, didn't want his viewers misled. He told his anchors to explain to the public what came next: "This is something we should not sanitize when we describe it." And Neal Shapiro, president of NBC News added, "If people can't watch, we've lost our ability to convey information."[66]

There had been a sea-change from two years previously. Not only had there been a war in Iraq—and a failure to find weapons of mass destruction—but three incidents in the previous two months had shocked the world with their own graphic images: in March, the terrorist attacks in Madrid and the killing, burning, and lynching of the four Blackwater contractors by a mob in Fallujah, and in April the release of the photographs from Abu Ghraib as seen on CBS's *60 Minutes II* and in the *New Yorker*. In the aftermath of the "European 9/11," the burning alive of four Americans, and the gloating over their deaths by an entire crowd of Iraqis, and the additional horrors of seeing how far American personnel, themselves, were willing to go to torture and kill, yet another beheading, seemed, if not standard fare, at least not quite as perverted as the act had seemed two long years before. Reuters sent the unedited videotape of Berg's killing to its subscribers around the world. Although it appears that no major news outlet in the United States or Arab countries showed the beheading or its aftermath, Reuters sent the tape saying "it was not its place to make editorial choices on behalf of its clients."[67]

"It is as though, rather suddenly, the gloves have come off, and the war seems less sanitized, more personally intrusive," wrote Michael Getler, ombudsman at the *Washington Post*.

Some critics were still not persuaded that media should air any portion of propaganda videos made by terrorists. "Any news outlet—or any private individual, for that matter—who makes available footage of the actual beheadings is, to my mind, an accessory to the crime itself," said Tom Kunkel, dean of the College of Journalism at the University of Maryland. "Those are the individuals who are essentially finishing the work of the terrorists, by delivering their grisly 'message.'" But not only were mainstream media carrying clips of the beheadings, in greater and greater numbers online surfers were "digging past the mainstream news sites to find the raw footage," observed the *Los Angeles Times*, "for reasons that may include a simple desire to keep up with the news, morbid curiosity or salaciousness." "The reader is in much more control of what he or she sees because of availability of photographs on the Web," *Time* managing editor Jim Kelly noted. "In some respects, we're not the gatekeepers of violent images that we might have been" in years past.[68]

In May 2004, "Nick Berg" was the second most popular search request on Google, following "American Idol," and the next month, the week engineer Paul Johnson, Jr. was beheaded, his name was the most popular search term on Google. Any news stories containing graphic violence—including the abuse at Abu Ghraib and the attacks in Fallujah—prompt an "astronomical" spike in photo and video viewing online, observed cbsnews.com news director Michael Sims. As a result, he noted, in recent months "we've really been forced to sit down and talk through the issues and decide for ourselves where the lines are. To tell the story, not sugarcoat it, but not be offensive."[69]

By the end of June, with the beheading of South Korean translator Kim Sun-il, three hostages had been beheaded in two months. Grim footage was run and rerun, especially when there were no new updates to feature. "We talk about this all the time," admitted John Stack, vice president for news gathering at Fox News. "We always want to be responsible. We also have a tremendous void to fill. Sometimes we're blessed with an abundance of video." Others too saw the images as a potential audience grabber. Images of the men kneeling in front of their executioners "popped up repeatedly as teasers to TV news programs and on Internet news sites," according to the *Los Angeles Times*, and every time ABC Radio talkshow host Sean Hannity cut for a commercial, up cued the soundbite of "Kim's gut-wrenching pleas for his life."[70] And when the Saudi terrorists gave the United States 72 hours to comply with their demands before beheading Paul Johnson, Jr., cable news breathlessly ticked down the time remaining. Certainly, in those cases, media had become publicists for the terrorists.

By the beginning of August nearly two dozen people had been kidnapped since Nick Berg's execution and many of the hostages had been videotaped, although not all had been killed. The greater number of abductions and the greater number of videotapes presented a new dilemma for news outlets. "It's nothing new anymore that hostages are being taken," said Ballout at Al Jazeera. "This is becoming somewhat monotonous. It's not like before." CNN, which had shown the video and audio of Kim's pleading through his tears for his life, also noted the videos piling up. "Because of the number of incidents we have been forced to report, sadly, in recent weeks, we are less likely to show that kind of extract again," said Chris Cramer, managing director of CNN International.

News outlets wrestled with the on-the-one-hand and on-the-other. Nakhle El Hage, the director of news at Al Arabiya, told the *New York Times* that, while he would refuse to air "anything that can be considered propaganda for terrorists," the previous day his network had aired a tape of kidnappers who claimed to be holding six foreign truck drivers. But Hage noted that while the channel had broadcast the portion of the tape where the abductors listed their demands and deadline, it did not air those portions of the tape where the kidnappers invoked Allah in their fight against the United States.

There was news value in the tapes. "I believe, as a journalist, it's newsworthy if a party says, 'We have kidnapped five or six people, here are our conditions,'" said Hage. The executive editor of the *New York Times* agreed. "I just think it's a slippery slope to craziness, to try to calculate what some madman is calculating about how you play a picture or a news story," said Bill Keller. "If what they're really looking for is to send a frisson of anxiety to the Western world about the perils of operating in Iraq—and that very well may be part of their motivation for posting these pictures—that still doesn't seem like a very persuasive argument for suppressing the pictures."[71]

Countdowns and promo teasers and audioclips of screams before heading into commercials are clearly way too many steps too far down the road toward sensationalism and horror porn. But condemning that crude brand of fear-mongering does not necessarily clarify where responsible journalists should draw the line in how they deliver the news of terrorist attacks.

In an article in *AJR*, MaryAnne Golon, picture editor at *Time* magazine, is quoted. *Time*, she argued, had published a number of photographs that were not easy images to look at: a close-up of a dead Iraqi in the desert, Kozyrev's image of Ali Abbas, and another picture of a raw wood coffin with bloodstains where a head would have lain. Golon took pride in the decisions to run those—as well as the decision to run an image of an American soldier carrying a wounded comrade on his back. But there were images that readers didn't see. They didn't see a photo by VII photographer Christopher Morris, for example, of a "road-clearing mission"—soldiers literally clearing the road of body parts of dead Iraqis. One image from that series, however, of two soldiers dragging a civilian by his legs into a ditch, ran on *Time*'s website and in a book *Time* published, *21 Days to Baghdad*. Managing editor Jim Kelly defended that choice. To run the photo in the magazine would not only have been disrespectful to the families of the Iraqis who were killed, "I had stuff that I thought was more germane to what was going on that week." But "to use one of those images in a book that's more than 100 pages long, I don't have a problem with that."[72]

Some daily journalists have suggested that their role is only to tell the news; it's not to tell their audience what to do about the news—that's the role of commentators and editorial writers. But a decision to only tell "part" of a story, to "spare" the public some of the most difficult bits of the news, is, in effect, a decision to direct an audience about what to do. If Americans, for example, don't have an equal opportunity to see injured Iraqis as injured US troops, they will have a faulty impression about who is suffering in the war—and they also will not understand the reactions of those from other countries who may be seeing images of the injured civilians. If media parent the public, they are not only censoring the news, they are editorializing about it.

Where's the line? Should there be an absolute prohibition, as Kunkel argued, or should there be mainstream access to the videotapes generated by the terrorists?

Does writing about it tell the story sufficiently? Or are images essential? Are photographs "facts" or are they "illustrations"? There remain Holocaust deniers, despite the thousands of photographs and films easily available. But for the rest of us, what do those images of Bergen-Belsen and Auschwitz add to our understanding of Nazi Germany that we didn't know from watching *Triumph of the Will?* Do the concentration camp images prompt us to avert our eyes and close our minds or do they inspire us to care more? "Some will say wasn't the attack on the WTC and Pentagon enough? Didn't that convey enough about the reality of terrorism? No, I don't think that the footage of either attack did for the simple reason that most of what the media presented was objects colliding (planes into buildings) or objects collapsing (the towers falling)," said journalist-blogger Jim Lynch. We need to see graphic images. "Most of the video from the WTC was quickly cleaned up so as to not show people falling from the buildings. It was typical of our media to do that to spare the public's sensibilities. The end result is that it distanced a lot of us emotionally from the reality of what happened: the murder of thousands of people."[73]

There are some, however, who feel burdened by the information embedded in painful images. They may feel outrage at the terror they see, but also incapable of helping ameliorate the crisis—what can they do, as ndividuals, to arrest such horrors? The photos' message of suffering is met with helplessness, and that turns into a withdrawal from the message and the messenger. "Compassion is an unstable emotion. It needs to be translated into action, or it withers," wrote Susan Sontag in her last book, *Regarding the Pain of Others.* "If one feels that there is nothing 'we' can do—but who is that 'we'?—and nothing 'they' can do either— and who are 'they'?—then one starts to get bored, cynical, apathetic."[74]

And while it may well be true that no single donation given or letter written will make much of a dent, Oxfam or Amnesty International would disagree with the premise that learning about others' bad news must ultimately lead to apathy. In the aggregate, money and public attention (as measured in part by letters and emails) can have a significant impact on policy and opinion.[75] And so can voting and other forms of civic engagement.

That is why there are some academics and journalists who are increasingly committed to the educational field of "Media Literacy." The long-standing principle behind Media Literacy is that we all need to know how the media work. We swim in a sea of news and information, words and pictures every day. Much of it washes over us, but it all leaves a significant imprint—and both consciously and subliminally influences our notions of what we care about, about what we think is important, about what we do with that information. Recently, the proponents of Media Literacy have come to understand that they need to additionally make explicit the links between media consumption and civic participation. The field of Media Literacy has come to directly address Sontag's concern. Educators and journalists have learned that if you teach students and the larger public to understand how media package the news and also teach them the tools of civic participation—voting, writing, speaking out, getting involved—they won't feel helpless, alienated or cynical. Instead, they become engaged, they let themselves feel concern and compassion, they assimilate difficult news and graphic images by taking public action based on the knowledge they have gained.[76]

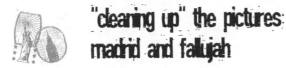

On March 11, 2004, at 7:30 a.m.—in the middle of rush hour—13 backpack and gym bag-laden bombs detonated on a train outside of Madrid, killing 190 people and injuring close to 1,800. Spanish Foreign Minister Ana Palacio blamed the Basque separatist group ETA, but soon arrests and a video claiming responsibility tied the bombing to al Qaeda. On March 14, Spain's Socialist Party won an upset in the country's general election—voters turned on the government in part for its handling of terrorism.

A photograph, taken by Pablo Torres Guerrero of *El País* of the bombing in Madrid on March 11, 2004, appeared on front pages around the world. *El País* ran it as-is, huge, across the entire front page. But editors elsewhere struggled with what to do about a bloody severed arm visible on the train tracks in the image. In London, the *Times*, the *Daily Telegraph*, the *Sun*, and the *Daily Mail* airbrushed the body part out, replacing it with stones. The *Guardian* changed its color from red to grey, making it almost impossible to identify. The *Independent* and the *Daily Mirror* got around the problem by printing the image in black and white. "For most of us," noted the *Guardian*, "the true awfulness of these scenes were edited out, deemed unfit to view."

Images, not words, were what the papers found so troubling. In its same leader column that observed that images were being edited, the *Guardian* gave an especially vivid verbal description of that scene at the train station: "It was like a modern version of the gruesome wartime images painted by Goya. A Spanish commuter train torn apart. A headless body lying on its front. A three-year-old child burned from head to foot. Amputated legs and arms scattered on station platforms, pieces of human flesh on the road, mobile phones bleeping on the bodies carted off, the injured weeping helplessly on the pavement."[77]

Professional photographers were aghast that the papers resorted to photo-shopping the pictorial evidence. The *Digital Journalist*, the premiere online magazine for news photographers, wrote in its editorial in its April edition:

Newspapers are supposed to present the news in an honest context. This was a news photograph. It was not a photographic illustration. If the newspapers felt that the photograph might cause readers distress, they had the option of using another one. This is a massive breach of journalistic ethics. You may not "clean up" a news photograph to suit your audience. . . . If these newspapers are serious about credibility the editors who authorized this manipulation should be fired on the spot."[78]

In the US, there wasn't any "clean up," but there was some heavy-handed editing of the image. The *New York Times*, the *Los Angeles Times*, and *USA Today* cropped the photo so the bloody limb couldn't be seen. *Time* magazine used it as a double-page spread but strategically dropped its headline on top of the arm. The *Washington Post*, however, like *El País*, ran it unaltered, large, above the fold.

And then there was *Newsweek*. *Newsweek* featured other photographs, more horrific still. Lynn Staley, associate managing editor at *Newsweek*, chose a photograph of a lone dead victim ravaged in a passenger car. "The opener of the body of the woman in the wreckage was one of the most beautiful, haunting, and amazing images that we had seen . . ."[79]

The image of the severed arm that had blown out of the train, the image of the dead woman sprawled, blindly staring upwards in the midst of unidentifiable debris, were the kind of pictures that no one had ever shown from New York City's Ground Zero. News outlets were trying to come to grips both with what their audiences could bear but also with what needed to be told. The *News Photographer*, the publication of the American National Press Photographers Association, wrote an editorial about the manipulation of Guerrero's photograph:

An image must establish the truth and context of a newsworthy moment. An altered image is a lie.

We believe that the public is ill served when elements within the frame are reduced or removed in an attempt to soften the horror of the moment. If one unaltered image is too graphic for public consumption, find another. One must not alter a graphic image in an attempt to protect public sensibilities.

Removing a bloody body part from a photograph sends the public an untrue and unfortunate message. Removing a victim's remains from a photograph sends the message that someone who died is anonymous. Removing a person's blood-soaked limb from a photograph tells the public that someone who died is invisible.

The victims of terrorism must never be anonymous. The victims of terrorism must never be invisible.[80]

The Spanish now call the events of that day the 11-M attack—for the 11th of March. But the bombing in Madrid was more than a European iteration of 9/11. Not only did the attack remake Spanish politics, it remade the coalition in the "War on Terror" declared by President Bush. Spanish voters moved into line with the

French and German view that the "War on Terror" had nothing to do with the war in Iraq. Most Europeans were now joined in their belief that the war in Iraq was a distraction—and that it had made global terrorism worse.

Twenty days after the bombings in Madrid, another shocking attack occurred, and pictures of it went round the world. On March 31, an Iraqi mob killed, burned, dismembered, hit with shoes and hung from a bridge four US contractors. All at once, Fallujah looked disturbingly like Mogadishu, Somalia, circa 1993. Once again a population Americans thought they had sent military forces to help had turned against them. Instead of a dead US soldier being dragged through the streets of Somalia, there were four charred bodies sprawled in the street or lynched from a bridge. "This day could become a hugely symbolic one in the course of the Iraq war," said *Washington Post* executive editor Len Downie.[81]

American media decided that this event needed to be shown to the public. "One of the things that people in this country have not understood," said David Gelber, a producer for CBS *60 Minutes*, "is how angry Iraqis are at us, and if 200 Iraqis go crazy and start killing Americans and . . . hanging them from bridges, I think it's incredibly awful stuff to look at." But, he continued, "If we don't let people know that that impulse is there, then we're depriving our audience of a full sense of the intensity of the feelings there."[82] Many major US papers ran on their front page the color photograph that juxtaposed the smiling, cheering crowd with the dismembered corpses. "Iraqis Revel in U.S. Deaths," read *USA Today*'s headline. Others, such as the *Los Angeles Times*, decided to run the photograph inside the paper. Either way, the still images prompted angry emails to editors around the country.

On TV, the US networks largely forbore to run the video that had been taken as well, deeming it too graphic. How did the Europeans cover it? In Germany, ZDF News showed the tape of the riot scenes but not any bodies. In London, Channel 4 News broadcast an electronically blurred body being dragged through the street. In Paris, LC1 television showed the footage of the bodies without pixelating them. And Al Jazeera? The Arab network didn't show the burnt corpses. At a panel discussion in New York City in April 2004 sponsored by the Dart Center for Journalism and Trauma, Al Jazeera United Nations correspondent Abderrahim Foukara said that his network hadn't shown the images because it was "shying away from showing the real gore" in Iraq. Why? Foukara said the network was reacting to the controversy that had erupted after it showed images of dead American soldiers the previous year.[83]

In part the differences in what European media showed reflected the Europeans' longer-standing and greater distaste for the Iraq war. It was not a coincidence that the most graphic airing of the Fallujah images was in France. But differences in how the European media cover the world spoke as well, speak, as well, some thought, to Europeans' greater feelings of engagement in world affairs—and their greater vulnerability. "When I left university," Channel 4 broadcaster Lindsey Hilsum mused in an interview:

> I worked in a home for refugee children. And they were so much better informed than British children. And it was because they felt vulnerable in the world and they knew that what big powers did could change their lives. And that's what we feel in Europe now. We need to know this stuff because we don't identify entirely with the most powerful nation. We identify partly with those who have no power because we have little power. We are a small island off the coast of Europe and therefore it's not quite the same. If you feel you are subject to history then you care more. It matters more. They could be coming for you next.[84]

 ## losing control of the image: official photos, snapshots, and cameraphones

Three days after the Iraq war's start in March 2003, US Defense Secretary Donald Rumsfeld and US Lieutenant General John Abizaid tried to chill American television networks' interest in bringing to air an Iraqi video of battered prisoners and dead American soldiers. "After days of buoyant images, reporting enters a second and more ominous act," noted the headline of a *New York Times* article. Rumsfeld cited the Geneva convention governing the treatment of prisoners, and stated that any network that carried the images would be "doing something that's unfortunate." Abizaid told a news briefing in Qatar that "the showing of these pictures is absolutely unacceptable."

Lester Holt, the MSNBC anchor, said: "I've seen them. They are beyond disturbing, and I'd be lying if I said I wasn't still physically shaken by them."[85] CBS, NBC and CNN ran portions of the videotape that included the POWs in the evening, after holding off during the day at the Pentagon's request; ABC and Fox News only aired still images of the POWs captured from the video. The *New York Times*, the *Washington Post*, and *USA Today* chose not to run any photos of the POWs the next day, although as the prisoners' next of kin became notified, some ran the images in succeeding days. The *Washington Times* and the *New York Daily News* ran images of the POWs on their front pages, and the *Chicago Tribune* and *Los Angeles Times* ran them inside on the first day. "We've run pictures of prisoners taken by both sides," said *Los Angeles Times* editor John Carroll. "It's a war, and we're supposed to cover the whole thing, not just part of it."[86]

As they wrestled with what to do, the salient question for the media became less whether the enemy committed a war crime in taping the prisoners and "exposing them to public curiosity," and more about where the line in news coverage should be, between what is "necessary and sufficient" and what NBC said was "gruesome and exploitative." Charles Gibson, anchoring ABC's desk in New York, told Ted Koppel, embedded with the Third US Infantry Division, that it would be disrespectful to show the bodies of dead soldiers of either side. "I must tell you, Charlie, I disagree with you a little bit," said Koppel. "We need to remind people in the most graphic way that war is a dreadful thing."[87]

As Philip Kennicott parsed the decision in the *Washington Post*, it came down to this: some media believed that

> the images were more a matter of illustration, something supplemental and dis-
> cretionary that wasn't necessary to fully cover the capture of American soldiers. The
> *fact* was the capture and possible execution of some POWs; the images were a graphic
> addendum. And so most American news organizations chose to keep viewers at one
> descriptive remove. They would tell viewers what was on the tape, but not show it.

Those images that the American news outlets wouldn't show, however, others were putting out there. Al Jazeera aired the entire videotape and Matt Drudge ran several grab shots of unidentifiable dead American soldiers on his website. ArabNews.com, the website for an English-language newspaper out of Saudi Arabia, ran a large box on its homepage saying "Click here to see photos U.S. media won't show you." According to John Bradley, the managing editor of the outlet, 80 percent of the more than 1 million hits came from North America. The DrudgeReport.com site, however, published some of the more gruesome shots that Arab News forbore to show.[88]

Almost exactly four months later, at the end of July, the US government released through the provisional authority in Baghdad photographs taken of the dead faces of Uday and Qusay Hussein, the two sons of Saddam Hussein killed in a firefight with Americans. The authorities distributed the images via CD-ROM to reporters. The CDs also, helpfully, included X-rays of the wounds Uday Hussein suffered in a 1996 assassination attempt which were said to have helped doctors confirm his identity. The next day journalists were allowed to view the bodies, and the following day videos of that viewing, which included full-body shots of the two men, were also distributed.

Rumsfeld, who had been very critical of Iraq releasing pictures of dead Americans during the war and hostile to American media that decided to show the images, defended the US government's actions in putting out to the global public photographs of the two mutilated faces: "This is an unusual situation. This regime has been in power for decades. These two individuals were particu-larly vicious individuals. . . . They are now dead. . . . The Iraqi people have been waiting for confirmation of that and they in my view deserve having confirma-tion of that."

As the macabre photos aired around the world, debate swirled not only about whether they should have been released but whether they constituted proof of Uday and Qusay's deaths. For many Iraqis the most convincing evidence was not the American photographs, which in the digital age could clearly be photoshopped, but a videotape of a masked man that aired on Al Arabiya television. The man, claiming to be from Fedayeen Saddam which Uday had run, said: "We pledge to you Iraqi people that we will continue in the jihad against the infidels. The killing of Uday and Qusay will be avenged."

Five months later a third kind of government-generated image grabbed headlines —this time a tape made by an American combat camera crew of a submissive, bedraggled Saddam Hussein submitting to a doctor's probe of his mouth and a search for lice in his hair. During the war, back in March and April, identical video clips of Saddam speaking on Iraqi TV took on Rashomon-like meanings. "You'd have the same picture and it would be three different truths," said publisher Dorothee Walliser. "On Italian TV, Saddam would be alive: There's the picture. On US TV, Saddam would be dead, implying it was a false video or one of his doubles. On French TV, it would be unconfirmed."[89]

But on December 13, 2003, US soldiers captured Hussein hiding in a hole in the ground. "Here was a man who was photographed hundreds of times shooting off rifles and showing how tough he was," said Donald Rumsfeld on *60 Minutes* the next evening, "and in fact, he wasn't very tough, he was cowering in a hole in the ground, and had a pistol and didn't use it . . . In the last analysis, he seemed not terribly brave."[90] But it was that intrusive videotape, as Hussein received his medical checkup, that most damaged his aura of indomitability as it was broadcast around the world—even as some deplored its invasion of Hussein's privacy. (A sentiment that would only be more vociferously heard when the cellphone images of his hanging became available.)

So—a video from Iraqi TV of US POWs and dead soldiers, morgue shots of Hussein's sons courtesy of the US authorities, a videotape of Hussein's medical once-over, and a cellphone clip of Saddam's execution. Add to that Secretary of State Colin Powell's use of satellite photos and images that he said came from "intelligence sources" and unnamed "defectors" in his televised live session as he made the administration's case for war against Iraq in front of the UN Security Council in February 2003. Then, in 2004 the publishing of a photograph of flag-draped coffins taken by a civilian contractor as the caskets were being readied to fly home. And the snapshots taken in Abu Ghraib that emerged a few weeks later in late April 2004.

Photographs were clearly bringing some of the most important stories of the "War on Terror" back to those at home. In fact in some cases, when there weren't pictures, there wasn't a story. Consider Abu Ghraib. Beginning in the spring of 2003, the International Committee of the Red Cross gave US officials verbal and written reports on Iraqi prisoner abuse by US troops, including details of mistreatment at Abu Ghraib. In January 2004, a soldier in the prison reported abuse to his superiors, prompting a criminal investigation by the US military.

But the story only erupted on April 28, 2004, when *60 Minutes II* broadcast snapshots of the torture and humiliation. A rumor surfaced that President Bush had chastised Defense Secretary Donald Rumsfeld for not telling him about the pictures until after they aired. Although human rights groups had been warning of the use of torture for months and some news had trickled out, it was only after the release of the digital images that the White House and global media attention became riveted.

What made the Abu Ghraib photographs so disturbing was not only the obscenity of the acts on view—for one can argue that much of war is obscene—but that the photographers who took the pictures were, at least to some degree, participants in the torture and abuse. That fact made us, the public, co-conspirators of sorts. As we saw the images, we effectively looked through the same camera lens as those soldier-photographers. Other photographs—think of a series of three from 2001 by *New York Times* photographer Tyler Hicks of a Taliban prisoner being shot dead by Northern Alliance soldiers—were also disturbing: we saw the man's face as he pleaded for his life, we saw his body jump with the impact of the shots hitting his chest. But in those images we were outsiders, clearly not part of the charmed circle of the Afghan troops. We were left after seeing that series with breathtaking questions about the photographer's bravery—what happened to him after he took those images? Was he safe? Did they notice?[91] We were left after seeing the Abu Ghraib images with the desire to take a shower, to wash our hands, to purge ourselves somehow from the unclean feeling of being part of a foul crime.

As Americans saw the Abu Ghraib photos of dogs being sicced on the prisoners, they flashed back to the images from the US Civil Rights era of dogs being set on black marchers by sheriffs and police in the American South. Arab media reacted with rage at the evidence of torture and sexual abuse, European media acted with revulsion at the snapshots of smirking American soldiers giving thumbs-up. The partially clad and wired man on the box became the model for political cartoons the world over that morphed the Statue of Liberty into a hooded horror. Many international viewers, who formerly didn't share the perspective of the Islamic world, found themselves in agreement with the *Tehran Times* when it wrote that the Abu Ghraib images were the reflection of "the entire criminal operation being conducted in Iraq." If the images from Fallujah of gleeful Iraqi faces dancing around the bodies of the dead Americans had shocked the world, the Abu Ghraib photos of grinning Americans lauding it over their dead and tortured victims was an earthquake.[92]

US officials—as well as mainstream US and UK photographers and camera operators—no longer controlled the image of the "War on Terror."

Take a breath and skip ahead another year. Another kind of photography came to the fore.

Four days after the bombings in London on July 7, 2005, blogger Duncan Rawlinson posted his thoughts. "I couldn't help but notice how different my media consumption has been surrounding the terrorist attacks in London from September 11th," he wrote, "When my girlfriend came and hammered on my door on the morning of September 11th I turned on CNN and just watched. When I heard about the bombings in London I looked it up on Flickr, Nowpublic, Wikipedia, Wikinews to mention a few. It seems the editors/writers/journalists at the dinosaur blogs did the same. In fact, not only did these old school media folks go online for their news gathering, but they took citizen's media and ran front page stories with it."[93]

In the less than four years between September 11, 2001 and July 7, 2005, the ubiquity of digital cameras and cameraphones had turned millions into potential photographers. Mainstream media had also become more inclusive about what they would show. In the United States, many outlets had lost their fear that running grim images would by itself provoke charges of being unpatriotic, and the release of photos of flag-draped coffins and of those tortured and humiliated at Abu Ghraib—both sets of images taken by "amateurs"—cued media into looking for news images from sources other than professional photographers. Actually, "pick-ups," the journalistic term used to describe images gotten from eyewitnesses, have long been part of the media portfolio—many of the videos from the Asian tsunami, and photographs of the Columbia shuttle explosion and the Concord crash, all came from bystanders, as did George Holliday's videotape of Los Angeles police officers beating Rodney King, and Abraham Zapruder's recording of the assassination of President John F. Kennedy.

But now, both amateurs and professionals could be found with much the same equipment—a digital camera, a laptop and an internet connection. In fact in London, photographer Edmond Terakopian, after covering the bombing at the Edgware Road tube station, dashed to the nearest Starbucks to wire his photos back to his office. (His photograph of a British man, bandaged on his neck and head, blood on his face and shirt, but still carrying his folded newspaper tucked under his arm, subsequently ran on front pages around the world.) "Although all the cell phone networks were down," he said, the Starbucks "WiFi was still working."[94]

Technorati.com, which tracks blogs around the world, said the first cell-phone pictures of the London bombings were posted within minutes of the attacks. Flickr.com, a site that lets people post photographs free, had more than 300 bombing photos posted within eight hours of the attacks. Independent Television (ITV), the BBC, MSNBC, the *Guardian*, the *Times* of London, and other outlets posted messages on their sites soliciting pictures from witnesses as well as scoured picture-sharing blogs. World Picture News posted a solicitation for images on www.flickr.com offering to distribute any pictures to mainstream media outlets. Several of the photos which came through that channel were from a witness who photographed the Tavistock Square bus bombing from an office overlooking the scene—one ran as an exclusive as the entire front page of the *New York Post* (the photographer and WPN split the sale 50–50).

The BBC received around 30 video clips from bystanders and over 1,000 images attached to more than 300 emails. One was from Alexander Chadwick, who used his cellphone to photograph commuters on the track after evacuating the train which had been bombed near King's Cross station. The BBC immediately put the eerie green photo on its television feed, where the Associated Press saw it. AP then paid Chadwick to distribute it, with the result that it landed on newspaper front pages around the world—including those of the *New York Times* and the *Washington Post*.

Witnesses also emailed and posted video footage to media sites and blogs. Within half an hour of the attacks clips from the scene were up on television. One, minute-long, video taken by a cellphone from inside a subway car was grainy, jerky, and very dark. The clip was without sound but seemed to show the passengers as calm. The footage haphazardly zoomed in on windows that were broken and sometimes faded to black. But it was eyewitness, scene-of-the-crime stuff, and the three US networks, as well as Fox, CNN, and MSNBC, broadcast that video or ones like it repeatedly.

It was the immediacy rather than the quality of the cellphone images that seemed so compelling. "The news value outweighs the image quality issues in a case like this," noted Santiago Lyon, the Associated Press's director of photography. The breaking news value of the images mattered, but so too did the ineffable fascination of so many of them. Like the photos taken in Abu Ghraib, what made them so compelling was precisely their amateurness, that toss-away snapshot quality familiar to all casual photographers. That ordinariness made them seem real, truer somehow than if they had been sharp in focus and more intentionally framed and edited. They seemed *not to be* packaged; they seemed to exist outside the world of "spin."

The truth is desperately wanted. For all that images can now be manipulated as easily as words, for all that images can be taken from any perspective and given any caption, there is a certain naive power still in them that eludes words. *Life* magazine was right. Words are never enough. If they were then we wouldn't keep snapshots of our beloveds in our wallets and on our screen savers. We wouldn't watch, every anniversary, short snippets of film that have become inseparable from the history of those events—Zapruder's film of Kennedy's assassination, the footage of the landing on the moon, the videotape of the imploding of the World Trade Center towers. We wouldn't buy cellphones with cameras. We wouldn't have two millennia of paintings of Jesus, each trying to discover his likeness.

"Why do you do what you do?" *New York Times* photographer Ruth Fremson was asked about her work covering Afghanistan and other zones of terrorism and conflict. "There is a Chinese proverb that says 'Don't listen to what they say. Go see.' Curiosity about the world I am a part of and a desire to share what I've learned and seen with others is why I am a photojournalist," said Fremson. "If our readers learn something that they didn't previously know, if it stops them for just a moment, then I have been successful."[95]

Images have been used as legal evidence. But they also offer moral and emotional testimony more powerful than words. When we hear words in our own language we understand. When we see pictures we know.

 ## what do we need to see?
what do we need to do?

It's obscene.
Don't show it.
We can't take it.
You're an accessory to the enemy's crime.
We already know about it.
It betrays the feelings of the bereaved family.
Our children shouldn't see it.
You are helping terrorists recruit others to the cause.
You must show it.
This is what free speech means.
There is a difference between terrorism and showing terrorists' handiwork to others.
Unless we see it we can't fully understand it.
Those who support terrorists' political agenda need to see what they do in the name of honor.
We don't trust you to be accurate.
Let us judge for ourselves.
Never forget.

Those are the things we say about stories of violence and terror, about photos of people jumping out of tall building and images of children injured by bombs, about tapes of beheadings and images where body parts are littered among the devastation of a suicide bombing, about audiotapes where screams can be heard and video where kidnapped victims plead for their lives, about snapshots of those our side has tortured and morgue shots of those our side has killed. We say those things when the pictures and sounds and words are most graphic. We say those things when it is clearly the innocent and the outsiders who are at risk, who are hurt, who are killed. And we say those things most vehemently when those stories are of people we care about, people who are "us" or look like "us."

The public is the problem, argue journalists who have been out on the frontline. Audience members confuse their civic need for hard news with their desire to blissfully enjoy themselves. "There's a desire to ignore reality," noted James Hill, a contract photographer for the *New York Times*. Many "don't want to know what it really looks like. Because it's just too painful to deal with." Then there are the parents, who while tolerating violent movies and video games are "just horrified that their kid should be exposed to any real, honest-to-God violence in the world," said Cheryl Diaz Meyer, photographer at the *Dallas Morning News*, who, along with colleague David Leeson, won a Pulitzer for her work in Iraq.[96]

Richard Drew, who took the photograph of the Falling Man, commented that after its publication "Our readers e-mailed and phoned, and complained that they didn't want to see this over their morning cornflakes." To Drew, that wasn't a good enough reason not to put it in front of people. "This was a very important part of the story. It wasn't just a building falling down, there were people involved in this. This is how it affected people's lives at that time, and I think that is why it's an important picture. I didn't capture this person's death. I captured part of his life. This is what he decided to do, and I think I preserved that."[97]

Staci D. Kramer, a contributing editor for *Online Journalism Review* noted, "I know people would like to move on, like to forget or like to think they can remember without being reminded. My DNA doesn't work like that, perhaps because I have heard it before about the Holocaust. Why show the pictures? Why tell the stories? Why look for the truth? Why remember? Because not knowing and not remembering is oh, so dangerous."[98]

Before and after Madrid and Fallujah and London, there have been many, many terrorist attacks around the world: in Beirut and Beslan, the Democratic Republic of the Congo and Colombia, Pakistan and the Philippines. There are some moments that stand out to all of us—Benazir Bhutto assassinated in the attack on her convoy, the pale, damaged children rushed out of the school during the Chechen siege. And then there are other moments, other attacks, that at least for us, the audience, blur together in our mind's eye.

The stories and images—video and still—that we the public see we often consume as if there was no more challenge behind their creation than if they were manufactured by a factory that spits out packages of potato crisps. Tony Furlow, who at age 39 was already an 18-year veteran of photographing conflict for CBS, is aware of what it takes to be on the ground reporting on terrorism. We "have to pay a high price," he said. "Everything you cover has a different impact [on you]. Each story carries its own set of emotions."

The scenes of violence don't blur together for the journalists who cover them, especially for the photographers. Images that we the audience remember, images

174 *What Are the Images of Terror?*

that we the audience forget, images that we the audience never see—those that the producers and editors decide are too disturbing or graphic for us to take—all of those are shot live, up close, by videographers and photographers. "We see it in black and white, in a viewfinder." Furlow explained. "I look up, it gets hard. I retreat back to the viewfinder. It lessens the shock."[99]

Marco Di Lauro, a photographer for Getty Images, arrived in Jordan the day after the hotel bombings in November 2005. "The groom's best friend, 30-year-old Ramzi Nasser, told me that he had been outside the hotel smoking a cigarette with friends. The explosion took place as they were about to go back inside the banquet hall. He rushed in to search for his mother and father, with whom he had come to the wedding, and he found them dead, seated in exactly the same position in which he had left them just a few minutes earlier. As he told me all this, I was taking pictures of him," remembered Di Lauro. "It was not easy, and I had the distinct feeling of violating his privacy." Then he added, "There are times when I feel like a jackal feeding on the pain of others. Yet it is my hope that, by telling the stories of people who, quite often, might otherwise never be heard from, my work can serve as a lesson, heightening the awareness of those sitting comfortably in their chairs throughout the rest of the world, reading their newspapers."

Covering terrorism is emotionally challenging. It can also be life-threatening. On the road to Kabul one day in late 2001, a car full of journalists traveling in a convoy was ambushed, the journalists yanked out and summarily shot. Maria Grazia Cutuli, an Italian reporter and CBS employee, was one of those killed. Her body was retrieved from the roadside and brought to the morgue in Jalalabad, Afghanistan two days later. Gerald Herbert photographed her in a rough pine casket, her face pale and almost obscured by a white shroud and the fluffy white cotton that filled the coffin. Herbert said of his picture, which was published in the *Washington Times*, "The decision of whether to use this tragically graphic photo was difficult. I ultimately sided in favor of using it because I feel it is important for journalism educators, students, editors and reporters to understand fully the effects of risk-taking and loss of human life in covering such dangerous conflicts."[100]

On May 3, 2004, the Freedom Forum took out an almost full-page ad in the *Washington Post*. On top of the black background was a grid of small inch-and-a-half by inch-and-a-half photos. Under each photo was a name and news organization. "Last year," the headline read, "53 journalists died while reporting the news." Said the copy: "Today, in recognition of World Press Freedom Day, the names of these journalists will be added to the 1,475 names already inscribed on the Freedom Forum Journalists Memorial in Arlington, Virginia."

In Iraq alone, from the start of the US-led invasion in 2003 through 2005, journalists and those who support them were killed at a rate of one every 12 days, according to the Committee to Protect Journalists. In 2006 and 2007, journalists and other media workers died at a rate of one every eight days. Most of those who died were Iraqis. As a consequence hundreds of Iraqi journalists have fled the country since March 2003, Reporters Sans Frontières reported. Through the spring of 2008, according to RSF, 87 journalists had been kidnapped and 210 journalists and media assistants had been killed. And in those cases, RSF noted, Iraqi authorities have made only "an insignificant number" of arrests.

For us at home, those numbers don't make much of a impact, even if they are known. And the images of terror become just more pictures in our lives already wallpapered over and over again with images of all kinds. They settle into the background of our consciousness until one news image arrests us with some particular twist—the look on a face, a terrible motion, a dance of agony. Then we complain. How dare you force us out of our comfort zone? How dare you challenge us with horrors not in our own lives?

But as the Freedom Forum ad should remind us, the real question for those of us at home is not about what we do see, but what we don't. What are the stories that journalists have died covering? Where are the places that are too risky for reporters and photographers to go? "For the dozens of newspaper and television reporters trying to make sense of the place," *New York Times* correspondent Dexter Filkins wrote in 2004, "Iraq above all is a shrinking country. Village by village, block by block, the vast and challenging land that we entered in March 2003 has shriveled into a medieval city-state, a grim and edgy place where the only question is how much more territory we will lose tomorrow. On some days, it seems, we are all crowded into a single room together, clutching our notebooks and watching the walls."[101] Four years later the violence against journalists in Iraq hadn't abated. News organizations hired private security forces and Iraqi employees to go places Americans and British personnel could not. But safety remained elusive. As ABC News correspondent Terry McCarthy noted in mid-2008,

> We had a camera crew who were killed last year, unfortunately, in Baghdad. And with the permission of their families, we aired their pictures on air with a eulogy that night. Those pictures were picked up by local TV and, within hours, there was a huge crowd outside the house of . . . one of the crew, the soundman, who said, "We want to kill the whole family, because we didn't know that your son was working with the Americans." We had to quickly yank that picture off Iraqi TV. But it just shows you the risks involved not only for foreigners reporting there, but also for Iraqis themselves appearing on American television. That makes it very hard for us to tell their story properly.[102]

It used to be that war reporters were considered observers—as recently as the conflict in El Salvador in the 1980s, journalists could go back and forth between armed forces, reporting on both sides. They just took care to tape the words "TV" or "Prensa" in bold letters on their vehicles. It wasn't failsafe, but the operating notion was that journalists should get safe passage so they could get the story out, and both sides—all sides—wanted to get their stories out. When journalists tried that tape trick on their cars in Bosnia ten years later, the snipers in Sarajevo used the "TV" letters as a bull's-eye. ABC senior producer David Kaplan, part of an ABC contingent accompanying Milan Panic, the prime minister of Yugoslavia, to peace talks in Sarajevo, was hit by a bullet while in the back seat of the press van traveling from the airport to the UN Protection Force headquarters. The bullet smashed through the back closed doors, precisely between the T and the V taped on the van.

Since then, in wars across the globe, journalists have been among the first targeted. As armed factions left the rules of war behind, they had a compelling interest in keeping the media from reporting on their crimes. So, for example, among the first killed by the Hutus during the genocide in Rwanda were 14 local journalists. "The grim truth about this 'media strategy' is that it works," noted reporter Scott Anderson in the *New York Times Magazine*:

> How many people know, for example, that for the past decade Algeria has been ravaged by a war that has left an estimated 100,000 dead? Not many, because both sides in that conflict have taken turns murdering journalists: 60 at last count. After two rounds of a scorched-earth war in Chechnya that has left at least 5 percent of the civilian population dead and another 30 percent displaced, why does the rest of the world seem willing to accept President Putin's characterization of that conflict as a winding-down police action against "bandits" and "terrorists"? Because by helping turn Chechnya into a killing field for journalists—15 dead, by latest count, often at the hands of Russian soldiers—the Russian government can now characterize that conflict pretty much any way it wants to."[103]

We, the audience, can turn the page, click the remote on any story that doesn't engage us—or any story that we find too offensive or too threatening to our political, moral, and emotional equilibrium. But what we can't turn the page on are the stories and the images that never make it to air, to print, to radio. Beyond the stories that are so processed and packaged that the value of the news in them is itself in doubt, it's the stories that never even make it to the spin machine or through the 24/7 maw that we need to be up in arms about.

Many Americans and British don't seem to be noticing, for instance, that there is less and less coverage of the war in Iraq. By the summer of 2008, observed the *New York Times*, there were only half a dozen Western photographers covering the country, even though 150,000 American and 4,100 British troops remained engaged there. Why? Said reporters Michael Kamber and Tim Arango: because of the "danger, the high cost to financially ailing media outlets and diminished interest among Americans in following the war."

And there was one other key reason: smothering US military restrictions. The *Times* noted that it was increasingly difficult for photographers to cover the fighting:

> Journalists say it is now harder, or harder than in the earlier years, to accompany troops in Iraq on combat missions. Even memorial services for killed soldiers, once routinely open, are increasingly off limits. Detainees were widely photographed in the early years of the war, but the Department of Defense, citing prisoners' rights, has recently stopped that practice as well . . .
>
> New embed rules were adopted in the spring of 2007 that required written permission from wounded soldiers before their image could be used, a near impossibility in the case of badly wounded soldiers, journalists say . . .
>
> Two *New York Times* journalists were disembedded in January 2007 after the paper published a photo of a mortally wounded soldier. Though the soldier was shot through the head and died hours after the photo was taken, Lt. Gen. Raymond T. Odierno argued that *The Times* had broken embed rules by not getting written permission from the soldier.

It's turned into a brave new world of restrictions: "While embed restrictions do permit photographs of dead soldiers to be published once family members have been notified, in practice, photographers say, the military has exacted retribution on the rare occasions that such images have appeared. In four out of five cases that the *New York Times* was able to document, the photographer was immediately kicked out of his or her embed following publication of such photos."

But, noted the *Times* reporters, the US Marine Corps "denied it was trying to place limits on the news media," asserting that "security" not politics was behind its restrictions of the publication of images of the dead and injured. Observed Lieutenant Colonel Chris Hughes, a Marine spokesman, in regard to the July 2008 termination of the embed of freelance photographer Zoriah Miller for taking and posting online his photographs of marines killed in a June 26, 2008 suicide attack: "Specifically, Mr. Miller provided our enemy with an after-action report on the effectiveness of their attack and on the response procedures of U.S. and Iraqi forces."

Whatever the proximate cause of the restrictions—security, politics, or protection of the memory of the fallen troops—the result has been that those outside the theater of operations have had only a minimal ability to see how the Iraq war is being fought. In fact, reporters Kamber and Arango wrote, "after five years and more than 4,000 American combat deaths, searches and interviews turned up fewer than a half-dozen graphic photographs of dead American soldiers." Is that all the fault of problems of access and a de facto censorship by the US authorities? No, the *Times* admitted. "Most newspapers refuse to publish such pictures as a matter of policy."[104]

I believe both governments and most media need to change. What we need is a government and media that take responsibility for telling us without fear or favor about the terrorism in the world today *and* that challenge us to join them in taking some responsibility for solving it. "We can ask ourselves the reason for all this, how things could have gotten so far out of hand?" proposed Getty photographer Di Lauro. "How it is possible for our society and our way of life to produce people such as the husband and wife [suicide bomber] team of Ali Hussein Ali al-Shamira and Sajida Mubarak Atrous al-Rishawi, who voluntary deprived themselves of the most precious gift of all—life—in order to blow up not only themselves but dozens of innocent wedding guests, including women and children?"[105] What did we do? What did we not do? How can we engage with these questions about the causes of terrorism—beyond making a military response?

"When I started as a photographer, my goals were quite simple," said VII photographer Ron Haviv, "and I think that they have remained the same—my goals are to inform, to educate and to help change things when they need to be changed. I think that's something that probably most of my colleagues feel as well as we go about into the world, into these different conflict zones, into places where people in power are not paying attention to. . . . And with that in mind I feel that photojournalism—journalism as a whole, but photojournalism specifically because of the power of the image—really plays a very important role in this process of decision-making. Our ability to continuously remind people, to teach people, and to tell people over and over again what is happening, forces politicians many of the times to make decisions."

The place where terrorism occurs, said Haviv, is "no longer some faraway place. . . . It now affects you, the American, in New York City, in Los Angeles, in Iowa. It affects us all. We need to understand that. We need to educate ourselves because we need to vote for the right people to make the right decisions about foreign policy. The politicians need to know that we care about foreign policy in Afghanistan, that we care about foreign policy in Lebanon or wherever because we realize that we are . . . part of this very small community called the world."[106]

∽

I won't bore you with the details, but I'm not a religious person. I'm not even sure to whom or what I pray, but for those people, I've begun.
          Freelance photographer Martin Lueders, Oct. 30, 2001, in Pakistan[107]

IV

conclusion: packaging terrorism

April 4 is a powerful date in the calendar. On that date in 1968, the Reverend Dr. Martin Luther King Jr. was assassinated. And on that date in 1967, Dr. King gave perhaps his most important and least remembered major speech—an address to a meeting of Clergy and Laity Concerned at Riverside Church in New York City. Its title: "Beyond Vietnam: A Time to Break Silence."

"The world now demands a maturity of America that we may not be able to achieve," Dr. King declared to the packed audience. "We can no longer afford to worship the god of hate or bow before the altar of retaliation. The oceans of history are made turbulent by the ever-rising tides of hate. History is cluttered with the wreckage of nations and individuals that pursued this self-defeating path of hate."

Dr. King called for understanding: "Here is the true meaning and value of compassion and nonviolence, when it helps us to see the enemy's point of view, to hear his questions, to know his assessment of ourselves."

Dr. King called for change: "A true revolution of values will soon cause us to question the fairness and justice of many of our past and present policies."

Dr. King called for a re-evaluation of Western exceptionalism: "A genuine revolution of values means in the final analysis that our loyalties must become ecumenical rather than sectional. Every nation must now develop an overriding loyalty to mankind as a whole in order to preserve the best in their individual societies."

Dr. King called for action: "If we do not act, we shall surely be dragged down the long, dark, and shameful corridors of time reserved for those who possess power without compassion, might without morality, and strength without sight. Now let us begin."[1]

It is hard not to see parallels to the challenges we today face in the issues that Dr. King called out to his audience back in 1967. It is hard not to hear echoes of his speeches in the one made by Barack Obama in Berlin in the summer of 2008, 40 years after Dr. King's death: "The walls between the countries with the most and those with the least cannot stand. The walls between races and tribes; natives and immigrants; Christian and Muslim and Jew cannot stand. These now are the walls we must tear down."[2]

It is instructive to reflect on how we can apply Dr. King's appeals to our own circumstances. We too need to reconsider our hate, reflect on how others see us, strive towards greater justice, celebrate our own and others' diversity as integral parts of a larger whole.

The media are central to that process.

Media writ large are society's key conduit for information and catalyst for discussion and action. Honest and respectful communication among different sectors of society rarely occurs naturally. For this reason, open and pluralistic media (including "citizen journalists" of all kinds and stripes) are critical to fostering a dialogue about any issue and to ensuring that all voices in a community can be heard. Free and open airing of an issue ideally leads in turn to participatory governance where special interests are less able to singularly spin public debate and shape public policy.

But if those in power manipulate journalists, if those journalists don't protest against that manipulation—or willingly capitulate to it—the media can become just another arm of authority, a propaganda tool to distract, deceive, and betray the public. Media need to think independently. Too often the level of recognition that those in authority give to an issue aligns with the level of coverage media give to that issue. That's a problem.

At the end of the first chapter of this book, I rhetorically asked, "What have we learned about terrorism?" It's appropriate to ask now, "What have we learned about media?"

We've learned, oh so painfully, that information is power. As the opening page of this book asserted: it's not specific acts of terrorism that most matter in the post-9/11 world, it's what we are told to think about—and how we respond to—those acts of terrorism.

Too often what we are told about terrorism is what governments say. Pack journalism prevails.

Most media cover what everyone else covers. There are differences in audiences, in budgets, and in media platforms. There are differences among which news outlets are able to go live with audio and video, which struggle with 24/7 deadlines, and which are on air or online quickly, but at a sacrifice of thoughtful analysis and depth. There are differences in how news outlets prioritize stories and how well they cover them. There are differences in perspective and in how stories are sourced. British news media fold more analysis into reports than their US counterparts, and news organizations that have their primary outlets online proffer more commentary than other news platforms. But what few news outlets do is cover different "stuff."

Independent, ethical, and pluralistic media—ones that cross media platforms (print, broadcast, online, handheld) and political perspectives—are essential. Especially critical to that independence are investigative reporters who provide the unambiguous evidence and credible "content"—documents, sources, doggedly checked and rechecked details—that the public desperately needs for a functioning, civilized, open, and ultimately free society. So empowered, such media can help ensure transparency, accountability, and the rule of law. Indeed, insurgents, criminals, terrorists, and corrupt politicians understand very well that it is the months or years of digging by professional reporters, most of them supported by traditional news organizations, that expose lies and misdeeds. As a consequence, it must be a global priority to defend the freedom of those media around the world that dare to publish and broadcast investigative stories and dare to give voice to ideas outside the political and at times social or cultural mainstream.

The increasing concentration of ownership of the sources of news and information into fewer and fewer hands threatens the health of civil society. When media ownership is concentrated, those few owners exercise a great deal of control over the character of the national discussion. The fact that the news has become a profit—or loss—center for many owners means that cost considerations also lie behind decisions about what stories to cover, how much to cover them, and what angles to push. Too many important stories, too many essential stories are not getting covered because big government won't talk and big media won't look. It's difficult to get the major media to cover what they think won't sell, even when hot online blog sites, such as the Huffington Post, Michelle Malkin, Iain Dale's Diary, or Guido Fawkes' blog, or grassroots activist sites, such as Global Voices, Witness/The Hub, ActionNetwork, or Ushahidi are buzzing.

Ultimately the question becomes very basic: who controls news and information?

The powerful set the terms of the public debate on terrorism. Let me try to sum up how that happens, by again drawing on those studies, earlier discussed, that I and my colleagues at ICMPA as well as others have conducted.

As we discovered, while a terrorist attack may be the precipitating event for news coverage, the overwhelming amount of attention given to terrorism in the news relates to the political reaction to that event—and to the days and weeks and months of domestic policy debates that result. For all but the most spectacular terrorist attacks, the international news audience doesn't learn much beyond the initial (and often incorrect) vital statistics about who was killed and who was injured. Indeed, it's quite common for the public to never learn who the perpetrators of an attack were, what was their agenda, whether they were caught, or how the community is surviving (or not) after the event.

American and British coverage of terrorism, when viewed in isolation, usually seems straightforward, conscientious, and quite comprehensive. It is only when viewed comparatively—say against coverage of the same events by Arab media— that it becomes evident that US and UK media focus on policy agendas more than human suffering, on the statements of officials more than on graphic depictions of victims.

Most terrorist attacks in distant locations make the news to the extent that they do because the US and UK media judge that something about the terrorism represents a larger threat to the Western audience. Stories may focus on what an attack says about the power of the terrorists or what it says about the competence of the nation's political leaders or what it says about the need for outside governments to be involved, but they rarely focus on the victims and survivors. How much is told about the victims of terror is a barometer for how much media believe we can come to care about the particular event. If an attack is geographically or psychologically close then we hear the stories of individuals (as we did when the *New York Times* and the BBC told the personal narratives of those who perished in the World Trade Center or in the London transport bombings). But for more quotidian attacks, the voices of ordinary eyewitnesses are rarely heard, and when used, their words are primarily included to add drama and immediacy, rather than hard information or context. Indeed, information about an actual attack is often not only slight, but featured for a relatively brief period of time—typically only a few days. The trend stories, the policy stories, by contrast, linger on seemingly forever.

Suicide bombings, especially in Iraq, Afghanistan, and Pakistan, are a case in point. They are rarely highlighted in the news beyond the mention of who was killed where. Suicide bombings are often distilled down to a set of numbers that are presumptively meaningful, that presumably offer a bias-free evaluation of the violence or the politics. Then that litany of numbers is used as a way into trend stories: what does the attack or attacks say about the level of violence in the country—is it increasing or decreasing? What do the attacks say about the Iraqi or Pakistani governments' ability to function, about American or British policy towards the conflicts, about the strength of various factions within those countries?

The answers that are proffered track off from what politicians say. Politicians frame our understanding of terrorism. The nature of national security and intelligence policy and crises is such that relatively few people other than those within government can speak with any authority. The statements of presidents, home secretaries, the heads of security services, and military officers are therefore solicited to tell us both the breaking news and what to think about it all. Not coincidentally, using official sources from one's own country is also a way to "nationalize" an event—if media interview officials on their own side, often what happens is that the event is tied back to domestic affairs and connections are made to domestic precedents.

As a consequence, how government frames an event or policy becomes the standard way media talk about it—even when media disagree with the government's position. Even after US media began to challenge the Bush administration's response to September 11, for example, few considered the implications of the White House's repeated assertions that the opposite of terrorism is democracy. Commentators argued as to whether democracy could be exported or whether democracy could be a first-generation form of government for post-conflict societies, but few tried to argue another apposite relationship, such as the opposite of terrorism is non-aggression, or the opposite of terrorism is physical safety.

The fact that media take their cue from how government officials frame terrorism gives government tremendous power in directing the public debate. Framing the threat of terrorism in one way draws attention to certain strategic choices and opportunities, while masking others. Framing democracy as the opposite of terrorism, for instance, argues for political engagement in a country—and sufficient military force to compel political change.

Language too directs audiences what to think. To a tremendous degree, language shapes the terrorism issue, but our studies documented that media do little to clarify core terms of the discussion—starting with the word "terrorism." Almost all of the media debate has been focused on whether journalists should use the word, rather than on what those who use the term mean by it. Other studies noted that the word "terrorism" doesn't even have to be used for consumers of a news story to be cued to think about terrorism and to make value judgments about what has occurred and what should be done. Seemingly neutral words and combinations of words can powerfully package a message about terrorism, even when the coverage appears dispassionate.

Language can both obfuscate and impose meaning. Stories and sources often conflate disparate ideas, groups, events, and places by the use of umbrella words and phrases such as "terrorist," "madrassa," and "weapons of mass destruction," making miscommunication likely and misdirection possible. Word choices make a difference. ICMPA's studies observed that suicide attacks are more often discussed by using the generic terms "terrorism" or "terrorist" than by referencing specific perpetrators—a tendency which contributes to audiences' inability to make distinctions among terrorist groups and their agendas. "Iraq" is commonly referenced in discussions of a terrorist attack, even when the specific attack does not actively relate to the Iraq conflict—a tendency that reinforces the belief that the war in Iraq is an essential battleground for fighting terrorism elsewhere in the world. Television uses "scary" words like "terrorism" more often than print or online media outlets—a choice which undermines TV's ability to give its audience stories with depth, perspective, and context.

One could, in fact, neatly sum up the most essential element in our experience of terrorism in one phrase: fear-mongering. Fear-mongering by the terrorists themselves, by governments, by the media.

Terrorists may succeed in killing only a very few people, but the deliberate randomness of their targeting of civilians is what makes their violence so arresting. Everyone who is intimidated by their attacks becomes a victim. The real escalation in terrorism comes not only through greater numbers of attacks, but from wider attention to those that occur. The corollary to Rand expert Brian Michael Jenkins' famous words, "Terrorism is theater," is one that I make here: "Audiences are mesmerized by fear." Real as well as imagined terrorism is horrifyingly compelling—it is hard to watch and hard to turn away. Terrorists have become more sophisticated; those who want can design their attacks so as to attract a global audience. Terrorists consider their goals, then decide the appropriate packaging for their actions: a bombing of public transportation, an attack on civilian security forces, a kidnapping of a journalist or NGO officer, the beheading of foreigners or their domestic collaborators.

Governments need to be attentive to the safety and well-being of their citizens. But governments don't always respond proportionately to terrorist attacks. As *New York Times* columnist Paul Krugman wrote for example, the Bush administration misrepresented 9/11. "Instead of treating the attack as what it was—an atrocity committed by a fundamentally weak, though ruthless adversary—the administration portrayed America as a nation under threat from every direction."[3] Polls noted that the American public was willing to make great sacrifices to protect the United States against terrorism. The same polls noted that the public has been considerably less enthusiastic about making sacrifices to protect Iraqis or Afghanis. But representing America as profoundly beleaguered and linking the safety of Americans directly to the safety of Iraqis—by fear-mongering, in effect—the White House justified international and domestic policies that might otherwise have been considered indefensible. The Bush administration consistently framed terrorists as a monolithic "other" in an "us" against "them" binary relationship, leaving few opportunities for discussion about how to find common ground or even ways to distinguish among very different terrorist groups with quite different agendas—not all of which, of course, are "evil" or nihilistic. This was the flipside of fear-mongering, this talk about an "Axis of Evil" and comparison of present-day leaders to past political monsters. This was not just fear-mongering, but hate-mongering.

Too many media bought into the fear and hate. News-you-can-use coverage of terrorist attacks keeps audiences plugged into media accounts. As said earlier, most media find it irresistible to report doomsayer threats and defense and security arguments verbatim. This has the unfortunate effect of enabling policymakers to use threats of terrorism as powerful tools of public persuasion and as forceful rationales for policy initiatives. Yet paradoxically, media—American and British mainstream media—find it near-impossible to show and tell their audiences about the real consequences of terrorist attacks. Terrorists' threats, and the policies presumably crafted to meet them, can get uncounted column inches, airtime, and webspace, but graphic descriptions of what happens to people who actually are on the frontlines? Those are self-censored. There is a "squeamishness about the carnage that is war's chief byproduct," wrote media columnist David Carr about Iraq in April 2003 in the *New York Times*.

> During an era when popular culture is filled with depictions of violence and death, and the combination of technology and battlefield access for reporters has put the public in the middle of a shooting war, the images that many Americans are seeing are remarkably bloodless. The heroic narrative is shaped in part by what editors and producers view as a need to maintain standards and not offend their audience. But some cultural critics say that the relatively softened imagery has more to do with a political need to celebrate victory without dwelling on its price.[4]

Editors and producers, in other words, are responsible for packaging that antiseptic portrait of terrorism that most of us see. We can be made fearful, we can be taught to hate, but most American and British editors and producers cavil at showing and telling their audiences what the costs of terrorism and of fighting terrorism really are.

Fear-mongering and hate-mongering don't give the public sufficient information to be able to reason its own way to a response to real threats and actual attacks. And too often that's been the point of such tactics. Above all, the "War on Terror" has been a war for public opinion—and one played out through all the old media venues and the exponentially expanding new media ones. Terrorists as well as governments want to keep their own messages in the public's view: terrorists want as much notice for their actions as possible; governments want the public to see their policies as the appropriate ones for countering the terrorist threat. Then there are the media that want to tell a compelling story that will keep their audiences tuned in.

From our perspective on the years since September 11, 2001, we now can see that how the Bush and Blair governments played "terrorism" to look strong and decisive proved in many cases to be catastrophically counterproductive—both politically to those governments and strategically in their attempts to defeat terrorism.

From our perspective on the years since September 11, 2001, we now can see that media made appalling errors in covering terrorism. When Michael Getler was ombudsman at the *Washington Post,* he quoted the *Post*'s own guidelines in a column written in 2003: " 'We should always strive to satisfy our own standards and not let others set standards for us.' " Most news outlets, including the *Washington Post* at times, did not follow that advice. Accurate reporting demands determining responsibility. That includes critiquing one's own side, not just judging who's bad on the other side, and certainly not treating the assessment of the government— or any other actor for that matter—as sacrosanct.

Forty years after the day of Dr. King's assassination, April 4, 2008, the *New York Times* condemned in its lead editorial the "eighty-one spine-crawling" pages of "twisted legal reasoning" written in March 2003 by John Yoo, then a lawyer for the Justice Department, that "justify President Bush's decision to ignore federal law and international treaties and authorize the abuse and torture of prisoners."

The comments section to that editorial remained open for roughly 12 hours. In that time, 235 readers from around the country and around the world expressed their disgust both at the memo's content and at the lethal hubris of the Bush administration. Readers cried out in the same ways as Dr. King—they were deeply concerned about the implicit hatred expressed in Yoo's legal memorandum, worried about American deafness to the voices of others and its blindness to its own injustices, and dismayed about the future if radical revisions in policy were not made.

Among all those comments a few readers remarked on the apathy of the public: "Where is the outrage? Who seems to care?" wrote a reader from Maine. Some pointedly called out the media for their failures: "You provide strong evidence and arguments that members of this administration at best 'have failed to uphold the constitution of the United States', and at worst are felons if not war criminals. Where then is your call for accountability?" asked a reader from Palm Beach.

Or as a New Yorker bluntly asked, when we "sink to the same levels as Terrorists, are we not also Terrorists?"

One reader's comments frankly distilled the frustrations clearly felt by many others in the *Times'* audience. (I say "clearly" because the comments made were recommended by 78 other readers.) "I read a post somewhere saying the mainstream media's not giving this much play, and in truth, I don't really care about it, either. It's not that it isn't horrendous—it is. But so what? Bush and Cheney and Gonzalez and Yoo and Rove did something else that was horrendous. I mean, no one's going to DO anything about it, so why even waste time on outrage? Why even click on the headline any more. And the media senses this, and that's why it doesn't get much run. Outrage is great when there's a path to its satisfaction. Will we impeach someone, put him in prison, embarrass him to his face? No, we won't do such a thing," noted this reader from Los Angeles. "That's the real problem with this. And the unlikelihood of justice makes outrage unsatisfying and therefore depressing. So honestly, who cares about these torture memos and what happened in Iraq's prisons and the war profiteering and rendition and Guantanamo and the Patriot Act and warrantless wiretapping and the political persecution of US Attorneys and Katrina—because heads are not rolling."[5]

"If we do not act," said Dr. King, "we shall surely be dragged down the long, dark, and shameful corridors of time reserved for those who possess power without compassion, might without morality, and strength without sight." To act, one needs information and evidence together with the willingness to assume responsibility. We have had too little of either and as a result we are surely being dragged down a long, dark, and shameful corridor.

Where are the clarion voices like Dr. King's to be heard in the world today? From what podiums and pulpits and platforms do they call out to us? Citizens are raising their voices, but where is the accountability in the halls of government? Where can the information be heard in the media? Well, perhaps, the 2008 US presidential election has been in part a referendum on that—a referendum both on the politicians and on those who cover them.

This book notes a great irony: despite President Bush's avowal that the United States and its allies needed to fight his "War on Terror" by fostering democracy— "We seek the advance of democracy for the most practical of reasons: because democracies do not support terrorists or threaten the world with weapons of mass murder"[6]—democracy is not a prerequisite to peace: consider the relatively stable peace agreements between Israel and Egypt or Jordan. Nor does democracy inevitably bring an end to terrorism. Just ask Irish politician Conor Cruise O'Brien. But even if one were to accept the premise that states that hold free and fair elections are far less likely to host active terrorist populations, the years since 9/11 have amply demonstrated that you can't bring democracy to countries by conquering them. Democracy doesn't rise up, phoenix-like after a "liberation." The priority must be to build civil society institutions from the inside out and the ground up.

Perhaps the first civil society institution to foster is media. There's the irony. What we needed these past years was not to foster democracy through military engagement, because democracy was argued to be some cure-all for terrorism. What we needed was to foster democracy through supporting a pluralistic and diverse global media—a media that encompasses newspapers and television as well as radio, online and handheld sources, that understands the power of instant messages and the instantaneity of digital images, that agrees to listen to all voices and all perspectives, that comprehends the world's desperate need for transparency and accurate news and information, and that identifies spin, rather than parlays it for media's own agenda.

On March 31, 2008, the fortieth anniversary of the Reverend Dr. Martin Luther King Jr.'s last Sunday sermon, Taylor Branch, the great chronicler of the American Civil Rights Movement, spoke about King's legacy to an audience at the National Cathedral in Washington, DC. "The watchword of political discourse has degenerated from 'movement' to 'spin,'" Branch said. "In Dr. King's era, the word 'movement' grew from a personal inspiration into leaps of faith, then from shared discovery and sacrifice into upward struggle, spawning kindred movements until great hosts from Selma to the Berlin Wall literally could feel the movement of history. Now we have 'spin' instead, suggesting that there is no real direction at stake from political debate, nor any consequence except for the players in a game."

Branch challenged his audience: "SO what should we do, now that 40 years have passed? How do we restore our political culture from spin to movement, from muddle to purpose? We must take leaps, ask questions, study nonviolence, reclaim our history."

We must, in short, ask questions because we don't have all the answers, listen because we need to learn as well as teach, practice humanity because we ourselves want to be treated humanely.

First, we have to move beyond spin. We have to demand accountability by using that ultimate weapon of non-violence: our vote. That's how we can—and must—call government officials out on their packaging of terrorism, their betrayal of the public trust, and, in the United States, their utter corruption of the Constitution. "Our nation is a great cathedral of votes—votes not only for Congress and for president, but also votes on Supreme Court decisions and on countless juries. Votes govern the boards of great corporations and tiny charities alike. Visibly and invisibly," said Branch, "everything runs on votes."[7] What is the best check on spin? Our votes.

But in order to evaluate what we are being told, in order for us to understand that not just truth but our rights and liberties are at risk, in order to know what to vote for and what to vote against, we need information, we need to exercise our freedom of expression. We need a vibrant, spirited, diverse, and pluralistic media at home and around the world.

Appendix

icmpa studies of media coverage of terrorism incidents

What We Looked At

The International Center for Media and the Public Agenda (ICMPA), a center that I direct that bridges the Philip Merrill College of Journalism and the School of Public Policy at the University of Maryland, conducted a series of studies over several years to determine how American and British print (newspapers and magazines), broadcast (radio and TV), and online news outlets covered terrorism. In creating our studies, we knew we had to investigate coverage of different kinds of terrorism. So we looked at the coverage of suicide bomb attacks that seemingly occurred out of nowhere—against Kenyan, Egyptian, and Jordanian hotels, Balinese night-clubs and the transportation systems in London and Madrid, for example. And we looked at the coverage of suicide bomb attacks that occurred in the midst of ongoing fighting—in the Israeli–Palestinian conflict and in Iraq. We also looked at how media reported on different theaters of conflict in the "War on Terror"—Iraq and Pakistan and Afghanistan. Finally we looked at how media covered threats of terrorism—especially the threat of weapons of mass destruction—in South Asia in 1998, in North Korea and Iraq in 2002, and again in Iraq in 2003.

Beyond examining different "types" of terrorism, we also decided we needed to look at how journalists covered acts of terrorism before September 11, 2001, how they covered terrorism in the immediate aftermath of 9/11, and how they covered terrorism years five and six and more years later.[1]

At the end of each of the studies we conducted, we wrote up our analysis and formulated our conclusions. We found that some of the conventional wisdom about how terrorism comes to the attention of the public was borne out. In lots of ways terrorist attacks are treated no differently than any other international breaking-news event ("it just happened") and terrorist threats can be covered like other international trend stories (What's happening with AIDS? How serious is climate change?). But in other ways, newsrooms are reporting on terrorism—attacks that are dramatic, singular events, attacks that occur in the midst of a war zone, and threats from all over—differently than they covered violence in the past. We found much that surprised us.

Some of the results of those studies can be found on the ICMPA webpage—www.icmpa.umd.edu—or in the pages of *Foreign Policy* magazine's Passport blog: blog.foreignpolicy.com.

The second chapter of this book discussed the findings—and the surprises—uncovered in our studies. In nine sections, that chapter wrestled with a range of questions our studies were formulated to consider: How do media make sense of terrorism? How do media cover terrorist crises and the ongoing "politics" of terrorism? Are individuals or certain groups blamed or are social forces and polit-ical or religious agendas said to be at fault? What is the focus of coverage? Whose voices tell us the news? Whose stories do we hear? How do different media cover terrorism: Is British reporting on terror different than the American? Does it make a difference whether you get your news in print, on TV, or online?

For most of our studies, we used the Lexis-Nexis, Factiva, and Vanderbilt TV News archives to look at the US and UK print, TV, radio, and online news outlets. Using a keyword search of selected news outlets, we mined those data archives. Original "hard copies" of print outlets, grabs of online pages, and tape or MP3 files of TV and radio were used to assess images, video, and audio reports. A similar methodology was used for my study of media coverage of weapons of mass destruc-tion, prepared as part of the Advanced Methods of Cooperative Security Program at the Center for International and Security Studies at Maryland (CISSM) and funded by the National Science Foundation. That full published study can be found at www.cissm.umd.edu/papers/display.php?id=32.

☙

The following are the specific events, issues, and debates that were investigated for this book. As the text of *Packaging Terrorism* makes clear, however, many other events beyond those listed here were also considered and evaluated, as seemed necessary and appropriate. Yet because the focus of this book is the "War on Terror" as defined and fought by President George W. Bush, very few incidents were looked at outside of the regions of the United States, western Europe, the Middle East, and South Asia. Only a few terrorist attacks in East Asia and Africa were looked at, and this book does not include any analysis of media coverage of terrorism in

Latin America. An investigation of coverage of those regions would be a fruitful topic for a new and different work.

1998

1   MAY 5–26: Study of US and UK media coverage of several climactic events in South Asia, including India's first overt nuclear weapons tests on May 11–13, declarations from Pakistan about its nuclear readiness, and the run-up to six Pakistani nuclear weapons tests on May 28–30. This period also witnessed a flare-up in concern and controversy over lax security for Russian nuclear weapons—the "loose nukes" issue.

2001

2   MAY 1–DECEMBER 31: Study of US media coverage of the Israeli–Palestinian conflict, a period that included coverage of the ongoing "Second (or al-Aqsa) Intifada" and the June 1 suicide bombing of the Dolphinarium, a Tel Aviv club. Islamic Jihad claimed responsibility for the event that killed 21, including high school students. The period also straddled the September 11 bombing in New York City.

2001–2

3   SEPTEMBER 11, 2001 TO DECEMBER 31, 2002: Study of US and UK media coverage of Pakistan and Afghanistan. (see also 2006–7)

2002

4   MARCH 27: The suicide bombing in Netanya, Israel, of the Park Hotel dining room during Passover dinner that killed 30 and injured 140, including Holocaust survivors. Hamas claimed responsibility for the attack.

5   OCTOBER 11–31: Study of US and UK media coverage of the build-up to the war in Iraq and the debate over Saddam Hussein's use of terror and his possession of weapons of mass destruction, starting the day after the US Congress approved military action in Iraq, if Iraq "does not disarm," and including the intense public debate over WMD as a justification for preventive war. It also included the increased attention to the story of nuclear weapons development in North Korea, following the October 4 revelation by North Korean officials that the country had a nuclear weapons program using enriched uranium and the October 16 announcement by US officials that they had evidence of a nuclear weapons program in North Korea.

6   OCTOBER 12: The bombing in Bali, Indonesia of the Sari nightclub that killed 202 and injured 209. Three separate bombings occurred. First, an electronically triggered bomb hidden in a backpack ripped through Paddy's Bar, killing the presumed suicide bomber. Seconds later a much more powerful car bomb of close to 1,000 kg was detonated by remote control in front of the Sari Club. Almost simultaneously, a third bomb detonated in the street in front of the American consulate in Bali. This bomb caused no injuries, and only modest damage. The death toll for the Bali bombings remains the highest of any terrorist attack worldwide since September 11, 2001. (The bombing of the train in Madrid on March 11, 2004, killed 190 people and wounded close to 1,800.) Eighty-eight Australians were killed in the Bali attacks—the largest national group affected. As a result the event is sometimes called "Australia's September 11." Jemaah Islamiyah was believed to be responsible for the bombings; the group has ties to Al Qaeda.

7   NOVEMBER 29: The bombing in Mombasa, Kenya, of the Paradise Hotel that killed 15 and injured 26. Three suicide bombers detonated a car bomb outside the Israeli-owned hotel. The same morning a shoulder-fired missile attack unsuccessfully targeted an Israeli airliner taking off from Mombasa airport. There were more than 270 people on the plane. The Army of Palestine claimed initial responsibility for the hotel bombing; within days, Al Qaeda claimed responsibility on an Islamic website.

2003

8   MAY 1–21: Study of US and UK media coverage of hunt for Iraqi weapons of mass destruction, starting on the day of President George W. Bush's declaration of "an end to major combat operations" in Iraq. This timeframe also saw revelations about Iran's nuclear program and Russia's connection to it, beginning in earnest on May 8, with the Bush administration's demand that the International Atomic Energy Agency (IAEA) find Iran in violation of the Nuclear Non-Proliferation Treaty.

9   AUGUST 29: The car bombing in Najaf, Iraq, outside the Imam Ali mosque during prayers that injured dozens and killed over 125 people, including Shiite leader Ayatollah Sayed Mohammed Baqir al-Hakim.

10   OCTOBER 9: The attacks in Baghdad, Iraq, that killed 50 people, including a Spanish diplomat who was shot and killed and a car bombing at a police station in Baghdad's main Shiite neighborhood that killed at least 10.

11   OCTOBER 27: The car bombings in Iraq on the first day of Ramadan that targeted the Red Cross compound and several police stations. 40 people were killed and over 200 injured.

12   DECEMBER 14 AND 15: The car bomb attacks that exploded in and around Baghdad, including one at a police station in Khaldiyah, killing at least 17 and wounding 30. Saddam Hussein had been captured on December 13, but the news was released on December 14.

2004

13   MARCH 11: The series of coordinated bombings in Madrid, Spain, during the morning rush-hour commute. A series of 10 explosions on four commuter trains occurred in three stations. 190 people were killed and almost 1,800 were wounded. The Spanish government first charged the Basque separatist group ETA with the attacks, but later Al Qaeda claimed responsibility.

14   OCTOBER 7: The bombing in Taba, Egypt, of the Hilton hotel that killed 34 people and injured 105. Most victims were Israeli vacationers, but Egyptians and Russians also died. Israel charged Al Qaeda with involvement but a later inquiry by the Egyptian Interior Ministry into the bombings concluded that there was no Al Qaeda link.

2005

15   JULY 7: The series of coordinated bombings in London, England, in which three bombs exploded within 50 seconds of each other on three London Underground trains. A fourth bomb exploded on a bus nearly an hour later. Fifty-two people died in the attacks, not including the four suicide bombers, and about 700 were injured. (Later, a video statement from one of the suicide bombers was found that suggested a link between the bombers and Al Qaeda.)

16   OCTOBER 5: The suicide bombing in Iraq on the first day of Ramadan inside a Shiite mosque where police had been praying that killed 25 and wounded 87.

17   NOVEMBER 9: The bombings in Amman, Jordan, on the Grand Hyatt, the Radisson SAS, and the Days Inn hotels. Al Qaeda claimed responsibility for the attacks, which killed 60 people and injured 115 others. Three high-ranking Palestinian intelligence officials were among the dead.

18   NOVEMBER 10: The suicide bombing in Baghdad of a restaurant that Iraqi police frequented. 35 people were killed; Al Qaeda claimed responsibility.

19   NOVEMBER 18 AND 19:   A series of bombings in Iraq: first, several suicide bombings killed 74 worshipers at two Shiite mosques in eastern Iraq; then in Baghdad two car bombs went off near a hotel where many foreign ministers and Western journalists were staying, killing eight Iraqis; third, two car bombs went off at an Interior Ministry building at the center of the detainee abuse scandal.

2006

20   JANUARY 5 AND 6: A series of attacks in Iraq that killed around 150 people.
        The attacks included: a January 5 suicide attack at a Shiite funeral and
        a following car bomb that drove into the people fleeing after the suicide
        attack—the funeral was being held at the shrine of Imam Hussein; a January
        6 bombing of a group of Iraqi men waiting to be interviewed for jobs
        as policemen and a separate roadside bombing that killed 11 American
        soldiers near Karbala.

21   FEBRUARY 22: The bombing in Samarra, Iraq, that shattered the golden
        dome of the Al Askari mosque, one of the holiest Shiite shrines. Although
        no injuries occurred in the blast, the bombing resulted in violence over
        the following days. That same day, gunmen targeted 27 Baghdad mosques
        and killed three Sunni imams. Over the next several days sectarian rioting
        killed more than 170.

2006–7

22   JANUARY 1, 2006–DECEMBER 1, 2007: Study of US and UK media coverage
        of Pakistan and Afghanistan.

acknowledgments

Writing the acknowledgments is, in many ways, the very best part of writing a book. What makes writing them so wonderful is that one gets to say in public, in the very tangible form of print, how essential all kinds of people have been in all kinds of ways. One tries to thank people along the way—and in just that manner that one's parents have taught: look them in the eye and really try and be heartfelt—but lots of people inevitably get just a quick "thanks" before one moves on.

So this is fun.

As this is a book, the book people should come first, and I've been blessed with great book people. My editor Elizabeth Swayze came to me a while ago and asked if I might have an idea for a book to be part of her new International Communication Association (ICA) series, and I mused a bit and said, you know, I did. And with that very friendly beginning the process started. *Packaging Terrorism* has immeasurably benefited from her enthusiasm, her rigor, and her knowledge of the field. I also had the great good fortune of being cared for by executive editor Jayne Fargnoli, who took me on as her own and who has been a wonderful champion. She has made essential things happen, at critical stages in the process. Margot Morse patiently—and with humor—kept me in the communication loop and helped keep the book on schedule. Simon Eckley, Desirée Zicko, and Janet Moth helped make the book look and read as well as it does. And Maggie Fromm took on the thankless task of making sense of my footnotes. I can't blame any of them for the book's shortcomings, but they all are responsible for making it more than it otherwise would have been.

I'd next like to thank those at the University of Maryland, my base for the past seven years. Dean Tom Kunkel of the Philip Merrill College of Journalism at Maryland gave me room to develop courses that supported my interests, then helped me carve out time so that I could research and write, and then helped me create an international center that gave me and others a platform on which to stand and do our work. I owe Tom, and the university administration that made ICMPA and my role in it possible—President Dan Mote, Bill Destler, Ann

Wylie, Ellin Scholnick, Donna Hamilton, Phyllis Peres, Sapienza Barone—more than I am able to put into words. Then there have been my faculty colleagues who have supported me and the creation and work of my center. Linda Steiner and Carol Rogers have fed what I firmly believe are all the best students my way. Carl Stepp, Ira Chinoy, Haynes Johnson, Reese Cleghorn, Maurine Beasley, Jon Franklin, John Newhagen, Eric Zanot, Chris Harvey, Chris Hanson, Ray Hiebert, and Gene Roberts have tolerated my repeated visits to their offices, and my opening gambit that fooled none of them: "I just have a quick question for you . . ." Linda Ringer, Joyce Hutton, and Vanessa Lee have shepherded me with immense forbearance through the university's budgetary thickets, and Olive Reid, Marchelle Payne-Gassaway, and Stephanie Johnson have lifted amazing administrative burdens for me. Finally Dean Lee Thornton has been an extraordinary mentor, inspiration, and friend—she is all that I could wish to be as an intellect, a leader, and a human being.

The studies of media coverage of terrorism that form the backbone of this work were begun shortly after I moved to Maryland, just a few weeks before September 11, 2001. Many, many people over the years have worked with me on those studies—quite literally too many to thank, at least here. There are some, however whom I must single out by name: Nancy Gallagher, Anja Kuznetsova, Robert Lamb, Rafael Lorente, and Megan Fromm were invaluable editors and researchers. John Steinbruner stunned me with his trust and support and Mac Destler and Dean Steve Fetter with their welcome of me into the Public Policy school ranks. I have only wished I had the ability to be in two places at one time. Finally, if you were a student in my research seminar JOUR 470, I owe you a debt of gratitude.

Others, outside of Maryland, have helped beyond my ability to ever personally repay. Nayan Chanda has been the best of editors—for work along the way and for the book itself, he has been both a cheering squad and a tough taskmaster rolled into one. Moisés Naím has been the same, asking the best from me, believing it was there, and willing to put in his own time and effort to help me move to another level of analysis. Blake Hounsell has been another valued editor, working with me to bring others into the stories I've had to tell. Colleagues at the Dart Center on Journalism and Trauma have over the years helped me not only to understand violence and trauma in new ways, but to think about how media can best cover them. Joe Hight and Bruce Shapiro have been leaders in the fight for recognition of the importance of this field. I have learned a lot from their dedication to it. Deb Nelson has been a revelation to me in her direction of the Center. Deb is a brilliant writer and a brilliant editor, but she is also a tenacious fighter for right: for good journalism, for good management, for a better world. And Frank Ochberg, the founder of the Dart Center, the passionate scientist and humanitarian at the heart of it all, changed my life that day in 1999 when he sat next to me at dinner and turned and said: "I am starting something that I think might interest you."

There are many reporters, photographers, and others in the field whom I need to thank for their willingness to give me the benefit of their thoughts, in some cases over years of conversations, in other cases on just one pivotal occasion. Some I quote in this book, but I am indebted to them all: Eric Alterman, Mark Brayne, George Brock, Marc Charney, Ed Chen, Liz Colton, Mary Dejevsky, Leonard Doyle, Chris Elliott, Beth Frerking, Nik Gowing, Roy Gutman, Brian Hanrahan, Ron Haviv, Lindsey Hilsum, Steve Jukes, Gary Knight, Melissa Ludtke, Mary Kay Magistad, David Marash, Walt Mossberg, Lisa Mullins, Jonathan Munro, John Owen, Vin Ray, Richard Sambrook, Kevin Sites, and Jonathan Steele. There are others in academe, the foundation world, and international organizations who have critically helped shape my thinking on how media cover the world. These include: Stuart Allan, Alan Brinkley James Deane, Marvin Kalb, Emmanuel Kattan, Mark Kenoyer, Susan King, Andy Moravcsik, Eric Newton, Pippa Norris, Nancy Palmer, George Papagiannis, Pat Rosenfield, Rukhsana Qamber, Orville Schell, Phil Seib, Anne-Marie Slaughter, Marguerite Sullivan, Jordi Torrent, and Barbie Zelizer. And Sanjeev Chatterjee, an incredible documentarian and professor, was generous enough to turn his talents to taking occasional photographs during the 2008 Salzburg Academy on Media and Global Change session. One of those photos happened to be of me—and I thank him for its use on the hardback cover of this book.

I wrote this book while on sabbatical at the Salzburg Global Seminar, a circumstance made uniquely possible by my husband's role as president and chief executive officer. As much as I tried to represent living in an eighteenth-century palace overlooking a lake and the Austrian mountains as just a mirage beyond my computer screen, my friends and colleagues were on to me. And the truth is that I likely could not have written the book anywhere else. No other location would have given me both the privacy to hole up for hours and days and weeks on end, barely surfacing long enough to cook the family supper, as well as calm succor after burnout had set in. Whether through runs along the Salzburg canals or in candlelit dinners with experts from all fields from around the world, I never failed to regain my balance while living at the magical Schloss Leopoldskron. The famous anthropologist Margaret Mead was the lead faculty member for the first Salzburg Seminar held over 60 years ago, in the summer of 1947, that brought together over 100 students from across Europe and America. Mead spoke of the importance of Leopoldskron for the work of that first summer:

> The final choice of Leopoldskron as the site had very important implications for the success of the Seminar. . . . Under Max Reinhardt, the Leopoldskron had been carefully preserved as a period spot; the spacious rooms, the formal gardens, the terrace by the lake, presented a consistent stage set, an articulate architectural backdrop for a way of life devoted to the arts. In this setting students arriving to meet other students from the countries of their former enemies, students who had fought on opposite sides, students who had been active in the underground, were able to

meet in a mood which combined a sense of distance from real life, and a sense of the importance of the traditions of civilization. . . . The first shock as they found themselves sitting side by side with men whom two short years ago they might have killed, was softened as they saw themselves reflected back, in the dim lights, from the great mirrors. This gave them time to pause, to hesitate, to see themselves with a certain degree of detachment.[1]

I, like those faculty and students of Mead's era, was immensely fortunate in my choice of place, but I was also tremendously enriched by the people at Schloss Leopoldskron where I am writing now—both those who work here and those who travel through here. The Salzburg Global Seminar's program staff, led by Edward Mortimer, brought a dynamic set of issues and fellows and faculty to the Schloss that greatly enhanced not only my society but my understanding. Across the sectors, those who work here—Jochen Fried and David Goldman in the Education Programming Division, Angela Lee in the president's office, Cheryl Van Emburg and the administrative staff, Lynn McNair and Meg Harris and the development staff, Markus Hiljuk and the conference center staff, Rob Fish and Oliver Schinagl and the IT staff, Herr Kiesling, the kitchen and wait staff, Margit Fesl and the housekeeping staff, and each and every intern—were amazing in how they daily welcomed me and my family's intrusions into their work, looking after all of us in every way possible, from visas to dogsitting, from photocopying to befriending teenagers, from translating documents to making travel arrangements. In short, many of the burdens of our everyday life were lifted by others, and we were instead given the opportunity to take part in the programming that takes place here at the Seminar, programming that brings in world-famous names and unknown rising stars, all to work on the most important issues of our time—many of which had direct bearing on my work in this book. Countless large and small insights here would never have been realized without my unparalleled access to this intellectual richness and the liberty I gained to pursue it.

At my right and left hands in all my work of the past years have been my two ICMPA colleagues: my research director, Jad Melki, and my director of media education initiatives, Paul Mihailidis. No project that I dreamed up has been too big for them to contemplate throwing themselves into, no task has been too small or too menial for them to volunteer their help. They form the kind of a team that one dreams about working with: they are each academically rigorous, intellectually incisive, passionate about standards, curious about the next new thing, compassionately generous, emotionally mature, wittily irreverent. I would have been lost without them.

Family and friends have contributed home and hearth, welcoming me and feeding me on my research travels and on my repairing leases. My wonderful brother Scott, his amazing wife Daniela, his children Christine, Andrew, Ellen, and

Jonathan, have been one of those great resources for me—offering not only a place to hole up and raid the refrigerator (including all the dark chocolate hiding in the way way back) but a personal fan squad of supporters. My other family, Edgar James and Kathy Kinsella, Erin, Mara, also have allowed me a key to their home, free rein over their pantry, as well as a garden to get married in. Others in my extended family of friends, Bob Hauptman, Shanti Fry and Jeff Zinsmeyer, Victoria and Julia, Ann Beaudry, Scott Armstrong and Barbara Guss, Peter Herford, Elaine and Hirschel Abelson, have looked after me, championed me, encouraged me, questioned me, but never judged me. There are no better friends. And then there's my mother. My entire life my mother has been the motivation for all that I do. She taught me that there are no limits to what is possible. She taught me that women can do anything. She has modeled the greatest generosity of both spirit and resources of anyone I have ever known. I am, too often, a poor daughter, but she is the best mother in the world.

There are others who have made this year of writing literally possible. Sam, Duncan, and Clara Salyer—the three who put the light in their father's eye—have given their father so much and from a geographic distance that at times could be daunting. And Richard Davis, with tremendous consideration and at significant personal sacrifice, truly made this sojourn in Europe possible. I am grateful beyond measure to him.

But I really do everything in my life for three people: Walden, Sethly, and Stephen. This year they all bore with my upside-down days and my crabby ways, my shapeless T-shirts and sweats and my corralling of them to take on every chore. "Hey, who wants to ride a bike to the store?" "Hey, if you do the dishes you don't have to do the laundry—the other guy does!" Walden and Sethly, despite my haze of work, I noticed how you grew in all ways. You became more independent and responsible, but didn't lose your wonder at the changing light on the Untersberg or the fluffball ducklings in the stream. You learned how to hold a conversation with Sandra Day O'Connor and Kofi Annan, but remembered how to giggle and laugh (in German!) with the kids on the swim team. You came to care and learn about many of the world's most critical problems, but remained optimistic about the future and the role you can play in it. I am the luckiest of mothers and I love you.

And, finally, Stephen. There is too much to say, too much I feel, too much I owe. So let me just say thank you. Forever and always.

notes

Introduction

1   In fact there's an entire literature on how media tell "us" what to think—or actually tell us what to think about, beginning with the work on agenda-setting and framing by University of Texas at Austin Professor Maxwell McCombs and continuing through the work of George Washington University Professor Robert Entman. For a list of some of the most recent scholarship pertinent to media coverage of terrorism, see the following:

- McCombs, Maxwell. 2004. *Setting the Agenda: The Mass Media and Public Opinion*. New York: Polity.
- Entman, Robert M. 2003. *Projections of Power: Framing News, Public Opinion, and U.S. Foreign Policy*. Chicago: University Of Chicago Press.
- Graber, Doris A., Denis McQuail, and Pippa Norris. 2007. *The Politics of News: The News of Politics*. Washington, DC: CQ Press.
- Norris, Pippa, Marion R. Just, and Montague Kern, eds. 2003. *Framing Terrorism: The News Media, the Government and the Public*. New York: Routledge.
- Reese, Stephen D., Jr., Oscar H. Gandy, and August E. Grant. 2003. *Framing Public Life: Perspectives on Media and Our Understanding of the Social World*. Mahwah, NJ: Lawrence Erlbaum.
- Seib, Philip. 2006. *Beyond the Front Lines: How the News Media Cover a World Shaped by War*. New York: Palgrave Macmillan.
- Wolfsfeld, Gadi, 1997. *Media and Political Conflict: News from the Middle East*. Cambridge: Cambridge University Press.

I   What Is Terrorism?

1   Mann, James. 2004. *Rise of the Vulcans: The History of Bush's War Cabinet*. New York: Penguin, and Kakutani, Michiko. Standard Operating Procedure, by Philip Gourevitch and Errol Morris. *International Herald Tribune*. June 2, 2008. Available: http://www.iht.com/articles/2008/06/03/arts/booktue.php.

2   Transcript of remarks by President Bush on USS *Enterprise*, *U.S. Newswire*, Dec. 7, 2001.

3   Ibid.

4   See previous books by the author that detail the honeymoon period between the US media and US government officials (especially the President) in the aftermath of a crisis: Moeller, Susan. 1989. *Shooting War: Photography and the American Experience of Combat*. New York: Basic Books, and Moeller, Susan. 1999. *Compassion Fatigue: How the Media Sell Disease, Famine, War and Death*. New York: Routledge.

5   Walter Isaacson is the president and CEO of the Aspen Institute, a leadership institute focused on US foreign policy and national security. Isaacson was formerly the chairman and CEO of CNN and the managing editor of *Time* magazine.

6   Quoted in Kurtz, Howard. CNN chief orders "balance" in war news: reporters are told to remind viewers why U.S. is bombing. *Washington Post*, Oct. 31, 2001, p. C01.

7   Krugman, Paul. Fearing fear itself. *New York Times*, Oct. 29, 2007. Available: http://www.nytimes.com/2007/10/29/opinion/29krugman.html?th=&emc=th&pagewanted=print.

8   As the media studies that ICMPA conducted demonstrated, American and British media are not the only ones to take nationalistic or chauvinistic approaches to covering international news events. For an article that discusses this behavior in general see Moeller, Susan. "Regarding the pain of others": Media, bias and the coverage of international disasters. *Journal of International Affairs* (Spring/Summer 2006), pp. 173–96.

9   Are you ready? An in-depth guide to citizen preparedness. *Federal Emergency Management Agency*. Available: http://www.fema.gov/areyouready/terrorism.shtm. See also Brown, Michael. Letters to the Editor. *New York Times*, Feb. 14, 2003. Brown was the Undersecretary of Homeland Security for Emergency Preparedness and Response.

10 Chang, Kenneth, and Judith Miller. Threats and responses: Protective devices; duct tape and plastic sheeting can offer solace, if not real security. *New York Times*, Feb. 13, 2003. Available: http://query.nytimes.com/gst/fullpage.html?res=9E04E7DC143AF930A25751C0A9659C8B63&sec=health&spon=&pagewanted=print.

11 United Nationals General Assembly. Uniting against terrorism: Recommendations for a global counter-terrorism strategy. *Report of the Secretary-General*. 27 Apr. 2006. Available: www.unodc.org/pdf/terrorism/Global/en/3r60-825en.pdf. See also Mueller, John. 2007. *Overblown: How Politicians and The Terrorism Industry Inflate National Security Threats, and Why We Believe Them*. New York: Simon & Schuster.

12 *Are You Ready? An In-Depth Guide to Citizen Preparedness*. Federal Emergency Management Agency, p. 160.

13 *Are You Ready?* also discussed guidelines for Americans to protect themselves against technological and natural hazards, as well as against a possible NCB attack.

14 Full transcript of bin Laden's speech. *Aljazeera.net*. 2004. Available: http://english.aljazeera.net/English/archive/archive?ArchiveId=7403.

15 Sherwell, Philip. Bush takes a six-point lead after new bin Laden tape. *The Telegraph*, Oct. 30, 2004. Available: http://www.telegraph.co.uk/news/main.jhtml?xml=/news/2004/10/31/wus31.xml&sSheet=/news/2004/10/31/ixnewstop.html.

16 Suskind, Ron. 2006. *The One Percent Doctrine: Deep Inside America's Pursuit of its Enemies since 9/11*. New York: Simon & Schuster, pp. 335–6. In July 2004, Gary Trudeau's Sunday "Doonesbury" strip, had a series of images of a television. The bubbles of text coming from the TV read: "When George W. Bush first ran for president, he promised to be a uniter, not a divider. Three short years later, he's delivered! Today, Muslims

everywhere stand united in their anger toward America! By invading Iraq, Bush has created an incubator for a whole new generation of holy warriors! Moreover, by so carelessly squandering American's moral authority . . . He's done incalculable damage to her standing and interests around the world for years to come! May he be re-elected! God Willing! I'm Osama bin Laden, and I approve this message."

17 Steel, Ronald. Fight fire with fire. *New York Times*, July 25, 2004, Book Review, p. 13.

18 Leonard, Tom. BBC edits out the word "terrorist." *Telegraph*, July 12, 2005. Available: http://www.telegraph.co.uk/news/main.jhtml?xml=/news/2005/07/12/nbbc12.xml.

19 Trouble with the T-word? *BBC News* [database online]. Available: http://news.bbc.co.uk/newswatch/ifs/low/newsid_4680000/newsid_4680100/4680125.stm.

20 Gelfand, Lou. Newspaper careful in use of label "terrorist." *Minneapolis Star Tribune*, Feb. 3, 2002, p. 27A.

21 Ibid.

22 Getler, Michael. The language of terrorism. *Washington Post*, Sept. 21, 2003, p. B6.

23 Kurtz, Howard. Peter Jennings, in the news for what he didn't say. *Washington Post*, Sept. 24, 2001, p. C1.

24 Maguire, Sean. When does Reuters use the word terrorist or terrorism? Available: http://blogs.reuters.com/blog/2007/06/13/when-does-reuters-use-the-word-terrorist-or-terrorism/.

25 The CBC's guidelines can be found at: CBC defends ban on T word. Available: http://littlegreenfootballs.com/weblog/?entry=16716_CBC_Defends_Ban_on_T_Word&only. For ABC's guidelines, see Blair, Tim. ABC struggling for a defining statement in the war on terrorism. *Sydney Morning Herald*, Apr. 2, 2004. Available: http://www.smh.com.au/articles/2004/04/01/1080544628975.html?from=storyrhs.

26 Quoted in Conlan, Tara. BBC warns staff over "terrorism." *Guardian*, Dec. 16, 2005. Available: http://media.guardian.co.uk/bbc/story/0,,1668436,00.html.

27 Okrent, Daniel. The war of the words: A dispatch from the front lines. *New York Times*, Mar. 6, 2005. Available: http://www.nytimes.com/2005/03/06/weekinreview/06bott.html?ex=1267851600&en=631e2822853e2dc5&ei=5090&partner=rssuserland.

28 Lewis Carroll, *Through the Looking Glass*, 1871.

29 National Counterterrorism Center. 2008 Counterterrorism Calendar. Available: http://www.nctc.gov/site/index.html. A downloadable, print version is available at: http://www.nctc.gov/docs/ct_calendar_2007.pdf.

30 Absent a shared legal definition, "the term terrorism is widely misused," noted counter-terrorism expert Neil Livingstone. "It is utilized in its generic sense as a form of short-hand by governments and the media, and is applied to a variety of acts and occurrences." See Livingstone, Neil. 1982. *The War against Terrorism*. Lexington, MA: Lexington Books, p. 4.

31 Barr, Cameron W. In Mideast, one weapon of choice is a loaded word. *Christian Science Monitor*, July 31, 2001, p. 1.

32 Schulz, William. Security is a human right, too. *New York Times Magazine*, Apr. 18, 2004, p. 20. According to the website of the NCTC, US law, (Title 22 of the United States Code, Section 2656f(d)), defines "terrorism" as "Premeditated, politically motivated violence perpetrated against noncombatant targets by sub-national groups or clandestine agents, usually intended to influence an audience."

33 International Bar Association. 2003. *International Terrorism: Legal Challenges and Responses*. Ardsley, NY: Transnational Publishers, p. 2.

34 Schulz. Security is a human right too. See also Norris, Just, and Kern, eds. *Framing Terrorism*. They identify these situations as "one-sided" and "two-sided" conflicts. One-sided conflicts are those in which there is a broad consensus among the government, the public, and journalists about whether an act is terrorism; two-sided conflicts are those in which opinions about whether an act is terrorism is deeply divided. See especially part I.

35 The war on terrorism: Is there an alternative? *London Review of Books*, May 15, 2002. Available: http://www.lrb.co.uk/v00/n01/mult02_.html.

36 For the most comprehensive recent discussion of the definition of terrorism, see especially pp. 4–20 in Richardson, Louise. 2006. *What Terrorists Want: Understanding the Enemy, Containing the Threat*. New York: Random House.

37 Until September 11, the single deadliest terrorist attack was the 1985 crash of an Air India flight off the coast of Ireland, which killed 329. What 9/11 did was add a factor of almost 10 to that death toll, giving rise to a new term "catastrophic terrorism." But while much of the fear-mongering about terrorism has referred to scenarios of mass casualties in the wake of the detonation of a weapon of mass destruction, history suggests that there is a valuable distinction between casualty numbers and significance. A number of events in the recent past—the anthrax cases and the first bombing of the World Trade Center, for example—suggest that there doesn't have to be a high death toll for an event to have a major impact on both policy and the American psyche. See Quillen, Chris. A historical analysis of mass casualty bombers. *Studies in Conflict and Terrorism*, 25 (2002), pp. 279–92.

38 Actually, an earlier terrorism message sent to the entire world was the fatwah against Salman Rushdie. As NPR explained: "There was a flap over the word [terrorism] in 1989 when *The New York Times* editor A. M. Rosenthal attacked Christopher Hitchens for refusing to describe the fatwah against Salman Rushdie as terrorism. Hitchens had a good point, though. The fatwah may have been repugnant, but it was far from an act of indiscriminate violence; more like state-sponsored contract killing" (Bogaev, Barbara, and Geoff Nunberg. History of the term "terrorism." *Fresh Air*, NPR, Oct. 5, 2001). Ironically, the post-9/11 media missed much of the point of the new terrorism in their explanations of its origins. It wasn't, for example, that there was a fatwah against Salman Rushdie that mattered so much—there have often been death threats made against outspoken members of individual communities. What mattered, what was new and scary, was that the fatwah had been publicized to a global audience. Everyone in the world knew that there was a fatwah—in fact, everyone learned what a fatwah was—with the effect being that Rushdie had been put under a kind of global house arrest.

39 When terrorism is considered to be an international crime, the perpetrator can be tried under the principle of universal jurisdiction. A number of the international treaties on terrorism provide for universal jurisdiction. Cassese, Antonio. 2001. *International Law*. Oxford: Oxford University Press, p. 246.

40 See Laqueur, Walter. Postmodern terrorism. *Foreign Affairs* (Sept./Oct. 1996), and Purdum, Todd. What do you mean, "terrorist?" *New York Times*, Apr. 7, 2002, section 4, p. 1. Laqueur also observed that terror "is not an ideology or a political doctrine,

but rather a method—the substate application of violence or the threat of violence to sow panic and bring about political change." Laqueur, Walter. 2001. Left, Right and Beyond: The Changing Face of Terror. In J. Hoges and G. Rose, eds. *How Did This Happen? Terrorism and the New War.* New York: Council on Foreign Relations, pp. 71–82.

41　Maddocks, Melvin. "Terrorist"—A bomb-thrower of a word. *Christian Science Monitor*, Jan. 17, 1980, Opinion and Commentary, p. 23.

42　Jenkins, Brian Michael. Where I draw the line. *Christian Science Monitor*, May 1, 2006. Available: http://www.csmonitor.com/specials/terrorism/lite/expert.html.

43　The war on terrorism: Is there an alternative?

44　Auchmutey, Jim. The power of language. *Atlanta Journal and Constitution*, Oct. 21, 2001, p. 1D.

45　Furstenberg, François. Bush's dangerous liaisons. *New York Times*, Oct. 28, 2007. Available: http://www.nytimes.com/2007/10/28/opinion/28furstenberg.html?ei=5087&em=&en=62eaa390a911d2d4&ex=1193803200&pagewanted=print.

46　Bogaev, Barbara, and Geoff Nunberg. History of the term "terrorism." *Fresh Air*, NPR, Oct. 5, 2001.

47　Rice, Condoleezza. Dr. Rice addresses war on terror. Available: http://www.whitehouse.gov/news/releases/2004/08/print/20040819-5.html.

48　CNN.com. You are either with us or against us. Available: http://archives.cnn.com/2001/US/11/06/gen.attack.on.terror/.

49　The White House. Available: http://www.whitehouse.gov/.

50　For more on this point, see Mohamedou, Mohammad-Mahmoud O. Non-linearity of engagement: Transnational armed groups, international law, and the conflict between al Qaeda and the United States. Available: http://www.hpcr.org/pdfs/Non-Linearity_of_Engagement.pdf, pp. 17, 19.

51　Anderson, Sean, and Stephen Sloan. 2002. *Historical Dictionary of Terrorism.* London: Scarecrow Press, p. 1.

52　Jenkins, in Whittaker, D. J., ed. 2001. *The Terrorism Reader.* London: Routledge, p. 8.

53　Perez-Rivas, Manuel. Bush vows to rid the world of "evil-doers." Available: http://archives.cnn.com/2001/US/09/16/gen.bush.terrorism/.

54　Stevenson, Richard. Bush, in Britain, urges Europeans to fight terror. *New York Times*, Nov. 20, 2003, p. A1.

55　The war on terrorism: Is there an alternative?

56　President discusses global war on terror. Sept. 5, 2006. Available: http://www.whitehouse.gov/news/releases/2006/09/20060905-4.html. The insert "[Caliphate]" appears in the transcript released on the White House website. It is not an addition of the author.

57　Norman Podhoretz, the editor of *Commentary*, and a number of other neoconservatives have taken President Bush's name-calling one step farther with their invented word: "Islamofascism," noting that the United States has been fighting "Islamofascist ideology" since 9/11. Critics such as Paul Krugman have observed that "there isn't actually any such thing as Islamofascism—it's not an ideology; it's a figment of the neocon imagination. The term came into vogue only because it was a way for Iraq hawks to gloss over the awkward transition from pursuing Osama bin Laden, who attacked America, to Saddam Hussein, who didn't." See Krugman. Fearing fear itself.

58   Richardson. *What Terrorists Want*, p. 193.
59   The war on terrorism: Is there an alternative?
60   Simpson, Cam. Terror pipeline flows to Pakistan. *Chicago Tribune*, Aug. 12, 2006.
61   Mueller, John. 2007. *Overblown: How Politicians and the Terrorism Industry Inflate National Security Threats, and Why We Believe Them*. New York: Simon & Schuster.
62   O'Brien, Conor Cruise. 1983. Terrorism Under Democratic Conditions: The Case of the IRA. In Martha Crenshaw, ed. *Terrorism, Legitimacy, and Power: The Consequences of Political Violence*. Middletown, CT: Wesleyan Press, pp. 91–104.
63   Richardson. *What Terrorists Want*, p. 193.
64   Just consider the morass of the Israeli—Palestinian debate on the subject. Israeli officials have cited Palestinian "terrorism" as their rationale for policies which have included helicopter missile attacks against Palestinian buildings, "targeted assassinations," closures of Palestinian towns and villages and razing of the homes of militants. And Hamas and Islamic Jihad spokespeople have claimed that Israeli "state terror" has forced them into such strategies as suicide bombings and other attacks on Israeli soldiers and civilians. Both sides have emphasized context. Both sides have asserted that their actions are retaliatory; that they are not the perpetrators, but instead the victims. Both sides have also contested who are civilians—in other words who are legitimate targets of attacks: Israel argues that the settlers are civilians, while many Palestinian militants consider the settlers who have built homes on land seized in the 1967 war to be combatants, because they are the leading edge of Israeli occupation of the land and have been protected by the Israeli military. "One side invokes the murder of Israeli innocents by human bombs," wrote *New York Times* reporter Serge Schmemann, "the other speaks of the injustices suffered by the Palestinians. . . . This mingling of acts of murder with a desire for freedom has enabled the leaders on both sides to befuddle their people and their supporters, portraying suicide bombers as martyrs in a just struggle of national liberation, or casting the destruction of the institutions and symbols of Palestinian statehood as a war on terrorism." Schmemann, Serge. Beyond reason: The method of this madness. *New York Times*, Apr. 7, 2002.
65   Understanding terrorism: A *Harvard Magazine* roundtable. *Harvard Magazine* (Jan.–Feb. 2002), p. 38.
66   Burke, Jason. "Islamism" has no place in terror's lexicon. *Observer*, Aug. 26, 2007. Available: http://www.guardian.co.uk/alqaida/story/0,,2156384,00.html.
67   Video clip of President George W. Bush's speech used on CNN's show "Anderson Cooper 360 degrees," 7:00 pm. August 6, 2004. Video clip also transcribed by CNN, including transcription of the word "conscious" and the addition of the parenthetical "(sic)." The White House website transcribes the word as "conscience" See President's remarks to the Unity Journalists of Color Convention. August 6, 2004. Available: http://www.whitehouse.gov/news/releases/2004/08/20040806-1.html.
68   Milbank, Dana. Reprising a war with words. *Washington Post*, Aug. 17, 2004, p. A13.
69   Inside the administration the phrase "Global War On Terror," or GWOT, had been used to designate US military operations against terrorism. In May 2005, the acronym GWOT was succeeded by "The Global Struggle Against Violent Extremism," or GSAVE. GSAVE was dropped in its turn for the phrase "the Long War," first applied to the "War on Terror" in 2004 by Gen. John P. Abizaid, then the commander of the United States

Central Command (CENTCOM) for the Middle East, the Horn of Africa, and South Asia, and introduced as a new designation by President Bush in his 2006 State of the Union speech. "Our own generation is in a long war against a determined enemy." See Graham, Bradley, and Josh White. Abizaid credited with popularizing the term "long war." *Washington Post*, Feb. 3, 2006. Available: http://www.washingtonpost.com/wp-dyn/content/article/2006/02/02/AR2006020202242.html.

70 Said George Packer in the *New Yorker*: "In Iraq, America has run up against the limits of war in an ideological contest. The Administration is right to reconsider its strategy, starting with the language." See his article, Name calling. *New Yorker*, Aug. 8, 2005, p. 34.

71 Packer, George. Knowing the enemy: Can social scientists redefine the "war on terror?" *New Yorker*, Dec. 18, 2006, p. 63.

72 Slaughter, Anne-Marie. A defining moment in the parsing of war. *Washington Post*, Sept. 16, 2001, Outlook, p. B04.

73 Speech by Lord (Peter) Goldsmith, Salzburg Global Seminar, Austria, Sept. 2007.

74 Roth, Kenneth. The law of war in the war on terror. *Foreign Affairs* (Jan./Feb. 2004), p. 2.

75 Byford, Grenville. The wrong war. *Foreign Affairs* (July/Aug. 2002), 34–43.

76 The Foreign Office explained that the government wanted to "avoid reinforcing and giving succour to the terrorists' narrative by using language that, taken out of context, could be counter-productive." See Burke, Jason. Britain stops talk of "war on terror." *Observer*, Dec. 10, 2006. Available: http://observer.guardian.co.uk/politics/story/0,,1968668,00.html.

77 Understanding terrorism: A *Harvard Magazine* roundtable, p. 41.

78 Burke. Britain stops talk of "war on terror."

79 Hall, Macer. Brown: Don't say terrorists are Muslims. *Daily Express*, July 3, 2007. Available: http://www.express.co.uk/posts/view/12172/Brown:-Don.

80 Richardson. *What Terrorists Want*, p. 217.

81 Rieff, David. Brown drops "war on terror," redefining the fight. *International Herald Tribune*, July 22, 2007.

82 Associated Press. "Jihadist" booted from government lexicon. Apr. 24, 2008.

83 Moran, Terry. *ABC Nightline*, Feb. 22, 2006.

84 Barstow, David. Behind analysts, the Pentagon's hidden hand. *New York Times*, Apr. 20, 2008. Available: http://www.nytimes.com/2008/04/20/washington/20generals.html.

85 Burke. Britain stops talk of "war on terror."

86 Pincus, Walter, and Dan Eggen. 325,000 names on terrorism list. *Washington Post*, Feb. 15, 2006. Available: http://www.washingtonpost.com/wp-dyn/content/article/2006/02/14/AR2006021402125_pf.html.

87 Vice President's remarks at a Bush–Cheney '04 rally, Aug. 14, 2004. Available: http://www.whitehouse.gov/news/releases/2004/08/20040814-3.html. Earlier that month on the campaign trail in Iowa, President Bush also validated his doctrine of pre-emption: "We have more to do to protect us. Enemies who hate us are still plotting to harm us. Those who claim that America's war on terror is to blame for terror threats against the United States have a fundamental misunderstanding of the nature

of the enemy." See President's remarks in Davenport, Iowa, Aug. 4, 2004. Available: http://www.whitehouse.gov/news/releases/2004/08/20040804-5.html.

88   Marquis, Christopher. Rumsfeld warns against appeasement of terrorists. *New York Times*, June 5, 2004, p. A3.

89   President discusses global war on terror. Sept. 5, 2006. Available: http://www.whitehouse.gov/news/releases/2006/09/20060905-4.html.

90   Bush speaks to nation aboard warship. *United Press International*, May 2, 2003.

91   Ridge's comments, of course, ignored the fact that "biological and chemical weapons are not weapons of mass destruction," as the *Bulletin of the Atomic Scientists* defines them. "Terrorist weapons," yes, but their use "may cause hundreds, but probably not thousands, of deaths." As the *Bulletin* notes, "Subsuming these three types of weapons under the rubric of 'weapons of mass destruction' approaches the disingenuous." See Morrison, Philip, and Kosta Tsipis. Rightful names. *Bulletin of the Atomic Scientists* (May–June 2003), p. 77. See also Langley, Alicia. U.S. terror alert raised to second highest level; Intelligence assessments indicate al-Qaida in operational period. State Department, May 20, 2003. Available: http://www.globalsecurity.org/security/library/news/2003/05/sec-030520-usia02.htm.

92   Understanding terrorism: A *Harvard Magazine* roundtable, pp. 41, 103. Others have made similar observations. Terrorism "is a method for achieving a goal," agreed Professor Ronald Steel. "That goal is usually some kind of political change that is thwarted by other means. Terrorism is what the weak use to increase their bargaining power against the strong." (Steel, Ronald. 2004. Fight fire with fire. *New York Times*, July 25, 2004, p. 13.)

93   Paper chase. *Jurist: Legal News and Research*. Sept. 23, 2004. Available: http://jurist.law.pitt.edu/paperchase/2003_09_23_indexarch.php.

94   The terrorism link that wasn't. *New York Times*, Sept. 19, 2003, p. A26.

95   DeYoung, Karen. Powell says U.S. can balance human rights, war on terror. *Washington Post*, Aug. 2, 2002, p. A20.

96   Cushman, Jr., John. War's hidden cost. *New York Times*, Dec. 9, 2001, Week in Review, p. 14.

97   Russell, Alec. As Bush admits making mistakes over Iraq, Blair offers a new world vision. *Telegraph*, May 27, 2006. Available: http://www.telegraph.co.uk/news/main.jhtml?xml=/news/2006/05/27/wblair27.xml&sSheet=/news/2006/05/27/ixuknews.html.

II   How Is Terrorism Covered?

1   A reprise of this argument would be made in the run-up to the war in Iraq. As *New York Times* reporter David Barstow reported in his front-page story on the Pentagon's use of military analysts to sell that conflict to Americans, many of the 75 retired officers recruited as "message force multipliers" "shared with Mr. Bush's national security team a belief that pessimistic war coverage broke the nation's will to win in Vietnam, and there was a mutual resolve not to let that happen with this war." Barstow, David. Behind analysts, the Pentagon's hidden hand. *New York Times*, Apr. 20, 2008. Available: http://www.nytimes.com/2008/04/20/washington/20generals.html.

2   Herring, George. 2000. Preparing not to refight the last war: The impact of the Vietnam War on the U.S. military. In Charles E. Neu, ed. *After Vietnam: Legacies of a Lost War.* Baltimore: Johns Hopkins University Press. Available: http://www.hnet.org/reviews/showrev.cgi?path=12780982092531.

    Although many who lived through the 1960s and 1970s recollect vivid television images of blood and gore, the reality is that only a fraction of the Vietnam War reports on the nightly news showed violence and even fewer showed images of the dead or wounded. One study, cited by William Hammond of the US Army Center of Military History, showed that only 76 of more than 2,300 television reports about Vietnam over a five-year period depicted heavy fighting or casualties. Combat footage often was little more than puffs of smoke in the distance, and the worst images were mostly fleeting and not terribly graphic. "Only during the 1968 Tet and 1972 Spring offensives," noted author Daniel Hallin, "when the war came into urban areas, did its suffering and destruction appear with any regularity on TV." Hammond quoted in Sharkey, Jacqueline. Airing graphic footage. *American Journalism Review*, May 2003, p. 22. See also Hallin, Daniel C. 1986. *The "Uncensored War": The Media And Vietnam.* New York: Oxford University Press, and also http://www.museum.tv/archives/etv/V/htmlV/vietnamonte/vietnamonte.htm.

    For other background on the restraints on the American press during wartime, see Moeller, Susan. 1989. *Shooting War: Photography and the American Experience of Combat.* New York: Basic Books.

3   On the other hand, without independent media coverage, we all, the citizens of the world, would have had even less access to the truth of what happened during and after the "Great War" and the Grenada invasion. If the reporting of the professional journalists was too little and too late in many instances, it was far, far better than no news at all—or only news fed to the public by the states that were involved.

4   Britain under threat. *Economist*. Available: http://www.economist.com/world/britain/displaystory.cfm?story_id=9429130.

5   Koppel, Ted. And now, a word for our demographic. *New York Times*, Jan. 29, 2006, section 4, p. 16.

6   Interview with Walter Mossberg, 30 July 1993.

7   Myre, Greg, and Steven Erlanger. Clashes spread to Lebanon as Hezbollah raids Israel. July 12, 2006. Available: http://www.iht.com/articles/2006/07/13/africa/web.0712mideast.php.

8   CNN, July 11, 2006.

9   For four years following the invasion in early 2003, Iraq consistently led the news. "The world's obsession with Iraq has pushed to the margins many other scenes of mass violence," agreed Gareth Evans, the head of the Brussels-based International Crisis Group think tank. (Day, Julia. How the tsunami hogged the headlines. *Guardian Unlimited*, Mar. 11, 2005.) "One television news producer we met in the U.S. summed up the situation since spring 2003 this way: 'Look, we've got three foreign news priorities these days: Iraq, Iraq, Iraq' . . . And Iraq is not simply an American obsession. We've heard a similar refrain from news producers and newspaper editors again and again throughout Europe and elsewhere." (Gidley, Ruth. Brutal conflicts get scant

attention; Three "forgotten emergencies" take a back seat to Iraq and the tsunami coverage by media. *Houston Chronicle*, Mar. 10, 2005, p. A13.)

10 CNN, Nov. 10, 2005.

11 That presumes, of course, that one accepts the argument that WMD should be considered part of the conversation and debates about terrorist tactics. See Moeller, Susan. *Media Coverage of Weapons of Mass Destruction*. Center for International and Security Studies at Maryland (CISSM), 2004.

12 Please see the Appendix at the end of this book for a listing of those incidents.

13 In his speeches, President Bush detailed the terrorist agenda: "The enemy we face is brutal and determined. The terrorists have an ideology. They share a hateful vision that rejects tolerance and crushes all dissent. They seek a world where women are oppressed, where children are indoctrinated, and those who reject their ideology of violence and extremism are threatened and often murdered. The terrorists have aims. They seek to impose their heartless ideology of totalitarian control throughout the Middle East. They seek to arm themselves with weapons of mass murder. Their stated goal is to overthrow moderate governments, take control of countries, and then use them as safe havens to launch attacks against Americans and other free nations." President addresses American legion, discusses global war on terror. Feb. 24, 2006. Available: http://www.whitehouse.gov/news/releases/2006/02/20060224.html.

14 President discusses global war on terror at Kansas State University. Jan. 23, 2006. Available: http://www.whitehouse.gov/news/releases/2006/01/20060123-4.html.

15 President Bush discusses global war on terror. Apr. 10, 2006. Available: http://www.whitehouse.gov/news/releases/2006/04/20060410-1.html.

16 President discusses freedom and democracy in Iraq. Mar. 13, 2006. Available: http://www.whitehouse.gov/news/releases/2006/03/20060313-3.html.

17 President Bush and NATO Secretary General deliver remarks in Oval Office. Oct. 27, 2006. Available: http://www.whitehouse.gov/news/releases/2006/10/20061027.html.

18 The case for democracy. *Washington Post*, Mar. 5, 2006. Available: http://www.washingtonpost.com/wp-dyn/content/article/2006/03/04/AR2006030400933.html.

19 Strupp, Joe. PEJ survey: Journalists in Iraq defend coverage—dangers continue despite "surge." *Editor and Publisher*, Nov. 27, 2007. Available: http://www.editorandpublisher.com/eandp/news/article_display.jsp?vnu_content_id=1003678206.

20 Sciolino, Elaine. 10 bombs shatter trains in Madrid, killing 192. *New York Times*, Mar. 12, 2005, p. A1.

21 A dark day from which we will emerge stronger. *Daily Telegraph*, July 8, 2005, p. 23.

22 Suicide bomber kills 10 in Baghdad. NBC Nightly News, Oct. 9, 2003.

23 Bombing at Shiite mosque kills 36. *Los Angeles Times*, Oct. 6, 2005.

24 Carroll, Jill. Violence threatens Iraqi coalition. *Christian Science Monitor*, Jan. 6, 2006, p. 7.

25 *BBC World* (video), Apr. 14, 2007.

26 "Bombs detonated in three crowded subway trains and on a double-decker bus during the morning rush hour here Thursday, killing at least 37 people and injuring about 700 others in the deadliest terrorist attack carried out on British soil." Frankel,

Glenn. Bombers strike London at rush hour; at least 37 killed on trains, bus. *Washington Post*, July 8, 2005, p. A01.

27   "The available facts—the British venue, the soft targets with economic importance, the timing during the Group of Eight summit in Scotland and the relatively simple operational techniques—conformed almost precisely to the methods of what specialists describe as an evolving al Qaeda movement." Coll, Steve, and Susan B. Glasser. Attacks bear earmarks of evolving al-Qaeda: targets, timing both familiar. *Washington Post*, July 8, 2005, p. A01.

28   "Reverberations from the London bombings were felt almost immediately among transit systems in Washington and across the country yesterday as officials tried to fortify railroads, buses and trolleys that experts agree are vulnerable to attack by their very nature." Layton, Lyndsey, and Steven Ginsberg. Patrols on mass transit intensified but scattered. *Washington Post*, July 8, 2005, p. A01.

29   "The twisted, smoking wreckage of a red double-decker bus. The sidewalks slick with blood and body parts. Dozens of wounded people screaming in agony or stunned into silence." Frankel, Glenn, and Ellen Knickmeyer. "In my mind was: Am I dreaming? It was surreal." Survivors and rescuers recall day of dread. *Washington Post*, July 8, 2005, p. A01.

30   International crises—earthquakes and hurricanes, insurrections, famine—also have their virtual templates for reporting. In the case of a famine, for example, first, there will be no coverage until people are literally starving to death. Editors want solid, Ethiopian-style hunger stories. In the case of natural disasters, there is the need to regard the disaster as "a human tragedy of biblical proportions," and to characterize the event with phrases such as "unprecedented" and "single worst crisis in the world." If it's not the worst of its kind—at the very least this year or this season—then it doesn't get coverage.

31   Your world today. CNN, June 29, 2007.

32   Death toll from mosque attack rises to 81. CNN, Apr. 8, 2006.

33   Al-Ansary, Khalid, and Ali Adeeb. Most tribes in Anbar agree to unite against insurgents. *New York Times*, Sept. 18, 2006, p. A12.

34   Barstow. Behind analysts, the Pentagon's hidden hand.

35   Bumiller, Elisabeth. Threats and responses: The White House; Bush ties bombing at Bali nightclub to Qaeda network. *New York Times*, Oct. 15, 2002. Available: http://query.nytimes.com/gst/fullpage.html?res=9B01E5DE1F3AF936A25753C1A9649C8B63.

36   Katz, Yaakov, and JPost Staff. PM: Time for UN to sanction Iran. *Jerusalem Post*, Dec. 9, 2006. Available: http://www.jpost.com/servlet/Satellite?cid=1164881855295&pagename=JPost%2FJPArticle%2FShowFull.

37   Musharraf vows to up terror fight after attack. *Associated Press*, Sept. 14, 2007. Available: http://www.msnbc.msn.com/id/20770954/.

38   *Lou Dobbs Tonight*. CNN, Nov. 9, 2005.

39   *Los Angeles Times*, May 15, 2003.

40   Brook, Stephen. Financial Times wins newspaper of the year. *Guardian*, Apr. 9, 2008. Available: http://www.guardian.co.uk/media/2008/apr/09/pressandpublishing.

41   Bokhari, Farhan. Pakistan aims for nuclear acceptance. *Financial Times*, Aug. 27, 2008. Available: http://www.ft.com/cms/s/0/1ef5db2a-7456-11dd-bc91-0000779fd18c.html.

42 Editorial. The Iranian challenge. *Washington Post*, May 29, 2003, p. A24.

43 See Moeller. *Media Coverage of Weapons of Mass Destruction*. That study noted of US media coverage: "Conflating nuclear, chemical, and biological weapons amorphously together as 'weapons of mass destruction' often was a result of journalists keying off speeches and statements by President Bush, such as the following one about Iraq, delivered on Oct. 2, 2002, and transcribed in the New York Times:

> It [Iraq] has developed weapons of mass death. It has used them against innocent men, women and children.
> We know the designs of the Iraqi regime. In defiance of pledges to the U.N. it has stockpiled biological and chemical weapons. It is rebuilding the facilities used to make those weapons. U.N. inspectors believe that Iraq could have produced enough biological and chemical agent to kill millions of people. The regime has the scientists and facilities to build nuclear weapons and is seeking the materials needed to do so. (10/3/02)

The Bush administration's deliberate aggregating of a plethora of weapons systems and agents as well as of the nuclear interests of a wide range of nations tempted journalists to follow suit—to discuss widely divergent WMD issues in a single story, without taking sufficient care to distinguish one from another."

The study further noted: "Even if WMD terms were used distinctively and consistently, similar weapons systems were not always characterized similarly. Saddam's various purported WMD, for example, were reflexively characterized as offensive weapons, as have been North Korea's, while US and Israeli nuclear weapons systems have historically been characterized as 'deterrents.' "

44 Allen, Mike. Bush: "We found" banned weapons; President cites trailers in Iraq as proof. *Washington Post*, May 31, 2003, p. A1.

45 The events of that day not only received 24/7 coverage for days that followed, but the attacks continue to resonate powerfully years later, and not just for those who were physically present or personally affected. Rudy Giuliani, mayor of New York at 9/11, and the leading Republican candidate for the 2008 presidential nomination, so tied his campaign to his leadership in the weeks that followed the attack, that it became an issue for commentators—as *New York Times* columnist Gail Collins wrote in the fall of 2007, "Giuliani has finally figured out that he cannot simply keep muttering '9/11 . . . 9/11 . . . 9/11' until [the primaries in] February." See Collins, Gail. Rudy finds a new topic. *New York Times*, Oct. 6, 2007. Available: http://www.nytimes.com/2007/10/06/opinion/06collins.html?th&emc=th.

46 Barringer, Felicity. Pulitzers focus on Sept. 11, and the *Times* wins 7. *New York Times*, Apr. 9, 2002. Available: http://query.nytimes.com/gst/fullpage.html?res=9F04E4D6133DF93AA35757C0A9649C8B63.

47 Scott, Janny. A nation challenged: The portraits; closing a scrapbook full of life and sorrow. *New York Times*, Dec. 31, 2001. Available: http://query.nytimes.com/gst/fullpage.html?res=9505E7DA1730F932A05751C1A9679C8B63.

48 To hear *New York Times* editor Howell Raines explain the "Portraits of Grief" series, see this online video clip: http://www.nytimes.com/packages/html/national/portraits/20011207raines-video.html.

49   Leon Smith Jr.: Big-hearted driver. *New York Times.* Mar. 9, 2003. Available: http://www.nytimes.com/2003/03/09/national/portraits/POG-09SMITH.html?ex= 1192161600&en=8d0016af9227324b&ei=5070.

50   Aleksandr Ivantsov: "He was my everything." *New York Times.* Mar. 9, 2003. Available: http://www.nytimes.com/2003/03/09/national/portraits/POG-09IVANSTOF.html?ex= 1192161600&en=b6eade2b6af19334&ei=5070.

51   Scott. A nation challenged.

52   Dart Center for Journalism and Trauma. Best practices in trauma reporting: Narrative styles. Available: http://www.dartcenter.org/dartaward/best_practices/10.html.

53   Photo by Van Kesteren, Geert. *Newsweek,* Sept. 1, 2003, p. 21.

54   Both stories were aired on May 9, 2001.

55   Wilkinson, Tracy. Celebration of an escape turned into a death trap. *Los Angeles Times,* Mar. 29, 2002, p. A10.

56   Tremlett, Giles. Terror in Madrid. Mourning: Commuter town hit hardest where everyone knew a victim. *Guardian,* Mar. 13, 2004, p. 5.

57   Salisbury, Harrison. 1967. *Behind the Lines—Hanoi.* New York: Harper & Row, p. 195.

58   Two suicide bombings kill 40 in Baghdad. *Washington Post,* Nov. 10, 2005.

59   Richter, Paul. Door opened for new era of nuclear arms. *Los Angeles Times,* May 10, 2003.

60   Dewar, Helen. GOP blocks Democrats' effort to halt nuclear arms studies. *Washington Post.* May 22, 2003, p. A4, and Dewar, Helen. Nuclear weapons development tied to Hill approval. *Washington Post.* May 22, 2003, p. A5.

61   For example, many officials speak as if it would be possible to develop a nuclear weapon that can simultaneously destroy deeper targets than current capabilities permit *and* cause little or no collateral damage such as widespread radioactive fallout—and the media have often reported these claims as if such a weapon could actually be developed. In fact, increasing the yield and decreasing the collateral damage are two very different objectives: it would take a high-yield (i.e., more than 100 kt) nuclear weapon to destroy a hardened, deeply buried underground bunker—but a weapon exceeding 5 kt in yield would cause extensive collateral damage.

62   Walsh, Declan. "I don't think a human being can do this to someone." *Guardian,* Oct. 20, 2007. Available: http://www.guardian.co.uk/pakistan/Story/0,,2195610,00.html.

63   *The NewsHour with Jim Lehrer.* Nov. 10, 2005.

64   *The Situation Room.* CNN, Nov. 10, 2005, 3 p.m. See also *Rita Cosby Live.* MSNBC, Nov. 9, 2005, 9 p.m.

65   Butcher, Tim. Suicide bombers hit hotels in Jordan's capital. *Daily Telegraph,* Nov. 10, 2005, p. 16.

66   Burns, John. Gunmen kill 16 Christians in church in Pakistan. *New York Times,* Oct. 29, 2001, p. A1.

67   Struck, Doug. A survivor recounts horrors of N. Korea's prison camps; rebuke by U.N. Rights Commission reflects tougher U.S. stance. *Washington Post,* May 3, 2003, p. A20.

68   Editorial. Disinterring the truth. *Washington Post,* May 16, 2003, p. A28.

69   It isn't only in articles related to terrorism that such an approach is taken. A *New York Times* story looking at civilian casualties of the Iraq conflict listed a few of

those killed in the wartime bombing of "Chemical Ali's" neighborhood. 10 people were mentioned:

1   a girl in a "pink dress, Zeena Akram, 12."
2   "Mustafa Akram, 13, who loved to read books."
3   "Zain El Abideen Akram, 18, who so badly wanted to be a doctor like his father that when he was only 13 he would pester visitors by insisting on taking their blood pressure."
4   "Zainab Akram, 19, who loved fashion."
5   "Hassan Iyad, 10, who had begged his father to let him come stay at Grandpa's house."
6   "Ammar Muhammad was not yet 2 when his grandfather pulled him from the rubble and tried to give him mouth-to-mouth resuscitation, but his mouth was full of dust and he died."
7   "Noor elhuda Saad, an infant dressed up in a pink jumper."
8   "Wissam Abed, 40 . . . who was to be married in June."
9   "Dr. Ihab Abed, 34, who . . . came to her father's house because she was frightened."
10 "Khairiah Mahmoud was the mother of 10 and the grandmother of many more."

Five of the 10 mentioned were children, two more were just out of childhood at ages 18 and 19, one was described as a mother and grandmother, one as a medical doctor and a daughter, and the only adult man older than 18 to be mentioned was identified as going to be married in June. Santora, Marc. For family that lost 10 to allied bomb, only memories and grief remain. *New York Times*, May 11, 2003, section 1, p. 14.

70   Special sorrow for the young: Israelis lament number of children killed, hurt in bus bombing. *Washington Post*, Aug. 21, 2003; cover photo, *USA Today*, July 24, 2002.
71   Moeller, Susan. "Regarding the pain of others": Media, bias and the coverage of international disasters. *Journal of International Affairs* (Spring/Summer 2006), pp. 173–96.
72   Bali bomb victims recalled on 5th anniversary. Reuters. Oct. 12, 2007. Available: http://www.msnbc.msn.com/id/21261851/; Iraq bomber kills child and wounds 13 in playground. Reuters. Oct. 12, 2007. Available: http://www.msnbc.msn.com/id/21261815/.
73   The entire story was: "Today, a bomb hidden among toys blew up at a playground in northern Iraq. Two children were killed, 17 wounded." *Today*. NBC News, Oct. 12, 2007, 7 a.m.
74   Suicide bombings become daily occurrence in Iraq. CBS Evening News, Oct. 28, 2003; Series of bombings in Iraq kill at least 40 people. NBC *Today Show*, Oct. 29, 2003; Violence continues in Iraq despite daytime curfew. NBC Nightly News, Feb. 26, 2006.
75   ABC's unheralded Gibson emerges on top. *Washington Post*. May 17, 2007, p. C7.
76   There is an exception to that rule, however: when a suicide bombing is more than one of the all-too-common everyday variety. One example: the August 29, 2003, car bombing in Najaf. News outlets reported 95 dead immediately. That number rose to over 125. But in addition Ayatollah Muhammad Bakr al-Hakim was assassinated in the blast. Any time 95 or 125 people died in a car bombing—even in Iraq—it's going

to make the news. But the fact that the Ayatollah died kept the incident in the news and made it a Big Story. As a *New York Times* profile of him said:

> Ayatollah Hakim's death eliminated one of the few leaders of any stature who counseled against fighting the Americans, for now. While a critic of what he saw as the Americans' bungling administration, he helped temper those seeking to wage a holy war against them. . . . The alternative is readily apparent. Moktada al-Sadr, also the offspring of illustrious ayatollahs, has been a virulent critic of the American presence and stopped just short of calling for a holy war to create an Islamic state. His supporters are hoping to capitalize on the loss of his main counterweight to widen his appeal.

See Macfarquhar, Neil. After the war: A stilled voice; After cleric's assassination, fears for the future. *New York Times.* Sept. 2, 2003. Available: http://query.nytimes.com/gst/fullpage.html?res=9C07E0D71538F931A3575AC0A9659C8B63&n=Top%2fReference%2fTimes%20Topics%2fPeople%2fH%2fHakim%2c%20Muhammad%20Bakr%20Al%2d.

77 By several years into the Iraq war, it also became common for different media to identify different trends to feature. So, for example, the bombing on October 5, 2005, of a Shiite mosque on the first day of Ramadan was used in the *Guardian* as part of a story on Saddam Hussein's trial, in the *Los Angeles Times* as a way to tell a story about continued sectarian violence, and in the *Washington Post* as a side note to a story about changing the Iraq constitution. MacAskill, Ewan. Trial of Saddam likely to be postponed. *Guardian*, Oct. 6, 2005, p. 17; Roug, Louise. Bombing at Shiite mosque kills 36. *Los Angeles Times*, Oct. 6, 2005, p. A5; Finer, Jonathan. Iraq alters rule for vote on charter. *Washington Post*, Oct. 6, 2005, p. A22.

78 Pérez-Peña, Richard. The war endures, but where's the media? *New York Times*, Mar. 24, 2008. Available: http://www.nytimes.com/2008/03/24/business/media/24press.html?th&emc=th. Actually, coverage of the Iraqi policy debate in Washington dropped off between 2006 and 2008 even more significantly than coverage of the violence inside Iraq. First, the coverage dropped as a result of the White House winning the debate with Congress over the conduct of the war. Iraq had turned into "an incremental story," as ABC News correspondent Terry McCarthy noted. "The suspense has gone" (*Lehrer NewsHour*, PBS, Mar. 24, 2008). Then Iraq policy coverage dropped even more as the economic downturn and the presidential campaign usurped all the political news time and space.

79 383 stories came up for the month of October 2007 in the top digital news archive, Lexis-Nexis.

80 Yahoo! News, Oct. 12, 2007. Accessed at: http://www.news.yahoo.com.

81 Schell, Orville. Sending "liberal media" truism to the fact-checker. *New York Times*, Mar. 20, 2003, p. B7.

82 Welsh, Declan. 126 dead in suicide bombing as Bhutto returns to Pakistan. *Guardian*, Oct. 19, 2007. Available: http://www.guardian.co.uk/pakistan/Story/0,,2194786,00.html.

83 Bhutto blames deadly attack on al-Qaeda, Taliban. *Associated Press*, Oct. 19, 2007.

84 Sanger, David, and David Rohde. In Pakistan quandary: U.S. reviews stance. *New York Times*, Oct. 21, 2007. Available: http://www.nytimes.com/2007/10/21/world/asia/21musharraf.html?pagewanted=1&_r=1&th&emc=th.

85   Benazir Bhutto: "We want to save Pakistan." MSNBC, Oct. 22, 2007. Available:
      http://www.msnbc.msn.com/id/21412134/.
86   Dunn, Elizabeth W., Moriah Moore, and Brian A. Nosek. The war of the words: How
      linguistic differences in reporting shape perceptions of terrorism. *Analyses of Social Issues
      and Public Policy*, 5/1 (2005), pp. 67–86.
87   These lists of words had actually been generated by another set of students in another
      experiment. They had been asked to evaluate words for their association either with
      "us" or with "them"—with patriotism or terrorism. All the participants in every one
      of the experiments were American citizens.
          I've also streamlined Dunn's study methodology a bit in other ways. Dunn had her
      participants generally read either two or three stories, not just the targeted article. By
      doing that she hoped to distract the test-takers from focusing too much on the sub-
      ject of terrorism, and instead encourage them to believe that they were participating
      in a study about news coverage in general.
88   Kull, Steven. The press and public misperceptions about the Iraq war. *Words and Reflec-
      tions.* Available: www.nieman.harvard.edu/reports/04-2NRSummer/64-66V58N2.pdf.
89   Suellentrop, Chris. Al Jazeera: It's just as fair as CNN. *Slate*, Apr. 2, 2003. Available:
      http://slate.msn.com/id/2081057/.
90   Miller, Judith, and William Broad. Germ weapons: U.S. analysts link Iraq labs to germ
      arms. *New York Times*, May 21, 2003.
91   Sanger and Rohde. In Pakistan quandary. As the *Times* further reported: "It was also
      the source of the greatest leakage of nuclear arms technology in modern times."
92   *Insight Magazine*, Jan. 17, 2007.
93   Schlussel, Debbie. Barack Hussein Obama: Once a Muslim, always a Muslim. Available:
      http://www.debbieschlussel.com/archives/2006/12/barack_hussein.html.
94   Alter, Jonathan. *Newsweek.* Available: http://www.msnbc.msn.com/id/16842036/
      site/newsweek/.
95   Correction. *New York Times*, Jan. 27, 2007, p. A2. The story had a second life in
      December 2007 when the *Washington Post* ran a story reprising and dismissing
      many of the allegations, but neglecting to mention that other media, including CNN,
      had months previously entirely discredited the rumored Muslim ties to a radical
      Indonesian madrassa. The *Post*'s front-page article was pilloried in the blogosphere,
      as well as in its own newsroom. Ombudsman Deborah Howell criticized the editorial
      choices that were made, as did media critic Howard Kurtz, and political cartoonist
      Tom Toles lampooned it on the *Post*'s own editorial page. See MacGillis, Alec. Foes
      use Obama's Muslim ties to fuel rumors about him. *Washington Post*, Nov. 29, 2007.
      Available: http://www.washingtonpost.com/wp-dyn/content/article/2007/11/28/
      AR2007112802757_2.html.
          The digital reiteration of rumors and smear has meant that the Obama-is-a-
      Muslim rumor continues to live on. In a March 2, 2008, piece on *60 Minutes*,
      reported by Steve Kroft, an Ohio voter in one of the pivotal states in the primary
      election is asked what he thinks about the candidates. "I'm leaning towards Obama,"
      the voter says, "but there are a couple issues with him I'm not too clear on. I'm
      hearing he doesn't know the national anthem and wouldn't use the Holy Bible.
      He's got his own beliefs with the Muslim beliefs—a couple issues that bother me at

heart." (See http://www.huffingtonpost.com/2008/03/02/ohio-voter-on-60-minutes_ n_89476.html for post of the interview.) When Kroft said to the voter that the rumors about Obama were not true, the voter seemed puzzled, saying that he was just concerned over what he had been told.

See the end of this section for a discussion on the traction that smear campaigns can have—and why the rumors stick even when they've been shown to be false. As Salon.com writer Farhad Manjoo noted in the *New York Times*: "Journalists typically presume that facts matter: show the public what is true, and they will make decisions correctly. Psychologists who study how we separate truth from fiction, however, have demonstrated that the process is not so simple. . . . To determine the veracity of a given statement, we often look to society's collective assessment of it. But it is difficult to measure social consensus very precisely, and our brains rely, instead, upon a sensation of familiarity with an idea. You use a rule of thumb: if something seems familiar, you must have heard it before, and if you've heard it before, it must be true." Manjoo, Farhad. Rumor's reasons. *New York Times*. Mar. 16, 2008. Available: http://www.nytimes.com/ 2008/03/16/magazine/16wwln-idealab-t.html?_r=1&oref=slogin.

96   The Associated Press and Reuters. Pakistan cautious in pledge of support. *Seattle Times*, Sept. 16, 2001, p. A9. A *Seattle Times* story a month later revised the number of madrassas it said were "scattered through Pakistan" to 5,000: *Dallas Morning News* and *Newsday*, two schools of thought. *Seattle Times*, Oct. 28, 2001, p. A3. Said that article, "Some of the more radical madrassas have expanded their curriculum to also include instruction in how to use automatic weapons and explosives, skills that madrassa alumni have put to use in some of the region's 'holy wars.' What all the religious schools share in common is the conviction that the West, especially the United States, is a place of great moral and cultural wickedness."

97   Boxer, Sarah. When Afghanistan collapsed. *New York Times*, Oct. 2, 2001, p. E1.

98   Ehrenreich, Barbara. Veiled threat. *Los Angeles Times*, Nov. 4, 2001, p. M1.

99   Rivers, Caryl. When rage fuels world's "lost boys." *Boston Globe*, Feb. 24, 2002, p. E2.

100   Gingrich, Newt. Reflections on an America transformed. *New York Times*, Sept. 8, 2002, section 4, p. 15.

101   Friedman, Thomas L. Where freedom reigns. *New York Times*, Aug. 14, 2002, p. A23.

102   Sanger and Rohde. In Pakistan quandary.

103   Ibid.

104   The *New York Times*, however, is often a solid source for background coverage, particularly after a major breaking event. After the October 2007 Karachi bombing of former Pakistan prime minister Benazir Bhutto's convoy that killed over 130 people and wounded more than 500, the *Times* followed its page 1 stories on the bombing and its aftermath with strong stories on, for example, the background to Pakistani politics (see Kifner, John, David Rohde, Bill Marsh, and Renee Rigdon. Sorting out Pakistan's many struggles. *New York Times*, Oct. 21, 2007, available: http://www. nytimes.com/2007/10/21/weekinreview/21marsh.html?ref=asia) and US engagement in the region (see Cooper, Helene, and Mark Mazzetti. Backstage, U.S. nurtured Pakistan rivals' deal. *New York Times*, Oct. 20, 2007, available: http://www. nytimes.com/2007/10/20/world/asia/20bhutto.html?ref=asia).

105   Blustein, Paul. In Pakistan's squalor, cradles of terrorism. *Washington Post*, Mar. 14, 2002, p. A1. Other madrassas which do act as funnels for recruits into the Taliban and Al Qaeda also were frequently profiled—such as the Dar-ul Uloom Haqqani madrassa, for example, the oldest madrassa in Pakistan, which is famed for the toxic teaching of its faculty. Located only two hours north of the capital, Islamabad, the Haqqani madrassa is the alma mater of 90 percent of the Taliban leadership in Afghanistan.

106   A major study I conducted of media coverage of WMD showed how poorly the terms of discussion are defined. Even when WMD terms were used distinctively and consistently, similar weapons systems were not always characterized similarly. Were WMD, especially nuclear weapons, "deterrents," for example, or were they offensive weapons and indicators of a nation's "rogue" status? The response to that question and the media's reporting of it typically derived from the diplomatic relationships inherent in a particular situation. Saddam's various purported WMD, for example, were reflexively characterized as offensive weapons, as have been North Korea's, while US and Israeli nuclear weapons systems have historically been characterized as "deterrents"— although that automatic assumption about the US arsenal dramatically changed after Bush's enunciation of his doctrine of pre-emption, as the headline to a May 13, 2003, *Los Angeles Times* story noted: "Bush is seeking newer, smaller nuclear bombs; Cold War-era devices are too big to be a believable deterrent, and the US needs options to confront current threats." An earlier article in the *Los Angeles Times*, on May 13, 1998, when the world was turned to look at the nuclear testing in India and Pakistan, paused to note Israel's weapons capability. The story observed somewhat contradictorily: "US officials believe that Israel maintains 100 to 200 nuclear weapons as a deterrent to would-be attackers—and is ready to use them."

      The Bush administration's deliberate aggregating of a plethora of weapons systems and agents as well as of the nuclear interests of a wide range of nations tempted journalists to follow suit—to discuss widely divergent WMD issues in a single story, without taking sufficient care to distinguish one from another. While nuclear weapons experts prefer to use definitional terms that describe the attribute that matters (such as "low-yield" or "short-range"), many journalists distinguish weapons systems by employing more generic adjectival descriptions such as "smaller" vs. "larger," or "tactical" or "battlefield" vs. "strategic" (see Nelson, Robert. Nuclear bunker busters, mini-nukes, and the US nuclear stockpile. *Physics Today*, 56/11 (Nov. 2003), available: http://www.physicstoday.org/vol-56/iss-11/p32.html). This tendency can be seen in the May 2003 *Los Angeles Times* article: "The United States already had disposed of most of its smaller, or tactical, nuclear weapons, and US and Russian officials were busy negotiating to get rid of the thousands of strategic nuclear weapons as well." Stories may refer to terms such as "strategic nuclear weapons," "tactical nuclear weapons," and "low-yield nuclear weapons" without clarifying the differences (if any are meant) among them. Is a reporter quoting a government official or an independent scientist? The casual political "meaning" of terms such as "small nuclear weapons" or "battlefield nuclear weapons" is quite distinct from the scientific debate about the weapons systems' physical attributes and limits. Yet without the reporter providing definitions and signaling that scientists have sensitivities about the usage of certain terms and phrases, the audience is left clueless. There are, of course, always exceptions to the rule. In several stories in May 2003, for example, National Public Radio (NPR)'s Washington correspondent Tom Gjelten brought in scientists to clarify the science of the Congressional nuclear weapons debate and quoted Rumsfeld in the defense of his position—a type of coverage worth emulating.

107   *Nightline*. ABC News, Apr. 22, 2003.

108   Sengupta, Kim, and Patrick Cockburn. How the war on terror made the world a more terrifying place. *Independent*, Feb. 28, 2007. Available: http://news.independent.co.uk/world/middle_east/article2311307.ece.

109   Unconventional fears. *Philadelphia Inquirer*, June 4, 2002. See also the editorial, Ease the tensions. *Philadelphia Inquirer*, Dec. 27, 2001. Following President Bush's speech to the United Nations and his meeting with President Pervez Musharraf, papers also took up Bush's admonition. As the *Dallas Morning News* wrote: "The president further reminded delegates of al-Qaida's quest to obtain chemical, biological and even nuclear weapons. 'These same terrorists are searching for weapons of mass destruction, the tools to turn their hatred into holocaust,' Bush said." Jackson, David. U.S. will provide more than $1 billion in aid to Pakistan, Bush says. *Dallas Morning News*, Nov. 11, 2001.

110   See, for example, articles such as Rashid, Ahmed. US grows unhappier with Pakistan. *Wall Street Journal*, Dec. 2, 2002, p. A15.

111   Smith, Craig. North Africa feared as staging ground for terror. *New York Times*, Feb. 20, 2007, p. A1.

112   Dewar, Helen. Nuclear weapons development tied to hill approval. *Washington Post*. May 22, 2003; Drabble, Margaret. I loathe America and what it has done to the rest of the world. *Daily Telegraph*, May 8, 2003.

113   Gourevitch, Philip. 1998. *We Wish to Inform You that Tomorrow We Will Be Killed with our Families*. Farrar, Straus Giroux, 48.

114   Norris, Pippa, Marion Just, and Montague Kern, eds. 2003. *Framing Terrorism: The News Media, the Government, and the Public*. New York: Routledge, p. 13. The work of Michael Gurevitch, James Curran, Jay Blumler, and others such as Robert Entman has been essential is developing this field of communication studies. See, for example, the influential work by Jay Blumler and Michael Gurevitch. 1995. *Crisis of Political Communication*. London: Routledge, and the essential textbook, also by Gurevitch and co-edited by James Curran. 2005. *Mass Media and Society*. Oxford: Oxford University Press/Hodder Arnold.

115   Not only are the tactics learned from the advertising profession, but advertising and public relations firms are frequently employed (such as Hill & Knowlton, which has been hired by the governments of such countries as Kuwait and Guatemala). If a firm is a past master at selling the public the virtues of one brand of detergent or beer, the theory is that it can also sell the public—for a short time, at least—a particular government policy.

116   See Moeller, Susan. 1999. *Compassion Fatigue: How the Media Sell Disease, Famine, War and Death*. New York: Routledge, especially ch. 5 and p. 287.

117 Text of President Bush's Sept. 20 speech as prepared for delivery to Congress. *U.S. Newswire*, Sept. 20, 2001.

118 For discussion of how a "tribal" frame has been used as an explanation for Africa's problems, see such works as Lowe, Chris, et al. 1997. Talking about "tribe": Moving from stereotypes to analysis (available: http://www.africaaction.org/bp/documents/TalkingaboutTribeFeb2008Update_001.pdf); Hawk, Beverly, ed. 1992. *Africa's Media Image*. Westport, CT: Praeger; Wall, Melissa. The Rwanda crisis: An analysis of news magazine coverage. *International Communication Gazette*, 1997, pp. 121–34; Alozie, Emmanuel C. What did they say? African media coverage of the first 100 days of the Rwandan crisis (available: http://www.idrc.ca/en/ev-108206-201-1-DO_TOPIC.html).

119 Brokaw, Tom. NBC Nightly News, Oct. 7, 2004.

120 Adams, Noah. *All Things Considered*. NPR, June 4, 2001.

121 Oppel, Jr., Richard. Up to 130 killed in Iraq, drawing a Shiite warning. *New York Times*, Jan. 6, 2006, p. A1.

122 *Daybreak*. CNN, Mar. 18, 2004.

123 Kirkup, James. Britain allows Iranians in to study nuclear science at university. *Daily Telegraph*, Oct. 29, 2007, p. 13.

124 Conan, Neal. Progress in reconstruction of Iraq. *Talk of the Nation*. NPR, May 12, 2003.

125 Wakin, Daniel. Iran's chief, in Lebanon, urges quick U.S. exit from Iraq, but favors vote. *New York Times*, May 14, 2003, p. A14.

126 Times Wire Services. U.S. Wants Nuclear Declaration on Iran. *Los Angeles Times*, May 9, 2003, part 1, p. 27.

127 Conan, Neal. US–Iran relations. *Talk of the Nation*. NPR, May 12, 2003.

128 The House makes its decision: "Let us take this stand against terror." *New York Times*, Oct. 11, 2002, p. A14. Anderson, Nick, and Richard Simon. Wary Congress moves toward a vote on Iraq. *Los Angeles Times*, Oct. 10, 2002, part 1, p. 1.

129 *The Early Show*. CBS News, Oct. 22, 2007.

130 Grey, Stephen. Lance Corporal Matt Croucher hurls himself onto Taliban grenade. *Sunday Times*, Mar. 30, 2008.

131 Oppel. Up to 130 killed in Iraq.

132 Woodruff, Katie, Lori Dorfman, and Liana Winett. Frames on children and youth in US newspapers. Delivered at "Media Matters: The Institute on News and Social Problems," Sept. 29–30, 1995, p. 6.

133 Peterson, Scott. Remains of toxic bullets litter Iraq. *Christian Science Monitor*, May 15, 2003, p. 1. Nordland, Rod. WMDs for the taking? *Newsweek*, May 19, 2003, p. 30.

134 For a much more detailed accounting of how the media cover international affairs, see Moeller. *Compassion Fatigue*.

135 Ricchiardi, Sherry. Over the line? *American Journalism Review*, Sept. 1996, p. 27.

136 Favorite Jefferson quotes. Available: http://etext.virginia.edu/jefferson/quotations/jeff6.htm.

137 *All Things Considered*, NPR, Aug. 20, 2001.

138 Kurtz, Howard. For Blair and Bush, no Fleet Street credibility. *Washington Post*, June 16, 2003, pp. C1, 7.

139   Rycroft, Matthew. The secret Downing Street memo. Reproduced in *New York Review of Books*. June 9, 2005, p. 71. For a wide range of citations on the memo, see the links in http://en.wikipedia.org/wiki/Downing_Street_memo.

140   Complete text of the Downing Street memo can be found at: http://www.downingstreetmemo.com/memos.html.

141   Clark, Matthew. Why has "Downing Street memo" story been a dud US? *Christian Science Monitor*, May 17, 2005. Available: http://www.csmonitor.com/2005/0517/dailyUpdate.html.

142   Daniel Okrent, the public editor for the *New York Times*, spoke out on the evening news program the *Lehrer NewsHour* about why he thought the memo didn't get more attention: "I have two thoughts on it. The first is that it was seen as in the context of Tony Blair's reelection campaign and the people who were covering it were covering politics, they were covering foreign politics. The people who were assigned that story weren't the people who would be engaged in looking at the walk-up to the war in Iraq." The June 8, 2005 transcript is available at http://www.pbs.org/newshour/bb/media/jan-june05/ombuds_6-8.html.

143   Getler, Michael. News over there, but not here. *Washington Post*, May 15, 2005. Available: http://www.washingtonpost.com/wp-dyn/content/article/2005/05/14/AR2005051400705.html. There were those who believed that the memo did not show a manipulation of the intelligence, in fact those who argue that the memo shows how seriously the British government took the notion of WMDs and their possible use.

144   Warrick, Joby, and Ellen Nakashima. Senate votes to expand warrantless surveillance. *Washington Post*, Aug. 4, 2007. Available: http://www.washingtonpost.com/wp-dyn/content/article/2007/08/03/AR2007080302296.html.

145   A *NewsHour with Jim Lehrer* transcript. *Online NewsHour*. June 8, 2005. Available: http://www.pbs.org/newshour/bb/media/jan-june05/ombuds_6-8.html.

146   Howell, Deborah. To readers, terror and war underplayed. *Washington Post*, July 8, 2007, p. B6.

147   The Pulitzer Prizes. Available: http://www.pulitzer.org/.

148   ABC Nightly News, Feb 23, 2006; CNN, Jan 5, 2006.

149   Okrent, Daniel. All the news that's fit to print? Or just our news? *New York Times*, Feb. 1, 2004, Week in Review, p. 2.

150   Peterson. Remains of toxic bullets litter Iraq.

151   Knickerbocker, Brad. US sees renewed role for nukes in military arsenal, *Christian Science Monitor*, May 27, 2003, p. 2.

152   Sandhana, Lakshmi. Greenery on alert. *Christian Science Monitor*, May 1, 2003, p. 12.

153   Bumiller, Elisabeth. Keepers of Bush Image Lift Stagecraft to New Heights. *New York Times*, May 16, 2003, A1; Keller, Bill. The Thinkable. *New York Times Magazine*, May 4, 2003.

154   Wertheimer, Linda. Ambassador Wendy Sherman of the Albright Group, and Anthony Cordesman of the Center for Strategic & International Studies discuss containment strategies of nuclear weapons programs. *Saturday Weekend Edition*, NPR, May 10, 2003.

155   For a fuller discussion of US and UK media coverage of WMD, see Moeller. *Media Coverage of Weapons of Mass Destruction*.

156   NBC Nightly News is tracked here because it was the longtime leader in news ratings, first under Tom Brokaw, then his successor, Brian Williams, who took over in December

2004. Since spring 2007, ABC World News, anchored by Charles Gibson, has vied with NBC for the top slot. See Carter, Bill, and Jacques Steinberg. With anchors still settling in, NBC feels pressure at the top. *New York Times*, Mar. 1, 2007. Available: http://www.nytimes.com/2007/03/01/business/media/01nbc.html?pagewanted=print.

157   Note, however, that these raw numbers don't capture the length of the stories or where they appeared in the print periodical or in the newscast. The figures do, however, give a rough sense of how important the news outlet considered the story, especially in comparison to the coverage the outlet gave to other events.

158   Hawkins, Scott A., Stephen J. Hoch, and Joan Meyers-Levy. Low-involvement learning: Repetition and coherence in familiarity and belief. *Journal of Consumer Psychology*, 11/1 (2001), pp. 1–11.

159   Hasher, L., D. Goldstein, and T. Toppino. Frequency and the conference of referential validity. *Journal of Verbal Learning and Verbal Behavior*, 16 (1977), pp. 107–12.

160   Begg, I. M., A. Anas, and S. Farinacci. Dissociation of processes in belief: Source recollection, testimonial familiarity, and the illusion of truth. *Journal of Experimental Psychology: General*, 121/4 (1992), pp. 446–58.

161   Roggeveen, Anne L., and Gita Venkataramani Johar. Perceived source variability versus familiarity: Testing competing explanations for the truth effect. *Journal of Consumer Psychology*, 12/2 (2002), pp. 81–91. Another study by Kimberlee Weaver and others showed "that hearing the same thing over and over again from one source can have the same effect as hearing that thing from many different people—the brain gets tricked into thinking it has heard a piece of information from multiple, independent sources, even when it has not." Quoted from Vedantam, Shankar. Persistence of myths could alter public policy approach. *Washington Post*, Sept. 4, 2007. Available: http://www.washingtonpost.com/wp-dyn/content/article/2007/09/03/AR2007090300933_pf.html. And Weaver, Kimberlee. Inferring the popularity of an opinion from its familiarity: A repetitive voice can sound like a chorus. *Journal of Personality and Social Psychology*, 92/5 (2007), pp. 821–33.

162   Roggeveen and Johar. Perceived source variability versus familiarity.

163   Skurnik, Ian, Carolyn Yoon, Denise C. Park, and Norbert Schwarz. How warnings about false claims become recommendations, *Journal of Consumer Research*, 31(Mar.) (2005), pp. 713–24. Skurnik's article includes a listing of resources that address false information. Two on the web are: http://www.cdc.gov/doc.do/id/0900f3ec80226b9c and http://www.snopes.com/business/market/market.asp. Other scholars who have addressed this include:

- Grice, H. Paul. 1989. *Studies in the Way of Words*. Cambridge, MA: Harvard University Press.
- Hasher, Lynn, David Goldstein, and Thomas Toppino. Frequency and the conference of referential validity. *Journal of Verbal Learning & Verbal Behavior*, 16(Feb.) (1977), pp. 107–12.
- Jacoby, Jacob, Margaret C. Nelson, and Wayne D. Hoyer. Corrective advertising and affirmative disclosure statements: Their potential for confusing and misleading the consumer. *Journal of Marketing*, 19(Winter) (1982), pp. 61–72.

- Mandler, George. Recognizing: The judgment of previous occurrence. *Psychological Review*, 87(May) (1980), pp. 252–71.
- Schwarz, Norbert, Lawrence J. Sanna, Ian Skurnik, and Carolyn Yoon. Meta-cognitive experiences and the intricacies of setting people straight: Implications for debiasing and public information campaigns. *Advances in Experimental Social Psychology*, 39, ed. Mark Zanna. (2007).
- Skurnik, Ian, Nobert Schwarz, and Piotr Winkielman. 2000. Drawing inferences from feelings: The role of naive beliefs. In Herbert Bless and Joseph P. Forgas, eds. *The Message Within: The Role of Subjective Experience in Social Cognition and Behavior*. Philadelphia, PA: Psychology Press, pp. 162–75.

164 Quoted in Vedantam. Persistence of myths could alter public policy approach.
165 Ibid.
166 *On the Media*, Sept. 7, 2007. Available: http://www.onthemedia.org/transcripts/2007/09/07/04. And its not just Americans, of course, who come to believe misinformation. As *Washington Post* reporter Shankar Vedantam wrote:

> This phenomenon may help explain why large numbers of Americans incorrectly think that Saddam Hussein was directly involved in planning the Sept 11, 2001, terrorist attacks, and that most of the Sept. 11 hijackers were Iraqi. While these beliefs likely arose because Bush administration officials have repeatedly tried to connect Iraq with Sept. 11, the experiments suggest that intelligence reports and other efforts to debunk this account may in fact help keep it alive.
>
> Similarly, many in the Arab world are convinced that the destruction of the World Trade Center on Sept. 11 was not the work of Arab terrorists but was a controlled demolition; that 4,000 Jews working there had been warned to stay home that day; and that the Pentagon was struck by a missile rather than a plane.
>
> Those notions remain widespread even though the federal government now runs Web sites in seven languages to challenge them. Karen Hughes, who runs the Bush administration's campaign to win hearts and minds in the fight against terrorism, recently painted a glowing report of the "digital outreach" teams working to counter misinformation and myths by challenging those ideas on Arabic blogs.
>
> A report last year by the Pew Global Attitudes Project, however, found that the number of Muslims worldwide who do not believe that Arabs carried out the Sept. 11 attacks is soaring—to 59 percent of Turks and Egyptians, 65 percent of Indonesians, 53 percent of Jordanians, 41 percent of Pakistanis and even 56 percent of British Muslims.

167 Quoted in Passaro, Vince. Dangerous Don DeLillo, *New York Times Magazine*, May 19, 1991. DeLillo is the author of the 2007 novel *Falling Man*—a book that takes its title from Richard Drew's photograph of the man who fell from the North Tower of the World Trade Center on September 11, 2001.

III What Are the Images of Terror?

1 Winkler, Claudia. The "Guernica" myth. *Daily Standard*, Apr. 16, 2003. Available: http://www.weeklystandard.com/Content/Public/Articles/000/000/002/556paocc.asp?pg=2. Dowd, Maureen. Powell without Picasso. *New York Times*, Feb. 5, 2003, p. A31.

Edward Mortimer, the Director of Communications in the Executive Office of the United Nations Secretary General at the time, recollected of the occasion: "I am pretty sure that we had covered it up because we thought it would be embarrassing in the circumstances for him to have to speak to the world standing in front of it, and that we might be accused by US media or politicians of setting this up deliberately. I also think we took this decision preemptively—definitely not at his request nor, I think, at that of the US mission." Mortimer quoted from an entry in his diary that the cover-up of the Guernica tapestry was "an arrangement for which we took a lot of stick last week!" The UN had learned its lesson—the following week "Powell [again] came out & spoke at the improvised Sec Co stake-out—now carefully moved to the right so that the Guernica tapestry no longer has to be covered up." Personal email from Edward Mortimer, Dec. 20, 2007.

2   *NewsHour with Jim Lehrer* transcript. *Online NewsHour.* June 10, 2005. Available: http://www.pbs.org/newshour/bb/africa/jan-june05/kristof_6-10.html.

3   UN: Violence in DR Congo "beyond rape." RTE News, July 30, 2007. Available: http://www.rte.ie/news/2007/0730/rape.html.

4   *Charlie Rose Show.* PBS, Mar. 28, 2005.

5   Day, Julia. How the tsunami hogged the headlines. *Guardian Unlimited,* Mar. 11, 2005.

6   Von Gruber, Pamela. Special report. Emergency disaster response: The impact of the media, the military, and time. *Defense & Foreign Affairs Special Analysis,* June 16, 2005.

7   *Charlie Rose Show.* PBS, Dec. 22, 2005.

8   There is a tremendous amount of audience effects research. Two accessible overviews are: Fletcher, James. Audience research: Effects analysis. Found at the online site of the Museum of Broadcast Communications. Available: http://www.museum.tv/archives/etv/A/htmlA/audienceresee/audienceresee.htm; and Butsch, Richard. Class and audience effects. *Journal of Popular Film and Television,* Sept. 22, 2001. Available: http://www.encyclopedia.com/doc/1G1-79350859.html.

9   Moeller, Susan. 1989. *Shooting War: Photography and the American Experience of Combat.* New York: Basic Books.

10   This quote and others below related to media coverage of twentieth-century war come from Moeller. *Shooting War.*

11   Robertson, Lori. "We have a breaking story . . ." *American Journalism Review* (Oct. 2001). Available: http://www.ajr.org/Article.asp?id=49.

12   Shales, Tom. On television, the unimaginable story unfolds. *Washington Post,* Sept. 12, 2001.

13   King, Larry. Where Were You on 9-11? *Larry King Weekend.* CNN, Sept. 7, 2002. Available: http://transcripts.cnn.com/TRANSCRIPTS/0209/07/lklw.00.html.

14   Both Jennings and Fisher quoted in Sullivan, Patricia. ABE news anchor was a voice of the world. *Washington Post,* Aug. 8, 2005.

15   Palser, Barb. Not so bad. *American Journalism Review* (Nov. 2001). Available: http://www.ajr.org/Article.asp?id=2375.

16   Basheda, Valarie. An unforgettable picture. *American Journalism Review* (Oct. 2001). Available: http://www.ajr.org/Article.asp?id=52.

17   According to a story on the photo in *Esquire,* When Drew "was twenty-one years old, he was standing right behind Bobby Kennedy when Bobby Kennedy was shot in

the head. His jacket was spattered with Kennedy's blood, but he jumped on a table and shot pictures of Kennedy's open and ebbing eyes, and then of Ethel Kennedy crouching over her husband and begging photographers—begging him—not to take pictures." See Junod, Tom. The falling man. *Esquire.* Sept. 11, 2007. Available: http://www.esquire.com/features/ESQ0903-SEP_FALLINGMAN.

18   Howe, Peter. Richard Drew. *Digital Journalist* (2001). Available: http://www.digitaljournalist.org/issue0110/drew.htm.

19   The *New York Times* calculated the number of those who jumped by counting only what its reporters actually saw in the footage they collected, and it arrived at a figure of 50. *USA Today*, whose editors used eyewitness accounts and forensic evidence in addition to what they found on video, came to the conclusion that at least 200 people died by jumping—a count that the newspaper said authorities did not dispute. As *Esquire* noted, "if the number provided by *USA Today* is accurate, then between 7 and 8 percent of those who died in New York City on September 11, 2001, died by jumping out of the buildings; it means that if we consider only the North Tower, where the vast majority of jumpers came from, the ratio is more like one in six." See Junod. The falling man.

   Another effort to wrestle with those who jumped was *9/11: The Falling Man*, a documentary about the Drew picture and the story behind it. The film is loosely based on Tom Junod's *Esquire*. The documentary debuted on Mar. 16, 2006, on the British television channel Channel 4, premiered in Canada on CBC Newsworld on September 6, 2006, and in the United States on September 10, 2007 on the Discovery Times Channel. It has been broadcast in over 30 countries.

20   Tugend, Alina. The simple act of getting to work was an ordeal. *American Journalism Review* (Oct. 2001). Available: http://www.ajr.org/Article.asp?id=51.

21   Junod. The falling man.

22   Interview with Jonathan Munro, London, July 29, 2004.

23   Junod. The falling man.

24   Rutenberg, Jim, and Felicity Barringer. After the attacks: The ethics. News media try to sort out policy on graphic images. *New York Times*, Sept. 13, 2001.

25   Halstead, Dirck. Bill Biggart's final exposures. *Digital Journalist.* (2001). Available: http://digitaljournalist.org/issue0111/biggart_intro.htm.

26   Unless otherwise noted, the facts and quotations in this account of the 9/11 flag-raising picture taken by photographer Thomas Franklin have come from the lengthy first-anniversary story published by Franklin's newspaper, *The Record*. Lisberg, Adam. Making of an image for the ages. *The Record*, Sept. 11, 2002, p. A26.

27   This quotation comes from an interview conducted with the firefighters by *Record* reporter Jeannine Clegg two days after 9/11. The three firefighters have refused all other interview requests since that time. Clegg, Jeannine. Flag-raising was "shot in the arm." *The Record*, Sept. 14, 2001, p. A5.

28   As quoted at http://www.arlingtoncemetery.net/fireman-01.htm.

29   Mahibir, Karen. Historic moment captured in wax. *The Record*, Sept. 4, 2002.

30   Lisberg. Making of an image for the ages.

31   Mahibir. Historic moment captured in wax.

32   Edelson, Mark, and Sarah Franquet. Why didn't this photo win the Pulitzer Prize? *Palm Beach Post*, Apr. 27, 2002, p. 1E.

33 Ibid.

34 El-Nawawy, Mohammed. Whose "truth" is being reported? *Christian Science Monitor*, Apr. 8, 2003.

35 The timing of this account is pieced together from various records, including a *New Yorker* article by Jon Lee Anderson, which appeared in the April 14, 2003 issue, but was posted online on April 7, and a report by the Iraq Peace Team, a project of the Chicago-based independent grassroots group, Voices in the Wilderness, which visited Al Kindi Hospital on April 1, 2003. According to Dr. April Hurley's report of her conversation with Dr. Osama Saaleh, the director of the hospital, the bombing took place about 6 a.m. on March 30. The description of Ali's injuries is also derived from photographs the hospital took of Ali (and of his dead mother) before his hands and arms were amputated. The report and those images are available at: http://inlct.org/wade/iptreports/2003apr04/. *The Ali Abbas Story* by Jane Warren, (HarperCollins, 2004), contradicts this timing, stating that the bombing took place in the early hours of March 31.

36 Stephenson, Michele. *Edit.* Available: http://corporate.gettyimages.com/edit/source/article.aspx?article=123&page=8&bhcp=1.

37 Because of the practice of forward-dating, the *Time* magazine issue carried a cover date of April 14, 2003, but it appeared on newsstands a week earlier, on Monday, April 7. *Time* also agonized over its first photo showing a US casualty of war. "As a mass-market magazine we need to be aware of our public," Michelle Stephenson, *Time's* director of photography, said. "We felt it was important to show that [first casualty]. It wasn't bloody and it wasn't gory and maybe that made it a bit more palatable." DeFoore, Jay. PhotoPlus coverage: Shooting under fire. *Photo District News*, Nov. 6, 2003.

38 Carr, David, Jim Rutenberg, and Jacques Steinberg. Telling war's deadly story at just enough distance. *New York Times*, Apr. 7, 2003, p. B13.

39 Addley, Ester. Ali's story. *Guardian* (London), Aug. 1, 2003, p. 2.

40 Kheiber, Faleh, and Reuters. Photo of Ali Ismail Abbas. Available: http://www.digitaljournalist.org/issue0304/reutersf17.html.

41 Kelly, James. To our readers. *Time*, Apr. 21, 2003, p. 8.

42 Interview with Jonathan Munro, London, July 29, 2004.

43 Madore, James. Putting different faces on war. *Newsday*, Apr. 22, 2003, p. A48.

44 Interview with Lindsey Hilsum, London, July 28, 2004.

45 Your messages for Ali. *Newsround*, CBBC. Available: http://news.bbc.co.uk/cbbcnews/hi/chat/your_comments/newsid_2956000/2956519.stm.

46 Madore. Putting different faces on war.

47 Walter, Natasha. Women at war. *Guardian*, Apr. 17, 2003, p. 9.

48 Images noted in el-Nawawy. Whose "truth" is being reported?

49 Ibid.

50 MacArthur, John. Close encounters. *Washington Post*, Oct. 12, 2003, p. 4.

51 Aday, Sean. The G-rated war. *The Gadflyer*, Apr. 29, 2004. Available: http://stevemacek.blogspot.com/2004_05_01_archive.html. See also Aday, Sean. 2005. The real war will never get televised: An analysis of casualty imagery in American television coverage of the Iraq War. In Phil Seib, ed. *Media and Conflict in the Twenty-First Century*. New York: Palgrave Macmillan.

52 Stein, Jeff. Jessica Lynch: The untold paragraph. *Washington Post*, Nov. 19, 2003, p. C1.

53 Robertson, Lori. Images of war. *American Journalism Review* (Oct.–Nov. 2004). Available: http://www.ajr.org/Article.asp?id=3759.

54 McGrath, Charles. Bomb. *New York Times*, Apr. 13, 2003, pp. 15–16.

55 Interview with Jonathan Munro, London, July 29, 2004.

56 Others whose deaths were videotaped by terrorists included Eugene Armstrong, Kenneth Bigley, Nick Berg, Jack Hensley, Paul Marshall Johnson, Jr. (in Saudi Arabia), Ivaylo Kepov, Georgi Lazov, Fabrizio Quattrocchi, Kim Sun-il.

57 Yahya, Syed. Who killed Pearl? *Newsline* (Mar. 2002). Available: http://www.newsline.com.pk/NewsMarch2002/newsbeat1.htm.

58 Lane, Megan. The taboos still waiting to be broken. *BBC News Online Magazine*, Apr. 21, 2004. Available: http://news.bbc.co.uk/2/hi/uk_news/magazine/3639939.stm.

59 Leith, Sam. Outrage as CBS shows reporter's last seconds. *Telegraph*, May 16, 2002. Available: http://www.telegraph.co.uk/news/main.jhtml?xml=/news/2002/05/16/wcbs16.xml.

60 Lopez, Kathryn Jean. Airing Pearl: Reaction to CBS's decision to air the Daniel Pearl hostage video. *National Review Online*, May 17, 2002. Available: http://www.nationalreview.com/symposium/symposium051702.asp.

61 Pearl, Judea. Death images hide the truth of Danny Pearl. *New York Times*, June 18, 2002.

62 Steele, Bob. Pearl photo: Too harmful. Available: http://www.poynter.org/column.asp?id=36&aid=839.

63 Kennedy, Dan. The Daniel Pearl video. *Nieman Reports* (Fall 2002), p. 81.

64 Poland, David. Pearl photos: Too harmful? *Poynter Forums*, June 6, 2002. Available: http://www.poynter.org/forum/view_post.asp?id=2219.

65 Wright, Robin. Abductions in Iraq reflect new strategy, U.S. says. *Washington Post*, June 30, 2004, p. A14.

66 Smith, Lynn. Web amplifies message of primitive executions. *Los Angeles Times*, June 30, 2004.

67 Steinberg, Jacques. Kidnappings, beheading and defining what's news. *New York Times*, Aug. 1, 2004, p. 1.

68 Robertson. Images of war.

69 Smith. Web amplifies message of primitive executions.

70 Ibid.

71 Steinberg. Kidnappings, beheading and defining what's news.

72 Robertson. Images of war.

73 Lynch, Jim. Freedom, the internet and the murder of Daniel Pearl. Available: http://jimlynch.com/index.php/2003/08/11/7/.

74 See also Moeller, Susan D. 1999. *Compassion Fatigue: How the Media Sell Disease, Famine, War and Death*. New York: Routledge.

75 See Moeller, Susan. "Regarding the pain of others": Media, bias and the coverage of international disasters. *Journal of International Affairs* (Spring/Summer 2006), pp. 173–96.

76 The challenges of linking civic participation together with media literacy—or news literacy—is a major initiative of ICMPA at the University of Maryland. To

learn more about the global efforts go to: http://www.salzburg.umd.edu or http://www.icmpa.umd.edu.

77 Leader. Spanish bombs: To die in Madrid. *Guardian*, Mar. 12, 2004, p. 27.

78 Editorial. The case of the missing lamb. *Digital Journalist* (Apr. 2004). Available: http://www.digitaljournalist.org/issue0404/editorial.html.

79 Quoted in Irby, Kenny. Beyond taste: Editing truth. *Poynteronline*. Available: http://www.poynter.org/content/content_print.asp?id=63131&custom=.

80 The case of the missing lamb.

81 Editors on Fallujah. Newsdesigner.com, Apr. 4, 2004. Available: http://www.newsdesigner.com/archives/cat_fallujah_photographs.php.

82 Robertson. Images of war.

83 Ibid.

84 Interview with Lindsey Hilsum, London, July 28, 2004.

85 Rutenberg, Jim. A nation at war: The TV watch; after days of buoyant images, reporting enters a second and more ominous act. *New York Times*, Mar. 24, 2003. Available: http://query.nytimes.com/gst/fullpage.html?res=9C00EED71430F937A15750C0A9659C8B63&sec=&spon=&pagewanted=all.

86 Kurtz, Howard. Too painful to publish? *Washington Post*, Mar. 25, 2003, p. C1.

87 Rutenberg. A nation at war.

88 Kennicott, Philip. The illustrated horror of conflict. *Washington Post*, Mar. 25, 2003, p. C1.

89 Quoted in Friend, David. A war waged in images. *Digital Journalist* (Sept. 2003). Available: http://www.dirkhalstead.org/issue0309/dfriend.html.

90 Rumsfeld: In the end, Saddam "not terribly brave." CNN.com, Dec. 15, 2003. Available: http://edition.cnn.com/2003/WORLD/meast/12/14/sprj.irq.main/index.html.

91 Hicks, Tyler. Photograph. *New York Times*, Nov. 13, 2001, p. B1.

92 A June 6, 2004 CID investigation report summarized the photographic material from Abu Ghraib turned into the US government's Criminal Investigation Command: "A review of all the computer media submitted to this office revealed a total of 1,325 images of suspected detainee abuse, 93 video files of suspected detainee abuse, 660 images of adult pornography, 546 images of suspected dead Iraqi detainees, 29 images of soldiers in simulated sexual acts, 20 images of a soldier with a Swastika drawn between his eyes, 37 images of Military Working dogs being used in abuse of detainees and 125 images of questionable acts."

93 The day citizen media went mainstream. *Last Minute Blog*. Available: http://www.thelastminuteblog.com/?p=2610.

94 Terakopian, Edmond. London's darkest day. *Digital Journalist* (Aug. 2005). Available: http://www.digitaljournalist.org/issue0508/dis-terakopian.html.

95 Fremson, Ruth. Dispatches. *Digital Journalist* (Nov. 2001). Available: http://digitaljournalist.org/issue0111/fremson.htm.

96 Robertson. Images of war.

97 Howe, Peter. Richard Drew. *Digital Journalist* (2001). Available: http://www.digitaljournalist.org/issue0110/drew.htm.

98 Kramer, Staci D. The Sept. 11 media frenzy. *Online Journalism Review*, Sept. 12, 2002. Available: http://www.ojr.org/ojr/kramer/1031793726.php.

99   Quoted in Wenner, Kathryn S. Getting the picture. *American Journalism Review* (Oct. 2001). Available: http://www.ajr.org/Article.asp?id=2195.

100 Herbert, Gerald. Ambush. *Digital Journalist* (2001). Available: http://digitaljournalist.org/issue0112/herbert.htm.

101 Filkins, Dexter. Get me rewrite. Now. Bullets are flying. *New York Times*, Oct. 10, 2004, section 4, p. 1.

102 *Lehrer NewsHour*. PBS, Mar. 24, 2008.

103 Anderson, Scott. The target. *New York Times Magazine*, Dec. 28, 2002, p. 50.

104 Kamber, Michael, and Tim Arango. 4,000 U.S. deaths, and a handful of images. *New York Times*, July 26, 2008. Available: http://www.nytimes.com/2008/07/26/world/middleeast/26censor.html. A related slideshow of images is available at: http://www.nytimes.com/slideshow/2008/07/25/world/middleeast/20080726_CENSOR2_2.html.

105 Di Lauro, Marco. To die at your children's wedding. *Digital Journalist* (Dec. 2005). Available: http://www.digitaljournalist.org/issue0512/dis_dilauro.html.

106 Ozernoy, Ilana. Introduction. *Digital Journalist* (2002). Available: http://digitaljournalist.org/issue0208/rh_intro.htm.

107 Lueders, Marty. How it is. *Digital Journalist* (Oct. 2001). Available: http://digitaljournalist.org/issue0111/lueders.htm.

IV   Conclusion

1   An audio mp3 of the address is available: http://www.americanrhetoric.com/speeches/mlkatimetobreaksilence.htm.

2   A transcript of Barack Obama's speech made in Berlin on July 24, 2008, is available at: http://my.barackobama.com/page/community/post/obamaroadblog/gGxyd4.

3   Paul Krugman. Fearing fear itself. *New York Times*, Oct. 29, 2007. Available: http://www.nytimes.com/2007/10/29/opinion/29krugman.html.

4   Carr, David, Jim Rutenberg, and Jacques Steinberg. Telling war's deadly story at just enough distance. *New York Times*, Apr.7, 2003, p. B13.

5   Readers' Comments, There were orders to follow. *New York Times*, Apr. 4, 2008.

6   Speech by President George Bush, Feb. 4, 2004. Available: http://www.america.gov/st/washfile-english/2004/February/20040204181756ssorw0.4439203.html.

7   Branch, Tayler. The last wish of Martin Luther King, *New York Times*, Apr. 6, 2008.

Appendix

1   Literally dozens of books and journal articles were used as references in formulating ICMPA's studies. To name just a few of the most important not cited elsewhere:

   • Bennett, W. Lance, Regina Lawrence, and Steven Livingston. None dare call it torture: indexing and the limits of press independence in the Abu Ghraib Scandal. *Journal of Communication* (Sept. 2006), pp. 467–85.

- Picard, Robert. 1993. *Media Portrayals of Terrorism: Functions and Meaning of New Coverage*. Ames, Iowa: Iowa State University Press.
- Laqueur, Walter. 2003. *No End to War: Terrorism in the Twenty-First Century*. New York: Continuum.
- Nacos, Brigitte. 2007. *Mass-Mediated Terrorism: The Central Role of the Media in Terrorism and Counterterrorism*, 2nd edn. New York: Rowman & Littlefield.
- Palmer, Nancy, ed. 2003. *Terrorism, War, and the Press*. Hollis, NH: Hollis Publishing.

Acknowledgments

1 Report by Margaret Mead to the Harvard Student Council: "The Salzburg Seminar in American Civilization" (1947). Available: http://www.salzburgseminar.org/2007/history.cfm.

index